Macramé

Praise for *Macramé*

"In this book, Nghi Ho shares her vast wisdom about the power of knots and provides lots of fun and creative projects for macramé beginners to dive into!"

—**Fanny Zedenius,** founder of Createaholic and author of
Macramé: The Craft of Creative Knotting for Your Home

"An inspiring, skills–based book for modern makers looking to take their macramé knowledge and creatively to the next level."

—**Brydie Stewart**, founder of Mary Maker Studio

"A beautiful, inspiring book for anyone looking to dive into the art of knotting & macramé."

—**Isabella Strambio**, author of *Macramé for the Modern Home*

Macramé

The Power of Knots

Nghi Ho

CORAL GABLES

Copyright © 2023 by Nghi Ho.
Published by Yellow Pear Press, a division of Mango Publishing Group, Inc.

Cover Design: Elina Diaz
Cover Photo/illustration: Nghi Ho
Layout & Design: Elina Diaz

Mango is an active supporter of authors' rights to free speech and artistic expression in their books. The purpose of copyright is to encourage authors to produce exceptional works that enrich our culture and our open society.

Uploading or distributing photos, scans or any content from this book without prior permission is theft of the author's intellectual property. Please honor the author's work as you would your own. Thank you in advance for respecting our author's rights.

For permission requests, please contact the publisher at:
Mango Publishing Group
2850 S Douglas Road, 2nd Floor
Coral Gables, FL 33134 USA
info@mango.bz

For special orders, quantity sales, course adoptions and corporate sales, please email the publisher at sales@mango.bz. For trade and wholesale sales, please contact Ingram Publisher Services at customer.service@ingramcontent.com or +1.800.509.4887.

Macramé: The Power of Knots

Library of Congress Cataloging-in-Publication number: 2022946593
ISBN: (pb) 978-1-68481-108-3 (hc) 978-1-68481-280-6 (e) 978-1-68481-109-0
BISAC category code CRA055000, CRAFTS & HOBBIES / Knots, Macrame & Rope Work

Printed in China

Table of Contents

Introduction 11

Chapter 1 **Knot, Knot… Who's There?** 13

Chapter 2 **Tools & Materials** 25

Chapter 3 **Macramé Basic Knots** 37

Chapter 4 **15 Patterns & 4 Projects for Novice Artists** 85

Chapter 5 **15 Patterns & 4 Projects for Intermediate Artists** 129

Chapter 6 **15 Patterns & 4 Projects for Advanced Artists** 179

Resources & Acknowledgments 230

About the Author 231

Introduction

You've just moved to your new place and don't know what to do with it. It needs something. Or perhaps you have decided to give your place that needed makeover to finally make it feel like home. Maybe you just want to start something new that fulfills you and fits your modern lifestyle. Or, it could just be a case of wanting to try something that will allow you to tell the rest of the world who you really are. That "something" is macramé, and all you need to know about it is in this book, *Macramé: The Power of Knots*.

"But wait, I am not a crafty person and don't know anything about macramé."

"I don't know if I am creative enough."

"Macramé seems way too complicated, and it probably takes too long to learn."

Those might be some of the first thoughts popping into your head after reading the previous paragraph. And that is absolutely normal. In fact, those were my exact thoughts the first time I came across macramé.

My name is Nghi Ho, and I am a lifelong passionate crafter, a self-taught macramé artist, and a content creator. My love for crafting started at an early age. As a kid, I was amazed that, with a bit of creativity, a person could create something beautiful simply by using their hands. As an art major—and later, a graphic designer—I always worked in environments where creativity played a major role. But it wasn't until I found macramé that I realized what I really wanted to do in life: to be a macramé artist. I was instantly fascinated by its simplicity (making knots), especially the astonishing eye-catching pieces of art one could create.

Throughout my macramé journey, I've come across many macramé enthusiasts from every corner of the globe. And they have all helped reinforce what I believed all along: Macramé is a worldwide phenomenon! So, for as long as I'm able to, I will continue trying to inspire people by making sure they learn, enjoy, and grow in this amazing craft.

In *Macramé: The Power of Knots*, I guide you every step of the way and share with you all of my knowledge, experiences, and passion for this craft. I teach you every trick and provide you with all the tips to guarantee a smooth initiation into this art form, no matter what style you are into, what previous knowledge you have, or how crafty or creative you are. I enjoy a one-on-one mentoring style and easy-to-follow instructions, which I merge in this book with the aim of developing and improving your macramé skills.

From basic knots to never-before-seen macramé patterns and projects, from classic tools and materials to modern equipment that will take your macramé game to another level, from explaining its historic origins to displaying the trendy modern art form macramé is today, *Macramé: The Power of Knots* has it all. You can navigate this book as you please, but I suggest reading chapters 1 to 3 first to get a strong foundation. Then, after you've learned the basics and your confidence grows, you can start creating patterns or projects that match your level. It is always a good idea to review basic knots and patterns before beginning one of the many projects in the book. Allow me to inspire you and give you the confidence you need to become the macramé artist you want to be.

Chapter 1

Knot, Knot... Who's There?

Macramé is described as the art of knotting different types of cords or strings in order to create decorative pieces. The same way macramé could not exist without knotting, knotting would be impossible without, you guessed it, the knot!

Originally used by prehistoric humans to tie grass and limbs as well as to hold sticks and rocks, the knot was essential for the creation of tools, and consequently helped us evolve. During the Ice Age, knowing how to knot could mean the difference between life and death, as it meant *Homo sapiens* were able to tie rudimentary fences and roofs together to protect themselves from the freezing temperatures.

Knots took a more solemn role once different cultures began to use them as symbols. In ancient China, for instance, the Pan Chang Knot, also known as the Mystic Knot, began to be used as one of the eight symbols of Buddhism. With its seemingly endless pattern, the Pan Chang Knot symbolizes a cycle of life without a beginning or an end. The Celtic culture is also heavily influenced by knots. Their knots are believed to represent eternity in love, friendship, loyalty, or faith. The triquetra or the Trinity knot (as many people call it), is arguably the best-known Celtic knot. It represents the three main natural elements of air, water, and earth. On a more spiritual level, similarly to the Pan Chang knot, the Triquetra symbolizes life, death, and rebirth.

The art of knotting is a craft with a rich history and worldwide significance. It is an art form full of symbolism and tradition, loved by many due to its numerous additional benefits—from improving one's physical and mental health, social connections, and financial situation, to even aiding in caring for the environment and practicing sustainability.

Knotting is here to stay! And there is no more powerful evidence of that than macramé.

Macramé: The Power of Knots

Example of the Chinese Pan Chang knot.

Example of the Celtic knot.

A History of Knots

Macramé's actual origins have puzzled many for quite some time. However, researchers nowadays seem to collectively agree on placing the birth of macramé sometime during the thirteenth century, in Arab-ruled countries of northern Africa. The word macramé derives from the Arabic expressions *migramah* (fringe) and *mahramatun* (handkerchief), as well as from the Ottoman-Turkish word *makrama* (headscarf). Even then, Arab weavers were already using macramé techniques that we now consider standard. These artisans used methods of knotting and twisting threads to decorate and secure the ends of handmade fabrics. These pieces included items of clothing; accessories, such as shawls and bath towels; and more practical articles, like harnesses and decorative fringes used in livestock.

The art of knotting initially spread through Europe thanks to the Moors (Muslim inhabitants of regions in northern Africa), who after centuries managed to conquer and settle in most of the Iberian Peninsula. It is believed that macramé was introduced into Spain during the fifteenth century, reaching France and the rest of Europe sometime after that. During the sixteenth century in Genoa, a coastal city in the northwest of Italy, nuns started to favor macramé techniques over traditional labor-intensive needle work. Known for their refined work, these nuns used what was then known as *punto á groppo*, or knotted lace, to decorate altar cloths and religious vestments. Not long after, during the Renaissance period, an English monarch took a liking to this craft. Queen Mary II was so fascinated by and obsessed with macramé that she even taught it to her ladies-in-waiting at court, popularizing macramé among women of the time. However, the task of transmitting the art of knotting across continents was handled mainly by men. Bored European sailors, who were already very skillful at tying knots, regularly crafted handmade items (hammocks, lanyards, knife cases, footwear, belts, etc.) to kill time at sea. As an opportunity to make some extra earnings, they would sell these items upon arrival at their destinations. In this way, macramé was able to reach places as distant as South America and China.

Knot, Knot... Who's There?

Photo by Erik Speer, owner of @esspeer.

Macramé's popularity reached two major peaks during its history. The first occurred during the Victorian era in England. Massively popular among the middle-class women, macramé became an essential decorative element in most Victorian houses, as it perfectly matched the over-the-top style of this era. The printing boom that took place during the late nineteenth century also increased macramé's popularity. One book in particular, *Sylvia's Book of Macramé Lace* (published in 1890), taught many women how to knot macramé pieces such as items of clothing, bags, umbrellas, and curtains.

For most of the twentieth century, macramé disappeared from the map, only to come back into fashion during the late '60s and the '70s—its second peak. During this period, America was dealing with the Vietnam war, oil shortages, and economic strife, and of course, the rise of the "hippie" movement. Macramé aesthetic, due to its homemade and earthy vibes, perfectly fit the cultural and political ideology of that era's "flower children," and the craft became one of the anti-industrialism symbols of the movement. Beloved macramé designs of the time included bags, sweaters, flip-flops, and home decor items. The '70s is considered by many as the era that gave birth to modern macramé designs.

We live in a digitalized world nowadays. There is no argument about that. Vast amounts of information can be instantly accessed by anyone with an internet connection, anywhere in the world. Social media has allowed us to share who we are and what we like and dislike with people we've never met before. Online platforms have helped introduce macramé to people of all ages and ways of life. DIY craft spaces are available on most social media platforms, and online macramé tutorials and courses are growing exponentially in popularity. New and exciting materials are widely available in online macramé supply stores, allowing knotting enthusiasts to experiment and express themselves in ways they never could before. As was the

Photo by Kasha, owner of @kashascraftcreation

case in the past, modern macramé appeals not only to people with a certain taste or style, but to pretty much anyone with a creative itch. Some popular contemporary macramé designs include 3D realistic wall hangings, mixed-fabric freestyle compositions, and unique high-fashion clothing items of clothing. From traditional designs with a twist to powerful, bold new motifs, contemporary macramé artists are breaking the mold and taking the popularity of this old tradition to new heights with their artistic expressions.

The Benefits of Knots

Most people who get into macramé are usually unaware of all the additional benefits this craft brings to its makers. Macramé can be a fantastic method to improve your motor skills and mental ability. It is also a great way to relax and socialize. As mentioned before, it is a hobby that takes into consideration the environment and your own personal sustainability goals. And, of course, it's a fun way to express yourself artistically while generating some income along the way.

Health Benefits

Macramé can help increase the strength of arms, fingers, and hand muscles. As both hands are used in the process, it is a great way to build both your motor skills and bilateral dexterity. For those recovering from hand injuries or suffering from joint pain in their upper extremities, knotting has been proven to be very beneficial in its ability to help crafters regain strength and mobility. The act of tying knots also brings benefits to one of the largest and most complex organs in the human body: the brain. Learning a new skill enhances brain productivity and helps strengthen connections between brain cells and receptors. Expressing yourself artistically stimulates both hemispheres of your brain, which improves your focus and ability to think quickly.

Relaxation Aid

As is the case with other crafts, creating a macramé project can help you relax both body and mind. The repetitive nature of tying knots in macramé art pieces is believed to have therapeutic benefits. Herbert Benson, MD, a renowned mind and body expert from Harvard University, maintains that repetitive and rhythmic crafts like macramé can initiate what he refers to as the "relaxation response"—a calm feeling that's been scientifically proven to enhance health and reduce the risk of heart disease, anxiety, and depression. Engaging in macramé also allows you to get into what is commonly known as "being in the zone"—a state of mind that boosts satisfaction and happiness.

Sustainability

You will only need a few tools and supplies to create most macramé projects. Fortunately, materials used in the process tend to be naturally based, and there are always eco-friendly alternatives to be found. Cords and strings, for example, are mainly made from 100% cotton, and recycled options are widely available. Dowels, used as horizontal support on projects, can easily be replaced by fallen tree branches, which provide the perfect excuse to go for a walk in the park or around your backyard. There are also green options, if you feel like adding color to your creations. You could use natural coloring to dye your cords by using things like coffee, tea, beets, turmeric, berries, or leaves. Waste is not something you have to worry about with macramé. Pretty much everything can be reused. You could, for instance, use the cord trimmings or leftovers after your project to create little designs like tassels or key chains. They can also be used in decorative elements such as fluffy pom-poms.

Functionality & Versatility

There is an incredible number of basic knots used in macramé, and an almost endless number of ways to combine them with the purpose of creating patterns and projects. Mixing different patterns and using different materials will provide you with all the artistic freedom needed to achieve the specific style and look you desire. Don't be afraid to experiment and try new things. Aim for creations that are your own and that truly represent you! This will not only boost your creativity, it will also allow you to take your crafting skills to a new level. Macramé projects can be created for a variety of purposes. Decorative items seem to be some of the most popular ones. From purely decorative wall hangers and table runners to beautiful functional coasters, lampshades, and plant hangers, these are all great examples of how macramé is used to create different home decor elements. Fashion accessories and items of clothing is another area where macramé shows great diversity. Almost all kinds of jewelry (bracelets, rings, necklaces, earrings, etc.) can be made by tying knots. Bags are one of the prime examples of fashion products made using macramé techniques. With different materials and patterns used to create them, these bags are able to match any style and fashion trend.

Social Connections

Macramé is a hobby taken by many as a solo activity because it helps us relax and disconnect from the hectic world we live in. And to some extent, that's correct. However, macramé can also be a great way to create beautiful social connections. Giving gifts to people we love and care for is in our nature and helps us connect with each other. In this case, using your macramé projects as presents is an excellent option. Your handmade gifts will not only have your personal touch, they will also allow the recipient to remember you through them. Macramé is a fantastic activity to do as a family as well. There are plenty of simple projects that are perfect to do with kids. After a long, busy week, creating a little keychain or a colorful rainbow together can be a fun family activity that will make your bond even stronger. Social media nowadays offers another brilliant way to socialize through macramé. As it is a very trendy craft, a huge community exists online. Every major social media platform has people sharing their knowledge, experiences, and passion for this craft, which serves as a very effective way to meet fellow macramé lovers.

Income Opportunities

With persistence and love for the craft, of course, macramé is one of those hobbies that can turn into a viable entrepreneurial endeavor. It is not for everyone, and it will definitely not happen with overnight success. But once mastered, this skill can definitely generate some income. There are various ways you can profit with macramé. Most people start by selling their work online or at craft markets. You could also decide to open an online store to sell your art, as well as supplies and materials. Teaching macramé is another option (as an in-person class and/or through online courses). Finally, posting videos on social media platforms like YouTube or Instagram could be lucrative, too. If this is something you think you are interested in pursuing, make sure to choose a business venture that matches your financial ability. Some enterprises may require higher initial investments than others. As someone who has devoted all of her time and energy to macramé for a while now, my advice to you is to take it slow. This is just the beginning of a wonderful journey. Seeing macramé as a business at such an early stage may only spoil your overall experience. Make sure to first allow yourself to fall in love with this beautiful craft. And, most importantly, have fun with it!

Macramé FAQs

How Do I Set Up My Macramé Workspace?

Prior to starting your projects, it is very important to organize and set up your workspace. Keep all the tools and materials you need within reach, and arrange them in a way that allows you to move freely and comfortably. If you plan to work on projects sitting down, make sure you have an adequately padded chair to support your posture. Finally, check your lighting source to ensure it provides adequate light for working without straining your eyesight or compromising your attention to detail in projects.

Different setups are preferred for different projects. Depending on the type and size of the piece you plan to create, you may need to arrange your workspace horizontally (a flat surface to work on) or vertically (using a hanging setup like a clothes rack).

A **horizontal setup** is perfect for small projects, such as coasters, bracelets, and necklaces. Work atop a flat surface like a desk or dining table. In this kind of setup, a macramé board and pins are needed to ensure the cords are held in place while working on your piece.

Large projects like wall hangings, curtains, or dream catchers require a **vertical setup** workspace. Adjustable clothing racks are ideal for this. However, you can also work on the back of a tall chair, or even on a door. Be sure to use a setup that is high enough and allows you to work comfortably.

> **TIP:** Making a big macramé piece can easily take five to eight hours to complete. If you are planning to have a long macramé session, be sure to alternate between standing and sitting positions—be careful not to stay in one position too long. This will allow you to work on your piece for a longer period of time and prevent injuries. Long macramé sessions can put a strain on finger and hand joints as well. Be sure to stretch these extremities well before, during, and after your sessions. In addition, to avoid finger burns and blisters, consider using fabric gloves as protection. Take as many breaks as you need when completing time-consuming projects.

How Do I Keep My Knots Even?

Precise and tidy knots take some time to master. Practice knotting until your fingers get used to the movements. Over time, your fingers and hands will develop muscle memory based on the movements they repeat. To get consistently even knots, ensure there is always tension in the cords, and make sure your knots are perfectly aligned in the desired direction. Don't be afraid to untie and retie knots as many times as is necessary to perfect them. This is something every macramé artist goes through at the beginning.

How Do I Prevent Cords from Fraying?

One of the best ways to prevent fraying is by choosing a braided rope to knot with. It's a very sturdy type of cord that hardly ever frays while knotting. If you wish to use a different type of cord for your design, tie the ends of your ropes or strings with the Overhand Knot (see page 38). Taping or gluing the ends of the cords after cutting will achieve the same result.

How Do I Keep My Artwork Clean?

All macramé pieces will eventually get dirty. The best way to clean stains is to use a clean white cloth and a mix of cold water and mild dish soap to remove the dirt. Many eco-friendly detergents are available and safe to use on macramé materials. Always try the water-soap mix on the back of your piece first to ensure the detergent won't damage any fibers.

Decorative pieces tend to be static for long periods of time and get dusty after a while. To clean them off, you can use tape or a lint roller. Gently press the surface with the tape to remove any dust particles.

> **TIP:** To prevent damage, avoid using the washing machine to clean your artwork. This is especially important to remember if your pieces include decorative elements such as beads, charms, or tassels.

Can I Dye Macramé Cords at Home?

Nowadays, there are plenty of colored cords available in the market for textile artists. However, the effects you get when you dye cords yourself are incredibly beautiful and original. It is a fantastic way to put your own personal touch of creativity in your projects.

Cotton macramé cords are the best choice for dyeing. You can use synthetic dyes on cotton, but I encourage you to try dyeing your fibers with natural colorings. These include elements like coffee, tea, beetroot, or turmeric, amongst other options. Natural dyeing is not an easy process, but experimenting with it is fun and a great way to keep your projects eco-friendly.

Chapter 2

Tools & Materials

There are two main areas to consider before beginning to knot your macramé projects up: tools and materials. Investing in the right tools at the beginning will save you a great deal of hassle during the process, and choosing one material over another will accomplish different looks and feels within your projects. The more familiar you are with your materials, the easier it gets to add character and personal style to your creations. When I first started macramé, all I used was cord, a pair of scissors, and my hands. Then I learned about different tools, which made my journey so much easier. Using tools also elevated my knotting skills to new heights and gave me the confidence to immerse myself in more delicate and finer projects.

Tools

Scissors

A good pair of scissors can be your best ally or your worst enemy during a project. It is important to make sure your scissors are sharp. You will primarily use them to cut cords and trim fringes and tassels. Cutting with dull scissors will leave your cords frayed and your fringes and tassels uneven.

Comb/Brush

Use a comb/brush to get your fringes fluffy and soft after you finish your piece. I suggest using a pet brush with metal needle heads. The results are amazing, and your brushing time will be reduced significantly.

S–Hooks

These hooks will be your best friend when vertical knotting. S-hooks are very useful for hanging your projects while working on them, and you can never have too many of these hooks around.

Measurement Tape

When creating your artwork, you will need to take various measurements, particularly of the length of cords. Measurement tape makes this task very convenient, and fabric tape measures work like a charm.

Pins

Pins are used to keep your cords in place when you work on your pattern in a horizontal space. Sewing pins, push pins, or T-pins are perfect options to work with.

Glue

You will need to use glue on numerous occasions while working on and after completing your projects—for example, to secure the ends of knots, prevent fraying, or even to attach your piece to other items. I tend to use fabric glue in my macramé projects. If you're not able to find any near you, a glue gun will also do the job.

Tapestry Needles

These types of needles are needed if you are working on the net of a dream catcher or adding beads to your project. Tapestry needles are also helpful to tuck the ends of cords to the back to finalize your piece. Available in different sizes, these needles are generally made from metal or plastic. They have large eyes and dull points—the reason why they are referred to as ball-point needles most of the time. My tapestry needle of choice for macramé is one made of metal and with a large eye (USA size 13). It is strong enough to deal with hard cords, and the large eye is perfect to work with cords of medium thickness.

Clothes Rack

A clothes rack will help you work comfortably on projects that require a vertical setup. Some of these projects tend to have long fringes, and tying knots using long cords can be difficult and messy on a horizontal setting. Some of these pieces are big and take some time to complete. Get an adjustable clothes rack for easier maneuvering. It will allow you to alternate between working on your piece sitting down and standing up, which your back will benefit from.

Knotting Board

A knotting board is a board with slits in it to hold your cords while doing macramé. The use of a knotting board makes it easier to create knots because it holds the cords for you. Knotting boards are also useful to keep track of your measurements, and you can use pins to securely attach your work to the board. Knotting boards can be especially helpful when working with smaller pieces and projects that call for a horizontal workspace (coasters, bracelets, key chains, feathers, etc.). You can also make them yourself by using materials such as foam, cork, or, my personal favorite, rattan.

Materials

Cord

The variety of cords available for tying knots is great. There are natural-based cords such as cotton, hem, jute, yarn, and raffia, as well as synthetic options like nylon, paracord, acrylic, and polypropylene, among others. The list is long, but one type of cord seems to stand out above all others: cotton. Most macramé artists choose to work with it because it is an eco-friendly, widely available, and easy-to-handle alternative. Cotton is simply a great cord choice to use when getting started with macramé.

Choosing the right cord for your project is very important. Things to consider: whether you want a more natural or finer look, if your project will be a purely decorative piece or something to be used regularly, and also where you plan to place your work—whether it will be indoors or outdoors (see page 32 for more information about cords).

Dowels

For most wall hangings, you will need a dowel/stick to support your macramé piece horizontally. Dowels can come from wood, bamboo, or copper, and each adds a different look to your work. Remember that, especially for wall hanging projects, fallen branches can be excellent options.

Rings

Rings come in many sizes and are commonly made from wood, metal, or plastic. If you are planning to use a ring to hang something, consider the item's weight and choose your ring size and material accordingly. Wooden rings, for example, are a great way to provide your plant hangers with a natural look. Use smaller rings in decorative pieces like holiday ornaments or table mats.

Beads, Charms, & Crystals

Adornments are a fantastic way to add creativity and texture to your designs. Most macramé pieces go well with decorative elements made of wood and metal. In addition, stone and crystal are great choices if you are aiming for a more spiritual style.

Hoops

Made from metal and wood, hoops are the core of some of the most popular macramé projects (dream catchers, wall hangings, etc.). In contrast with the '70s round options, hoops nowadays come in a variety of fun and versatile shapes—moons, hearts, and stars, among others. They are also available in geometrical forms, with triangles, squares, and hexagons being the most popular. Personally, I find round-shaped hoops the easiest to use in terms of design. I recommend transitioning to the rest of the shapes once you are confident with your macramé skills and feel like challenging yourself.

Lobster Clasps

These are essential to create a very popular and easy-to-make macramé project: a keychain. Lobster clasps are mainly made from metal and come in many sizes and styles. They are widely used in bag straps as well.

Tools & Materials

Tools & Materials FAQs

Learning a new skill is inevitably accompanied by questions. This is highlighted even more if, in macramé, equipment is involved in the process. Here are some of the questions I have been asked the most frequently by macramé beginners regarding tools and materials.

What Tools and Materials Do I Need to Get Started with Macramé?

Easy! To get started with macramé, you will need the essentials: a good pair of scissors, a brush, some S-hooks, a tape measure, and some basic cords. Your nearest local craft store will have all you need to start practicing your knots and completing small projects.

After practicing your knotting skills and building up your confidence, I would consider getting the rest of the items shared in the tools list (see the "Tools" section on page 25). These more advanced tools will allow you to get into complex designs and ease your macramé sessions, saving time and improving the look of your final pieces.

Where Can I Shop to Purchase My Tools and Materials?

If you get hooked and plan on getting more involved in macramé, Etsy and Amazon are great options for purchasing affordable and quality tools and materials. As your macramé skills develop, you will likely want to scale up the size of your projects and immerse yourself in a variety of different ones. In that case, you will need to get your hands on a lot of good-quality cords. Plenty of options are available on those two platforms. Alternatively, there are lots of fiber artists who sell a wide selection of macramé supplies online as well. Some of my favorites are Createaholic (Sweden), The Lark's Head Shop (USA), and Mary Maker Studio (Australia). Make sure to check them out!

> **TIP:** To have the smallest environmental impact, opt for cords made of 100% recycled threads. If this is something you are interested in, check Hello Bobbiny, Unfettered Supply, or Ganxxet online to get your eco-friendly supplies. These cords would make sure you end up with an environmentally friendly piece that is as affordable as one made with regular, nonrecycled threads.

What's the Difference between Macramé String, Rope, and Cord?

Macramé makers have a wide variety of fibers available to knot with, but cotton is by far the most popular of them all. Cotton naturally comes in a creamy white color. However, it is available in many different colors, as it is a clean and hypo-allergenic fiber that is easy to dye. This fiber is favored over others because it balances thickness and softness very well. It is the ideal choice for beginners, as its minimal stretch will hold the structure of the knot perfectly.

While browsing the internet looking for cotton fibers, you will quickly realize that there are many terms used to describe them. The three main terms are string, rope, and cord. Though confusing due to their similarities, defining these terms is easier than you think. Learning their differences will not only allow you to choose fibers more accurately, but it will also prevent any disappointments after an online purchase.

String is a single strand of twisted fibers. Basically, it is lots of individual threads of cotton coiled together. Strings are very soft to the touch and can be brushed easily to create beautiful fluffy fringes.

Rope consists of individual strands of fiber twisted and grouped together. The most common ropes used in macramé are the 3-strand and 2-strand ropes (sometimes called 3-ply and 2-ply, respectively). Ropes tend to be stronger than strings, but are also more difficult to brush. Nevertheless, by brushing it, you will end up with a fun wavy fringe that is great for adding texture to your work.

Braided/Stash Rope is a special type of rope used for projects that require holding heavy weight. Its strands are tightly twisted, which makes them very difficult to unravel. It is a sturdy rope that keeps knots in shape. I do not recommend using this type of rope if you intend to brush it at some point. On the other hand, it works if you want the ends of your fringes to be clean and without any fraying.

Cord is a macramé term used to describe all types of threads in a general sense. In this book, for example, I will refer to strings, ropes, and other fibers as cords, when I have already specified the type of thread we are using in advance.

Tools & Materials

What Other Materials Can I Use?

Hemp and **jute** are fibers that work very well for projects aimed to have a more rustic look. High-quality organic fibers, hemp and jute can be a bit more challenging to work with. Both are reliable options if you want your projects to have character and last for a long time.

Yarn is not a material that people usually relate to macramé. However, yarn is ideal to add softness and fluffiness to decorative elements such as tassels. Yarn comes in many thicknesses—medium, bulky, and super bulky are most common. Be aware that yarn tends to compress itself, causing knots to end up being smaller than you expect. It is not a strong material, so disregard it for projects that are intended to support weight. An interesting type of yarn is T-shirt yarn. This peculiar type of fiber is mainly used in macramé clothing projects, as it is light and stretches with ease.

Synthetic rope is one of the best materials available for pieces intended to be outdoors. Synthetic rope will put up a fight no matter what mother nature throws at it. It is perfect to use when creating projects like hammocks, swings, parasol umbrellas, and plant hangers. With cords available in sizes as small as 0.5 mm thick, it is a very popular micro-macramé material used to create jewelry and accessories.

How Do I Choose the Right Materials for My Project?

For every project, you will need to consider the type of materials needed before beginning to knot your macramé. Choosing one cord over another will change the overall look and feel of your final piece. Using thick rope, for example, means bigger knots. Bigger knots often lead to large-scale, powerful artwork. If, on the other hand, you want a more elegant and delicate look, thinner cords are the way to go.

For micro-macramé and small pieces, opt for cords no thicker than 2 mm. Synthetic rope is a fantastic choice if you want to create jewelry-related projects and practice your fine knotting skills. Some small projects include key chains, bookmarks, and decorative ornaments.

Macramé: The Power of Knots

For medium-size macramé projects, you can use the most common cord size available, which is 3 mm to 5 mm in thickness. They are my go-to cords if I am making wall hangings, coasters, bags, table mats, or plant hangers.

For considerably sized projects, go for cords no thinner than 5 mm. Articles like umbrellas, swings, chairs, large wall hangings, or hammocks benefit greatly from the strength bigger knots bring to the structure. It also takes less time to finish a project when you use a thicker cord.

How Much Cord Will I Need?

One of the most frustrating situations you can encounter in macramé is running out of cord just when you are about to finish your project. I have personally had to deal with this issue a couple of times, and it wasn't pretty. To avoid putting yourself through this ordeal, be sure to follow the instructions and recommendations.

The amount of cord you need for a project will depend on the size of the piece, the type of knot, and the way in which you will arrange those knots. The general rule is to always cut four times the length of the finished piece. Let's say you are planning to knot a 1–m (3.3–ft) table runner. In this case, you will need to cut your cords 4 m (13.1 ft) long. Keep in mind that, for most projects, you are going to need to fold your cords in half and mount them to a dowel or anchor cord (see Lark's Head Knot/Reverse Lark's Head Knot on page 41). That being the case, cords will need to be cut at a minimum of 8 times the length of the final piece.

Based on my personal experience, I recommend cutting your cords 5–6 times the length of the final piece (10–12 times if your project is mounted). It is better to have too much cord than to end up with too little. Thanks to this rule, I have been able to add gorgeous fringes to some of my pieces that were not previously planned. Excess cord, as we mentioned before, can always be trimmed and reused.

TIP: Be sure to keep a record of the cord sizes and lengths you use for each project. It will be very helpful information that you can use as reference in your future designs.

CHAPTER 3

Macramé Basic Knots

This section includes 27 knots I consider essential to any macramé project you choose to create. You could start by learning and practicing all these knots one by one. However, that could end up being a bit tedious. Instead, I recommend first taking a tour through all the basic knots and then moving to the section on patterns (see page 85). From there, choose a pattern you are interested in creating, and then move back to learn the specific knots required to complete it. This will ease the learning process while allowing you to get familiar with different patterns at the same time.

Before we get into knotting, here are some terms and definitions you will encounter in all sections:

Working cord(s): Cord(s) used to tie your knots.
Filler cord(s): Cord(s) to which knots are tied.
Row: A horizontal line of knots.
Sinnet: A vertical line pattern or column of knots of a single type.
Chain: A vertical line pattern or column of knots of multiple types.

Overhand Knot

The **overhand knot** is a simple knot used to secure the ends of cords. Its primary use is to help prevent the fraying of the cord while knotting. It is also useful to decorate and add texture to your piece. You can tie this knot with one cord or with multiple cords at the same time.

Macramé Basic Knots

Step 1: Grab the cord below the point where you want your knot to be placed. Bring it up and fold it to create a circular loop.

Step 2: Take the same end of the cord and pass it back to front through the loop.

Step 3: Pull the end of the cord to tighten the knot.

Bundling Technique

For large-scale macramé pieces such as wall hangings, curtains, or backdrops, you will deal with lots of long cords at the same time. Trying to keep all the cords untangled can be challenging. To avoid getting frustrated, follow this **bundling technique**. It is one of the best methods for bundling your cords to keep them organized while working on your pieces.

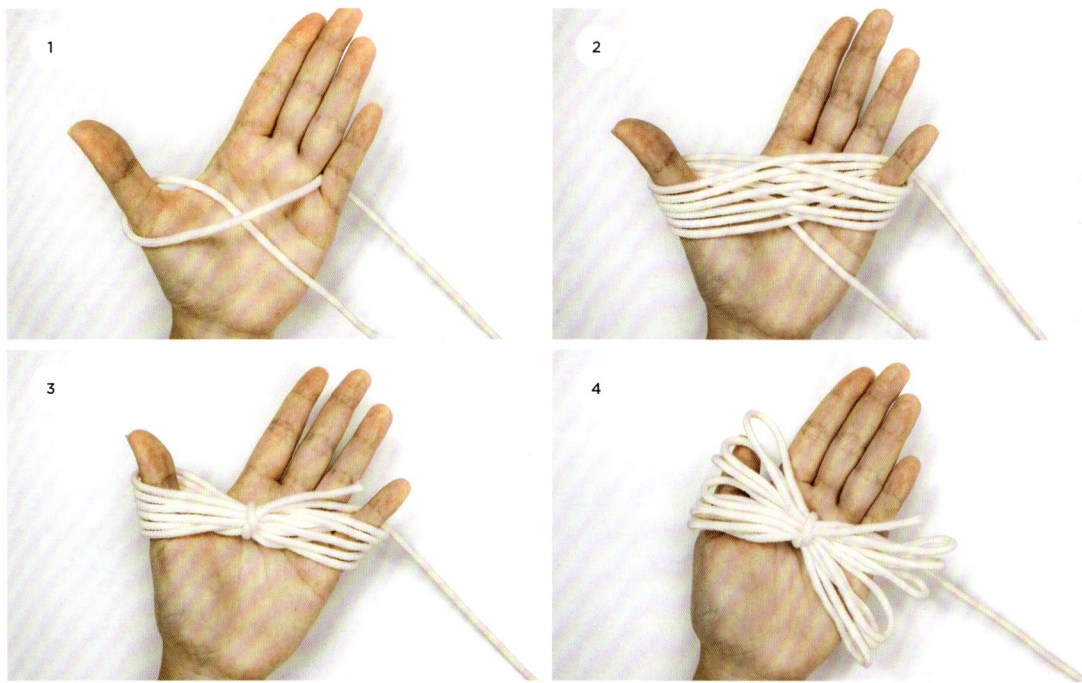

Step 1: Take the end of the cord and wrap it around your fingers as shown in the picture.

Step 2: Wrap the cord from finger to finger, creating an eight shape. Make sure the cords remain aligned at all times.

Step 3: To finish, take the end of the cord and use it to wrap and tie the bundle in the middle with an overhand knot. If you find it easier, use a rubber band to secure the bundle.

Step 4: Repeat this technique with every cord of the piece.

Arranging long cords with this technique will keep them organized and untangled. Working with them is very easy, too. Just pull the cord out of the bundle to allow more cord to be released.

Lark's Head Knot

The **lark's head knot (LHK)**, also referred to as the **cow hitch knot**, is what you use to mount the cords to your support at the beginning of most macramé projects. These knots can be tied to horizontal (dowel, branch, ring, or anchor cord) or vertical (filler cords) supports.

Horizontal Lark's Head Knots

Lark's Head Knot (LHK)

You will see the lark's head knot (LHK) often used in macramé projects with horizontal supports, such as wall hangings and plant hangers. After you mount the cord to the support, the bump of the knot will be visible at the front of the design (front-facing technique).

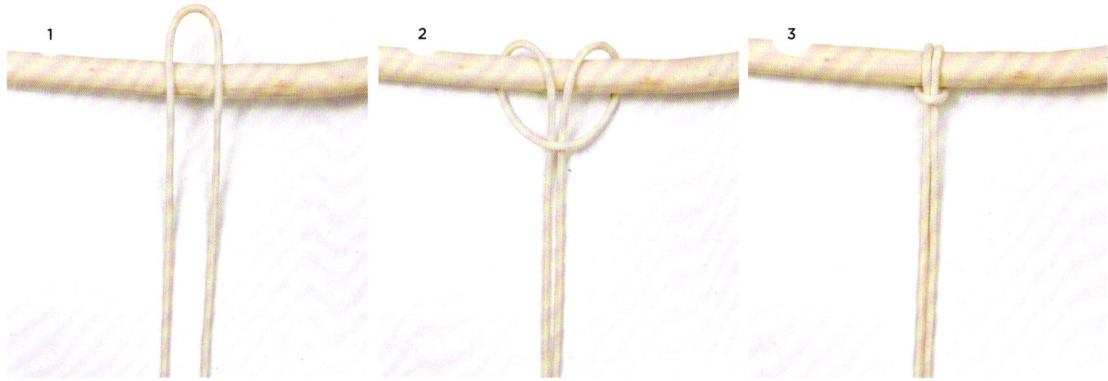

Step 1: Fold the cord in half and bring the loop in front of the horizontal support.

Step 2: Bring the loop behind the support and pass the ends of the cord through the loop.

Step 3: Pull down both ends of the cord to tighten the knot. Make sure the ends are even during the process.

Reverse Lark's Head Knot (RLHK)

The **reverse lark's head knot** (RLHK) is used in the same way as the LHK. The only difference is that, in this type of knot, the bump is hidden at the back of the design and not visible to people admiring the piece. To tie this knot, you will use the reverse-facing technique.

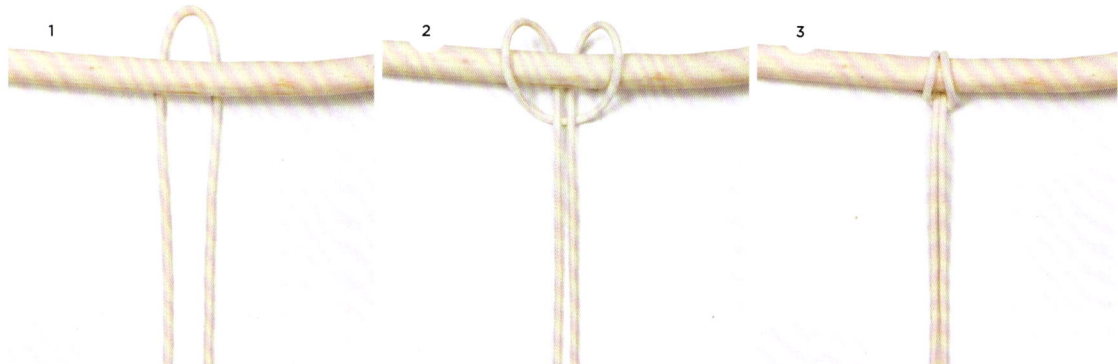

Step 1: Fold the cord in half and bring the loop behind the horizontal support.

Step 2: Bring the loop in front of the support and pass the ends of the cord through the loop.

Step 3: Pull down both ends of the cord to tighten the knot. Make sure the ends are even during the process.

Vertical Lark's Head Knots

Right-facing Vertical Lark's Head Knot (RFVLHK)

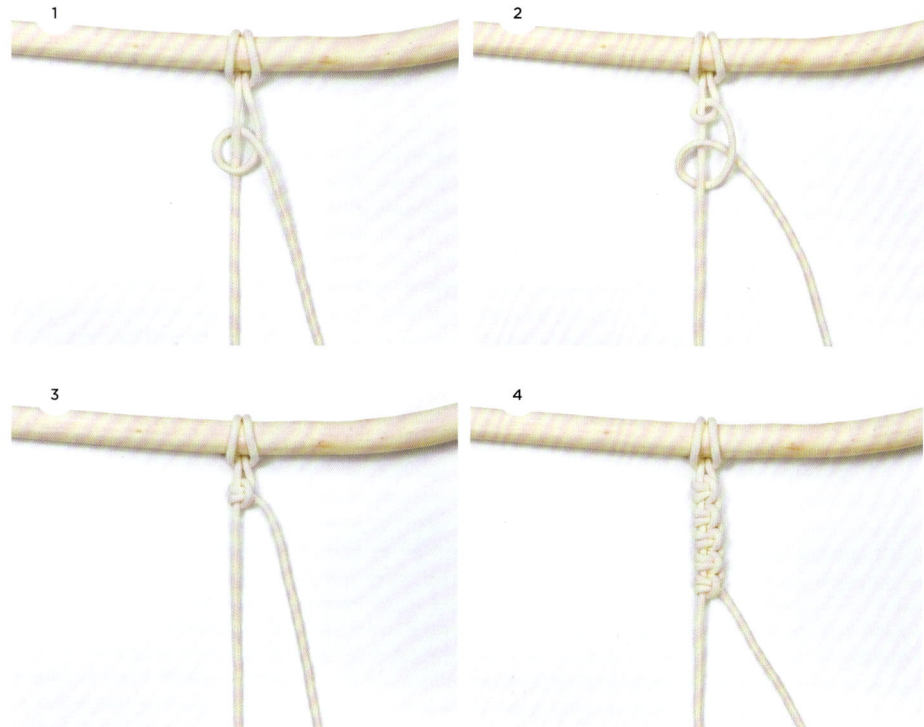

Step 1: Use the cord on the right as your working cord. Bring it over and wrap it around the filler cord on the left. Then, pass the working cord through the loop from back to front.

Step 2: Wrap the working cord around the filler cord again. This time, bring the working cord behind and wrap it around the filler cord. Then pass the working cord through the loop from front to back.

Step 3: Hold the filler cord straight and pull the working cord to tighten the two loops together.

Step 4: Repeat these steps until your chain of knots reaches the desired length. The **right-facing vertical lark's head knot** (RFVLHK) has visible bumps facing right.

Macramé Basic Knots

Left-facing Vertical Lark's Head Knot (LFVLHK)

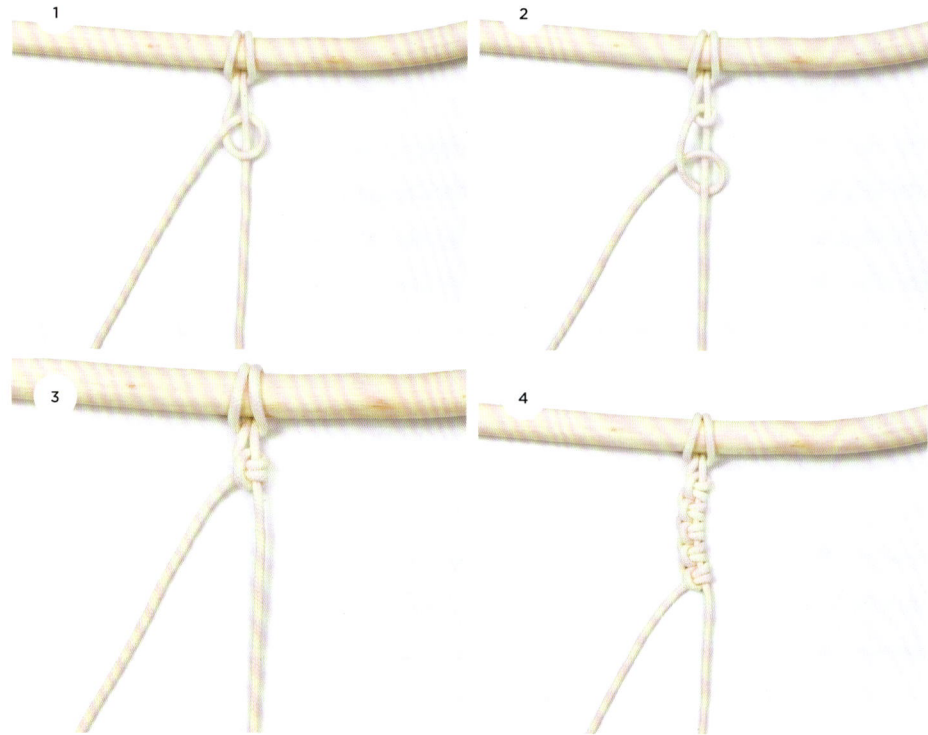

Step 1: Use the cord on the left as your working cord. Bring it over and wrap it around the filler cord on the right. Then, pass the working cord through the loop from back to front.

Step 2: Wrap the working cord around the filler cord again. This time, bring the working cord behind and wrap it around the filler cord. Then, pass the working cord through the loop from front to back.

Step 3: Hold the filler cord straight and pull the working cord to tighten the two loops together.

Step 4: Repeat these steps until your chain of knots reaches the desired length. The **left-facing vertical lark's head knot** (LFVLHK) has visible bumps facing left.

Alternating Vertical Lark's Head Knot

The **alternating vertical lark's head knot** uses a minimum of three cords: two outer working cords, and at least one inner cord(s). You can either use the right-facing or left-facing techniques to start this knot. For this example, I'll be using four cords (two working cords and two filler cords), and beginning with the left-facing lark's head knot (LFVLHK), followed by a right-facing lark's head knot (RFVLHK).

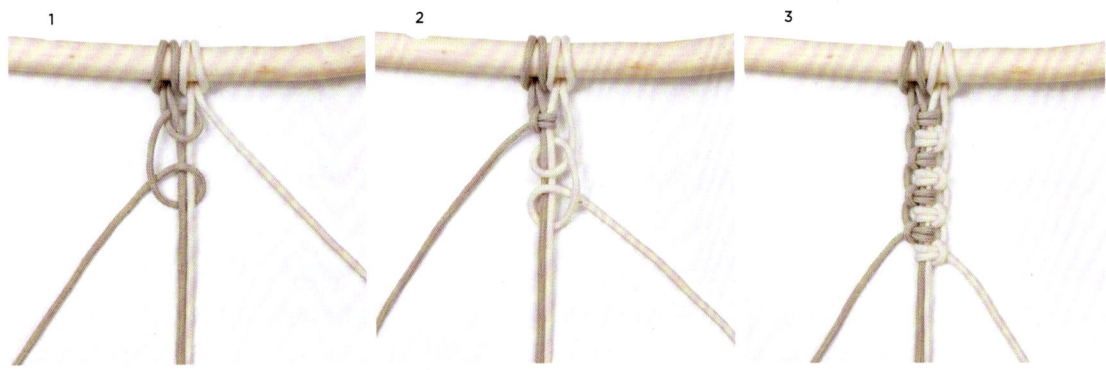

Step 1: Use the outer working cord on the left (gray) to tie an LFVLHK over both inner filler cords (gray and white).

Step 2: Now, underneath the first knot, use the outer working cord on the right (white) to tie an RFVLHK knot over the two inner filler cords.

Step 3: Continue the sinnet by repeating these steps as many times as needed. Keep the LFVLHK and RFVLHK close to each other in line. Make sure the linking pieces of cord between the same knots are even and straight.

Half Square Knot and Square Knot (SK)

The **square knot** (SK) is the most-used knot in macramé. Square knots are basically two alternating **half square knots** placed one under the other in a row. You can tie them facing left or right. Four cords are used to create the square knot (SK): two outer working cords, and two inner filler cords that remain static during the process.

For an outstanding-looking pattern or design, it is important to ensure all knots are consistent. To do so, the tension of the cord and arrangement of the knots are essential. As you will learn in this section of the book, the square knot (SK) is the foundation of many decorative knots.

Left-facing Square Knot (LFSK)

To create a **left-facing square knot** (LFSK), alternate a left-facing half square knot (LFHSK) with a right-facing half square knot (RFHSK) underneath. The bump in the left-facing square knot (LFSK) is noticeable on the left side (hence its name).

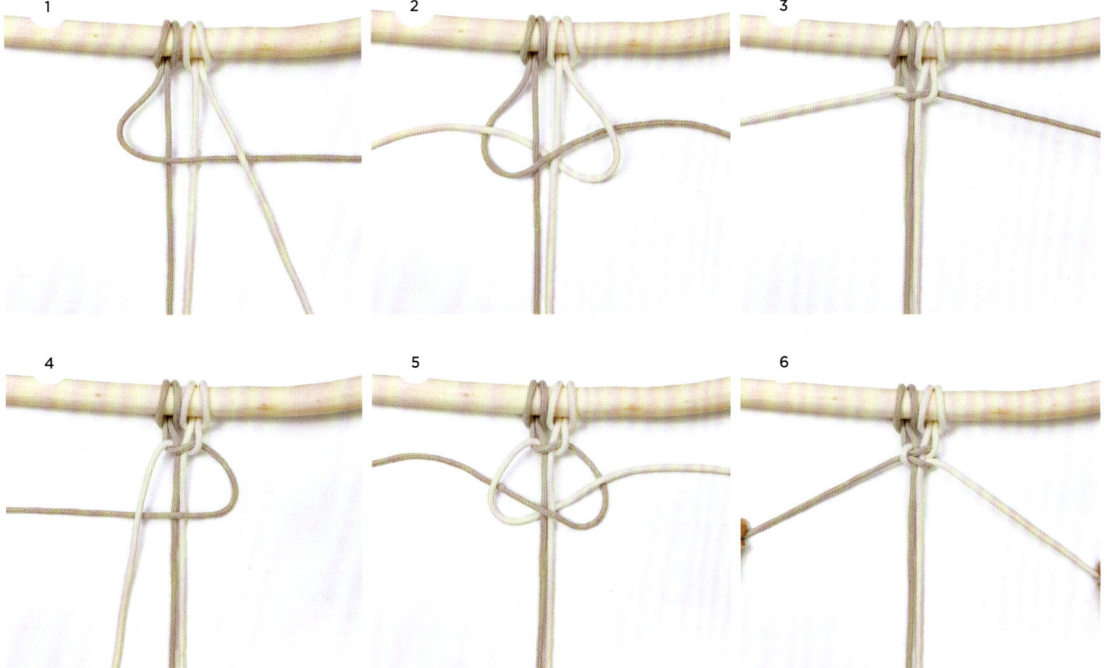

Step 1: Grab the left working cord (gray) and move it to the right, over both filler cords (gray and white) and under the working cord on the right (white).

Step 2: Bring the right working cord (white) toward the left, by passing it under both filler cords and over the working cord on the left (gray).

Step 3: While keeping the filler cords (inner white and gray cords) tense, proceed to pull both working cords. This is called a left-facing half square knot (LFHSK). Now we move on to the right-facing half square knot (RFHSK).

Step 4: The working cords have swapped places. Now, grab the right working cord (gray) and move it toward the left, passing it over both filler cords and under the working cord on the left (white).

Step 5: Bring the working cord on the left (white) under the filler cords and over the working cord on the left (gray).

Step 6: Keep both filler cords straight while pulling both working cords to tighten the knot. There you have it! This step completes the left-facing square knot (LFSK).

Right-facing Square Knot (RFSK)

Good news! If you know how to do a left-facing square knot (LFSK), you already know how to do a **right-facing half square knot** (RFSK). To create this knot, you will need to tie a right-facing half square knot first (steps 4–6 in the LFSK), followed by a left-facing half square knot (steps 1–3 in the LFSK). Notice how, this time, the bump is placed on the right.

Square Knot Sinnet (SKS)

You can start the **square knot sinnet** (SKS) either with a left–facing square knot (LFSK) or right–facing square knot (RFSK). In this example, I will begin by tying a left–facing square knot (LFSK).

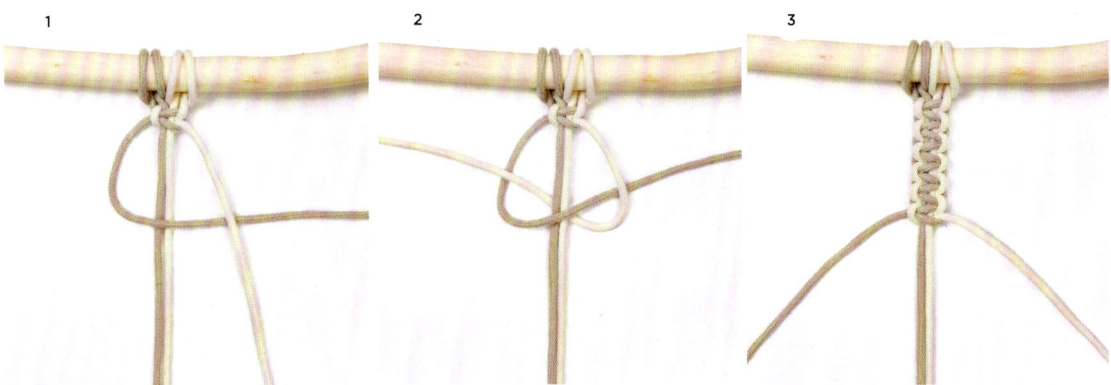

1 2 3

Step 1: Create a LFSK.

Step 2: Continue by tying another LFSK underneath the previous one. The SKS is created by tying the same SK over and over again.

Step 3: To finish this SKS, repeat LFSK knots until you reach the desired length. Remember to pull both working cords while holding the filler cords straight to create a beautiful and neat sinnet.

TIP: If you lose count, you can calculate the number of square knots you've made on the square knot sinnet (SKS) by counting the bumps created on the side you began knotting with. For example, if you start your square knot sinnet (SKS) with a left–facing square knot (LFSK), count the number of bumps on the left side of the sinnet. The number you come up with is the number of square knots (SKs) you have tied so far.

Macramé Basic Knots

Alternating Square Knot (ASK)

The **alternating square knot** (ASK) is very helpful if you want to practice knotting patterns. For this type of knot, you will need more than four cords. Most designs available use an even number of cords (six, eight, ten, etc.) to alternate with. This is because strings and ropes tend to be folded in half and mounted to horizontal supports. However, you could use an odd number of cords to create the alternating square knot (ASK). In this example, I will use four pairs of cords, eight cords total, to demonstrate.

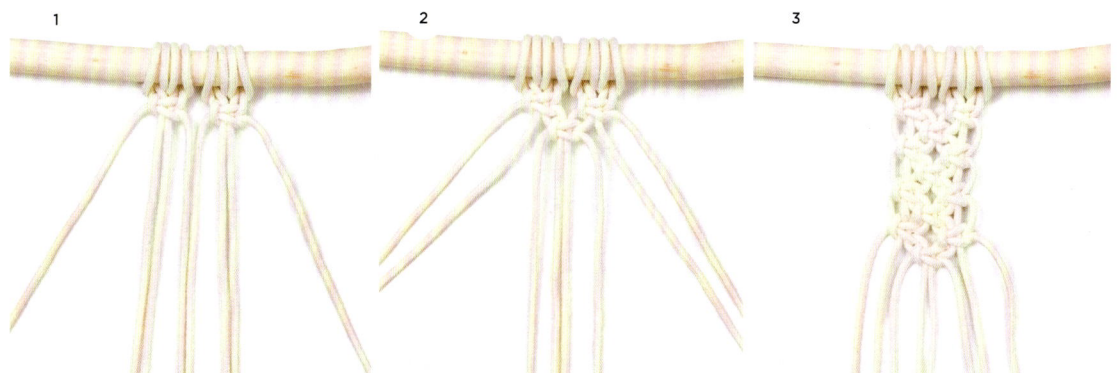

Step 1: Use the first two pairs of cords to create an SK. Then, use the other two pairs of cords to do the same. You will end up with a row formed by two SKs.

Step 2: For the second row, use the second and third pair of cords to create a single SK. The first and last pairs of cords, as you can see, remain unknotted.

Step 3: Repeat steps 1 and 2 as many times as you please, until you reach the desired length for your design.

Switch Knot (SWK)

The **switch knot (SWK)** is mainly used for decorative purposes. It is very common to see this knot in plant hangers. The switch knot (SWK) uses two square knots (SKs) with a twist. Quite literally!

Macramé Basic Knots

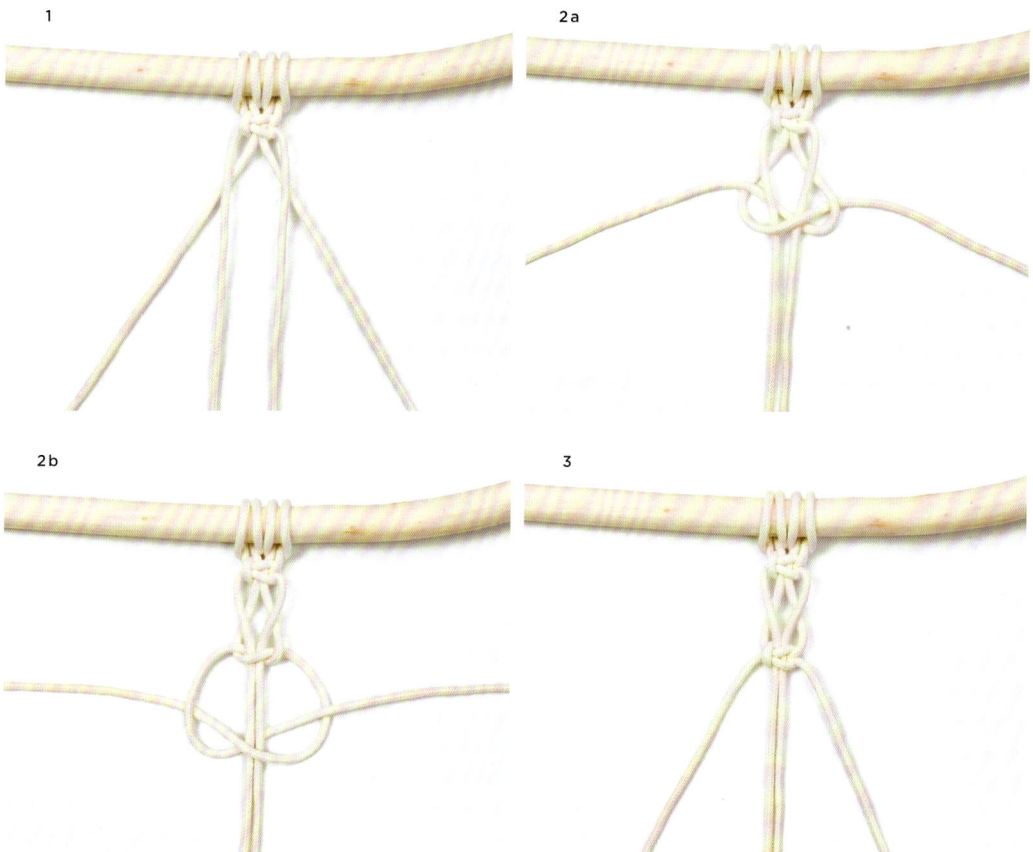

Step 1: To create the switch knot (SWK), begin by tying an SK. Then, grab the working cords (outer cords), and place them over the filler cords (inner cords). As you can see in the picture, we have "switched" the working cords for our filler cords. Now the filler cords become the working cords of the next SK.

Step 2: Before tying the next SK, leave a big gap (approximately 3–5 cm, 1.2–2 in). The gap between each knot and the next will depend on your design. Make sure the distance between your knots is consistent to achieve a neat-looking pattern.

Step 3: Continue repeating these steps until you've reached the desired length. Remember to "switch" working cords and filler cords after completing each SK.

Half Hitch Spiral

The **half hitch spiral** is the easiest way to add spiral elements to your projects. It is made by wrapping one working cord to one or several filler cords repeatedly. Depending on your design, the spiral could face left or right. This technique is commonly used in wall hanging or bracelet projects. The example in this book will use one working cord and one filler cord.

Left–facing Half Hitch (LFHH)

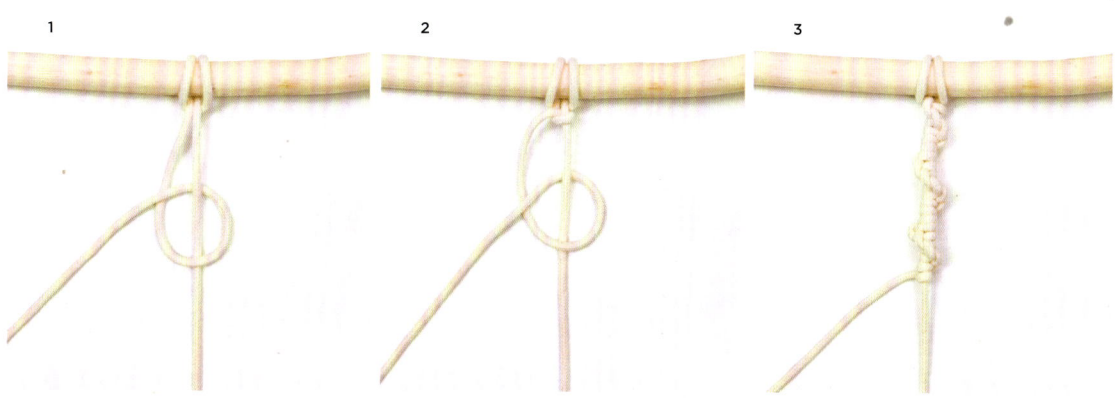

Step 1: Use the cord on the left as your working cord. Bring it over and wrap the filler cord on the right with it. Then, pass the working cord through the loop from back to front.

Step 2: While holding the filler cord straight, pull the working cord down to tighten the first **left–facing half hitch** (LFHH).

Step 3: Repeat the left–facing half hitch (LFHH) several times to create a spiral that twists from left to right. To get a tidy spiral, push the knots upward as you progress to keep them close and tied together.

Right-facing Half Hitch (RFHH)

To create a **right-facing half hitch** (RFHH), we use the same technique as in the left-facing half hitch (LFHH)—only, this time, we use the cord on the right as the working cord and the one on the left as the filler cord. The spiral created with the right-facing half hitch (RFHH) will twist from right to left.

Alternating Half Hitch (AHH)

To create an **alternating half hitch** (AHH), you begin by using a left-facing half hitch (LFHH) or right-facing half hitch (RFHH). The alternating half hitch (AHH), as its name indicates, alternates between these two techniques. In the example given below, the left-facing half hitch (LFHH) is used first, followed by the right-facing half hitch (RFHH).

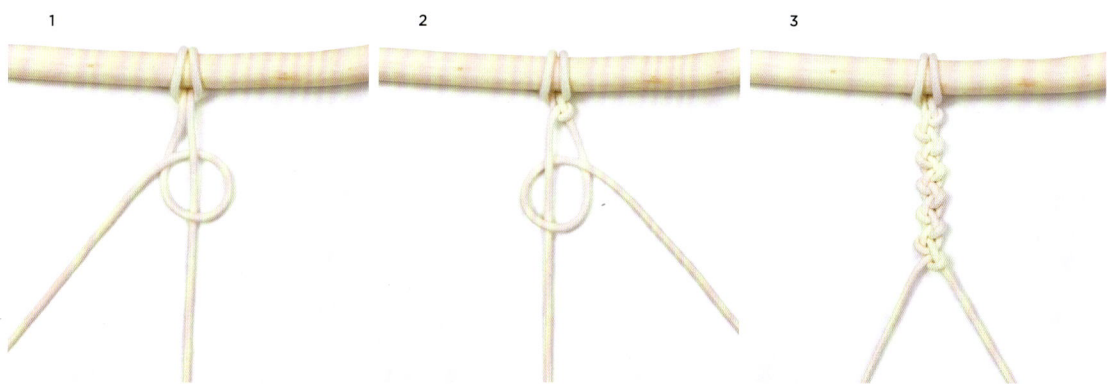

Step 1: Use the left cord as the working cord, tying an LFHH around the filler cord on the right.

Step 2: Now switch cords and tie an RFHH. Use the cord on the right as the working cord and the left one as your filler cord.

Step 3: Repeat the previous steps until you reach the desired chain length.

Spiral Knot

A **spiral knot** is made by tying the half square knot of your choice, left or right, repeatedly. The direction of the spiral will be determined by whether you start with a left-facing half square knot (LFHSK: steps 1–3 of the LFSK on page 48) or a right-facing half square knot (RFHSK: steps 4–6 of the LFSK).

Left–twist Spiral Knot (LSPK)

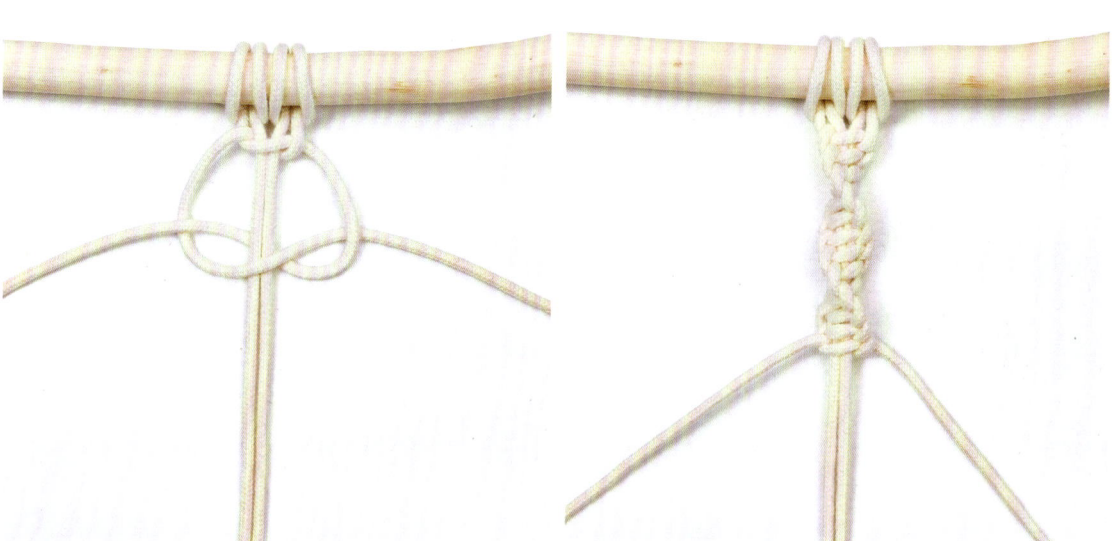

Step 1: Begin the **left–twist spiral knot** (LSPK) by making an LFHSK.

Step 2: Continue making several LFHSKs to form a spiral shape.

Right–twist Spiral Knot (RSPK)

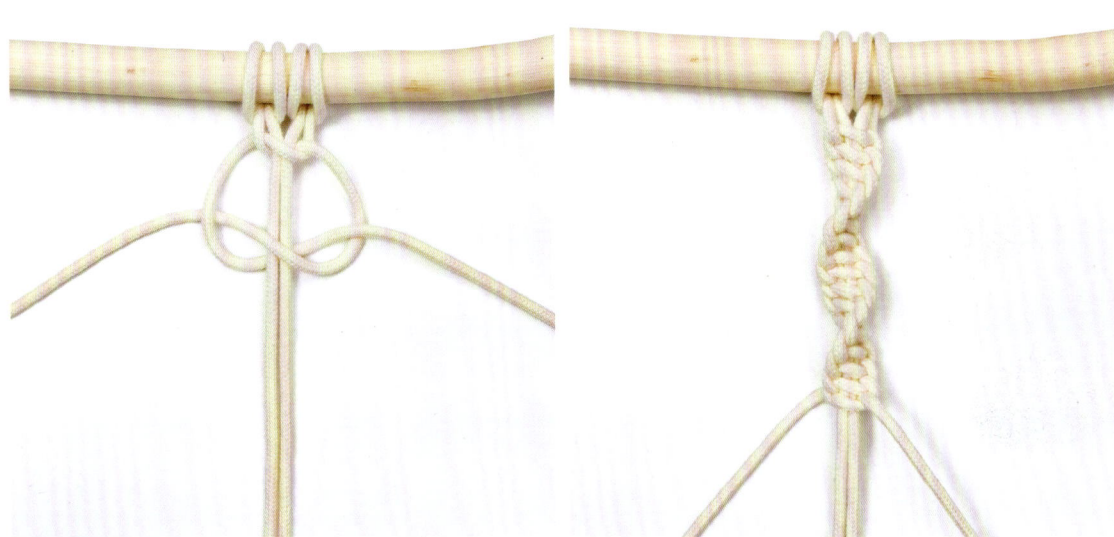

1

2

Step 1: Begin the **right-twist spiral knot** (RSPK) by making an RFHSK.

Step 2: Continue making several RFHSKs to form a spiral shape.

In the event that you drop your macramé piece, and now you don't know which side you were working on, you'll just need to continue knotting as you started at the beginning of the sequence.

TIP 1: Creating this knot can get confusing. The whole piece revolves, and all the cords move along with it. This means that the left and right working cords will switch positions naturally from time to time. The trick with the spiral knot is to always continue tying the knots as you began the sequence.

TIP 2: The tighter your knots, the tighter your spiral will be.

Double Half Hitch

Apart from square knot, the **double half hitch** (also known as the **clove hitch**) is another of the most used knots in macramé projects. This knot is created with the purpose of adding line patterns to your designs. These lines can be tied diagonally, horizontally, and less often, vertically. The double half hitch is, as its name implies, two half hitches (see page 54) tied one after the other. In this knot, the first cord works as the filler cord and the rest as working cords. The way in which you place the filler cord will determine the direction of the line pattern the double half hitches create.

As a beginner macramé maker, I personally struggled with this knot. And I was not alone, as many other artists I spoke to also found this knot tricky and confusing to make. That's why I have spared no detail in my explanation—so you are able to quickly and easily master this knot and realize that in reality, it is a piece of cake!

Diagonal Double Half Hitch (DDHH)–Left–to–right

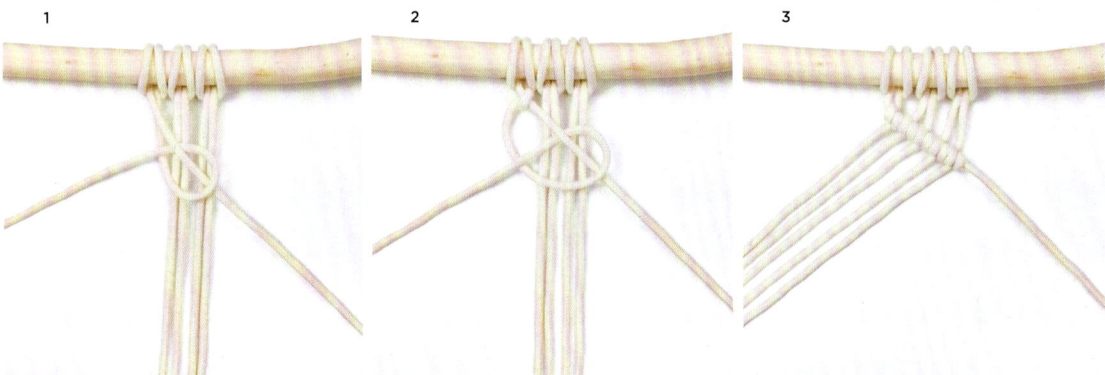

Step 1: Using the furthest cord to the left as your filler cord, place it down diagonally toward the right over the rest of the cords (working cords). Bring the first working cord (first cord to the right of the filler cord) up and wrap the filler cord with it. Then, pass the working cord front to back through the loop. Pull the working cord while holding the filler cord to tighten the first half hitch.

Step 2: To complete the second half hitch of your DDHH, take the same working cord, now placed to the left of the knot, and bring it up and over the filler cord. Use the working cord to wrap the filler cord once again, passing it through the loop front to back. Now, pull the working cord while holding the filler cord to tighten the second half hitch. Check that the half hitches are next to each other and both are evenly tightened. Congrats! You have completed your first DDHH.

Step 3: To create a diagonal line pattern moving down from left to right, repeat steps 1 and 2 with the rest of the working cords. Use the working cords one by one from left to right to knot DDHHs. Remember, your filler cord doesn't change during the process.

> **TIP:** Keep your filler cord slightly tense and without any bends during the whole process to create perfectly straight and even lines in your designs.

Diagonal Double Half Hitch (DDHH)–Right–to–left

If you are already familiar with the **diagonal double half hitch** (DDHH)–**left–to–right**, tying this knot is as easy as mirroring the previously explained steps in the opposite direction. This time, begin the process on the right, and tie your knots in reverse toward the left. If, on the other hand, this is the first time you have encountered the diagonal double half hitch (DDHH), please be sure to follow the steps explained in this section.

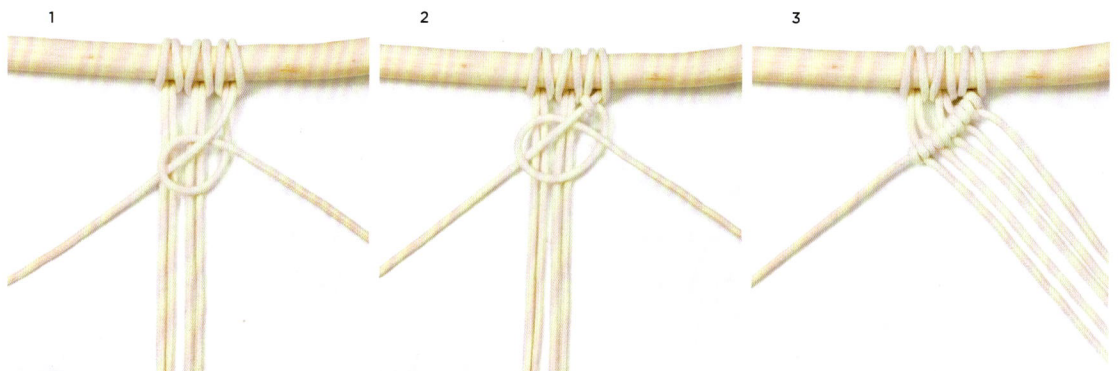

Step 1: Using the furthest cord to the right as your filler cord, place it down diagonally toward the left over the rest of the cords (working cords). Bring the first working cord (first cord to the left of the filler cord) up and wrap the filler cord with it. Then, pass the working cord front to back through the loop. Pull the working cord while holding the filler cord to tighten the first half hitch.

Step 2: To complete the second half hitch of your DDHH, take the same working cord, now placed to the right of the knot, and bring it up and over the filler cord. Use the working cord to wrap the filler cord once again, passing it through the loop front to back. Now, pull the working cord while holding the filler cord to tighten the second half hitch. Check that the half hitches are next to each other and evenly tightened.

Step 3: To create a diagonal line pattern moving down from right to left, repeat steps 1 and 2 with the rest of the working cords. Use the working cords one by one from right–to–left to knot the DDHHs. Remember, your filler cord doesn't change during the process.

Macramé: The Power of Knots

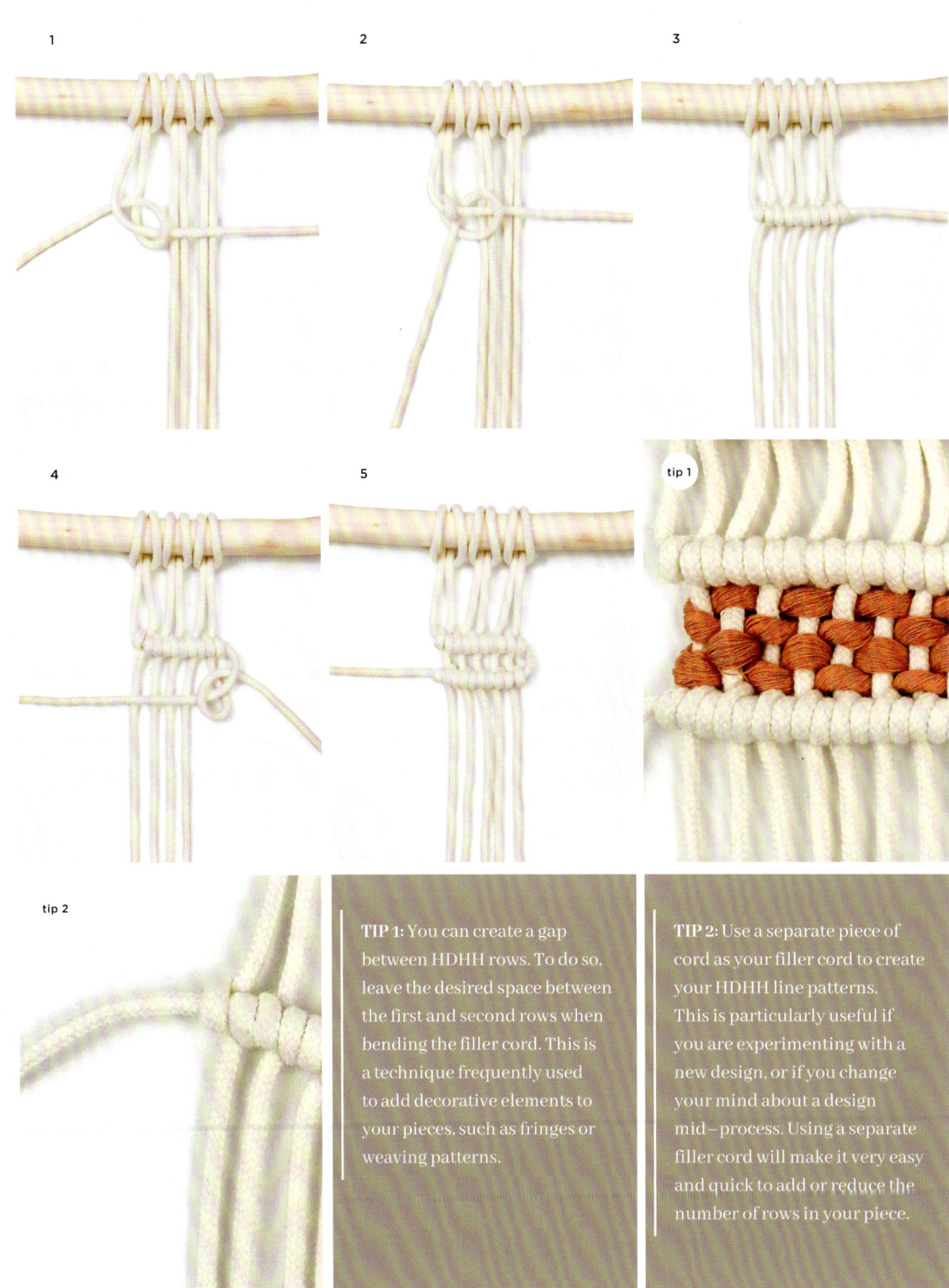

TIP 1: You can create a gap between HDHH rows. To do so, leave the desired space between the first and second rows when bending the filler cord. This is a technique frequently used to add decorative elements to your pieces, such as fringes or weaving patterns.

TIP 2: Use a separate piece of cord as your filler cord to create your HDHH line patterns. This is particularly useful if you are experimenting with a new design, or if you change your mind about a design mid–process. Using a separate filler cord will make it very easy and quick to add or reduce the number of rows in your piece.

Horizontal Double Half Hitch (HDHH)

Tying **horizontal double half hitches** (HDHHs) creates a horizontal line pattern in your design. The technique used to create this knot is the same as the technique used for diagonal double half hitches (DDHHs), only this time the filler cord is placed horizontally over the working cords. The filler cord in this knot, as it happens in the diagonal double half hitch (DDHH), can go from left to right or vice versa. In the example provided to demonstrate the horizontal double half hitch (HDHH), I'm going to place the filler cord first toward the right to explain a left–right pattern. Then, I will bend the same filler cord over to the left in order to explain a right–left pattern.

Step 1: To begin the HDHH, use the furthest cord to the left as your filler cord and place it horizontally toward the right over all the other cords (working cords). Bring the first working cord (first cord to the right of the filler cord) up and wrap the filler cord with it. Then, pass the working cord front to back through the loop. Pull the working cord while holding the filler cord to tighten the first half hitch.

Step 2: To complete the second half hitch of your HDHH, take the same working cord, now placed to the left of the knot, and bring it up and over the filler cord. Use the working cord to wrap the filler cord once again, passing it through the loop front to back. Now, pull the working cord while holding the filler cord to tighten the second half hitch. Check that the half hitches are next to each other and evenly tightened.

Before continuing with step 3, ensure your filler cord is still placed horizontally over the working cords. Failing to do so will result in an uneven line pattern.

Step 3: There should now be two half hitch knots sitting next to each other horizontally. This is a completed HDHH. Repeat steps 1 and 2 with the rest of the working cords to create a row of HDHHs. Use the working cords one by one from left to right. Remember, your filler cord doesn't change during the process.

Step 4: After completing your first row of left-to-right HDHHs, the filler cord should be the last cord to the right of the pattern. Then, take the filler cord and bend it over to the left, placing it horizontally over the working cords, underneath the first row of knots. This is the beginning of the second row of HDHHs. This horizontal line pattern will be knotted right-to-left this time.

Step 5: To complete the right-to-left row of HDHHs, follow the technique explained in the diagonal double half hitches (DDHH)–right-to-left section (see page 63). Ensure your filler cord is still placed horizontally over the working cords while knotting.

Macramé: The Power of Knots

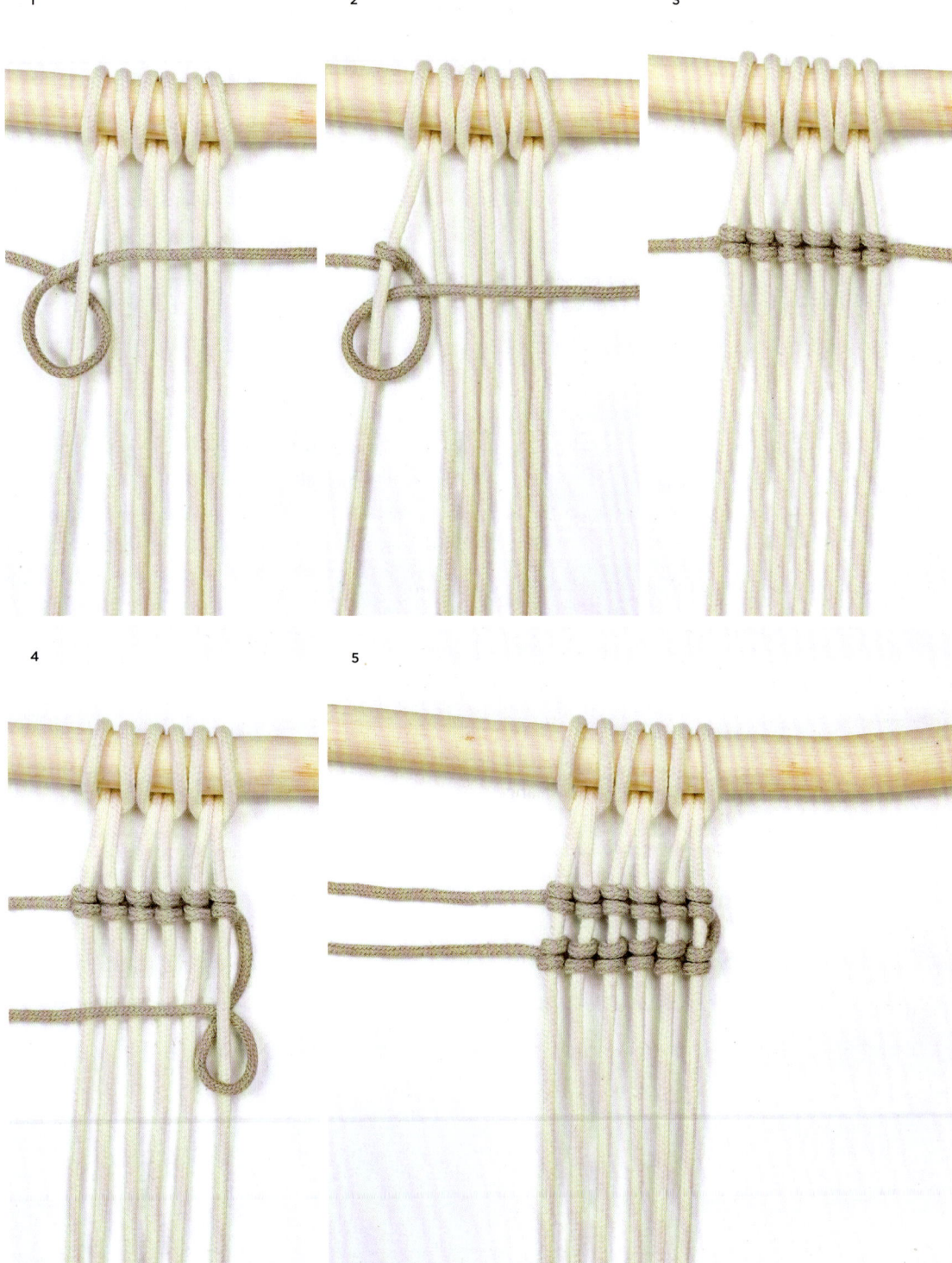

Vertical Double Half Hitch (VDHH)

A **vertical double half hitch** (VDHH) is created by tying **double half hitch** knots to a series of vertical filler cords to create horizontal line patterns. These rows, as it happens with all the double half hitches, can be approached from the left or the right. In the following demonstration, I will tie the first row of vertical double half hitches (VDHHs) using the left-to-right technique, followed by a second row of knots tied with the right-to-left method.

A separate piece of cord is used as a working cord to create these knots. The working cord tends to be a different color from the filler cords to add contrast and detail to your designs. You can even create a "depth effect" in your piece by using cords with different shades of the same color as working cords. This versatile knot will allow you to be very creative and add a personal touch to your artwork.

Step 1: Bring your working cord toward the right, passing it behind the first filler cord (first white cord on the left). Take the right end of the working cord and wrap it around the filler cord, passing it over itself and behind the filler cord once again. While holding the filler cord straight, pull both ends of the working cord gently to tie the knot.

Step 2: Use the right end of the working cord to wrap it around the same filler cord again, passing it back to front through the small loop created on the right. Pull both ends of the working cord in opposite directions, making sure the filler cord remains straight while tightening the first VDHH.

Step 3: Repeat steps 1 and 2 with the rest of the filler cords. Knot a single VDHH in every one of the filler cords with the working cord. Use the filler cords one by one from left to right. Make sure to tie the VDHHs evenly and in an orderly manner to create a straight horizontal row.

Step 4: After completing your first row of left-to-right VDHHs, take the right end of the working cord and bend it over to the left, placing it horizontally underneath the first row of knots. Now, continue with the second row of VDHHs. This time, the horizontal line pattern will be knotted right-to-left.

Step 5: To complete knotting the right-to-left line pattern, follow the steps of the first row of VDHHs (steps 1–3) in reverse.

Reverse Double Half Hitch

You might not have noticed it yet, but you have already knotted the **reverse double half hitch**. The reverse double half hitch and the double half hitch are basically the same knots. Take your double half hitch pattern and flip it around. Voila! What you see now is the reverse double half hitch. The main difference between these knots is the design of the line pattern created with them. To create the reverse double half hitch, tie the double half hitch backward, so the back side of the knot is displayed on the front. Both of these knots use the same number of filler and working cords and have the same number of variations: diagonal, horizontal, and vertical. In the example below, I demonstrate how to knot the diagonal version.

Reverse Diagonal Double Half Hitch (RDDHH)–Left–to–right

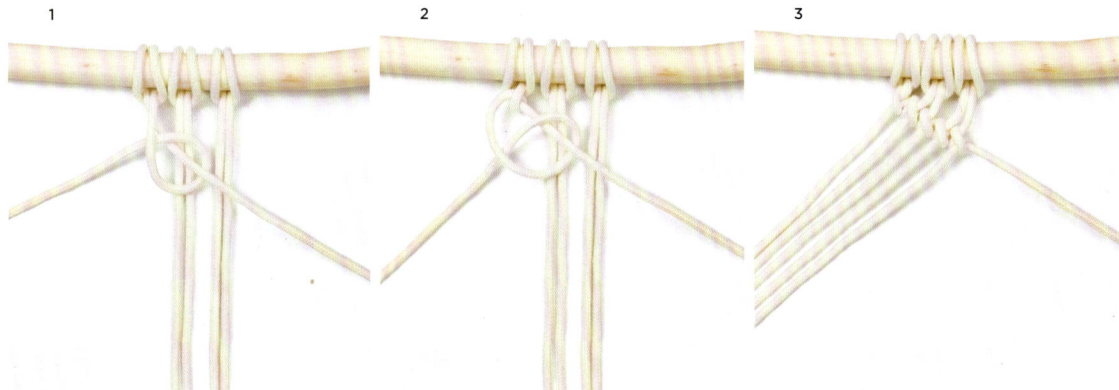

Step 1: Using the furthest cord to the left as your filler cord, place it down diagonally toward the right over the rest of the cords (working cords). Now take the first working cord (first cord to the right of the filler cord) and bring it over the filler cord. Grab the end of the first working cord, bring it up, and wrap the filler cord with it. Then, pass the working cord front to back through the loop. Pull the working cord while holding the filler cord to tighten the first reverse half hitch.

Step 2: To complete the second **reverse half hitch–left-to-right**, take the same working cord, now placed to the left of the knot, and bring it up and behind the filler cord. Use the working cord to wrap the filler cord once again, passing it through the loop front to back. Now, pull the working cord while holding the filler cord to tighten the second reverse half hitch. Check that the reverse half hitches are next to each other and evenly tightened. Your first RDDHH is now completed.

Step 3: Repeat steps 1 and 2 with the rest of the working cords, using them one by one to create a diagonal line pattern moving down from left to right. Remember, your filler cord doesn't change during the process.

Reverse Diagonal Double Half Hitch (RDDHH)–Right–to–left

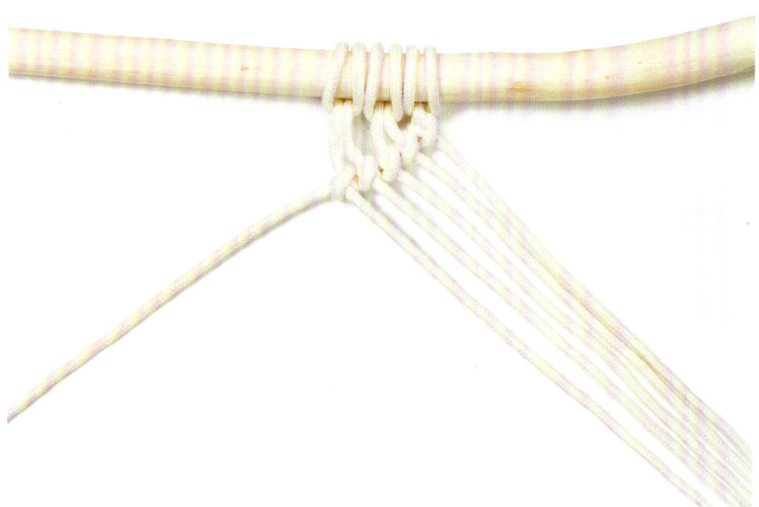

To knot a **reverse diagonal double half hitch–right–to–left**, the techniques of the reverse diagonal double half hitch (RDDHH)–left–to–right apply. This time, you want your line pattern to move down right-to-left. To do so, use the cord furthest to the right as your filler cord, tying your knots from right to left (follow steps 1 and 2 in the reverse diagonal double half hitch (RDDHH)–left–to–right in reverse).

Gathering Knot

A **gathering knot**, also called a **wrapping knot**, is a tying technique commonly used to finish pieces neatly. You will need a separate rope or string to secure and gather the cords in your project. The gathering knot works great at the bottom of a plant hanger, as it is a strong knot capable of holding the weight of the pot. This knot is also widely used in artwork designs that include clean ends. In wall hangings, for instance, the gathering knot helps create big fringes. To perfectly tie a gathering knot, follow the steps below. Take the separate piece of rope or string as your working cord and the cords belonging to your piece as filler cords.

Macramé Basic Knots

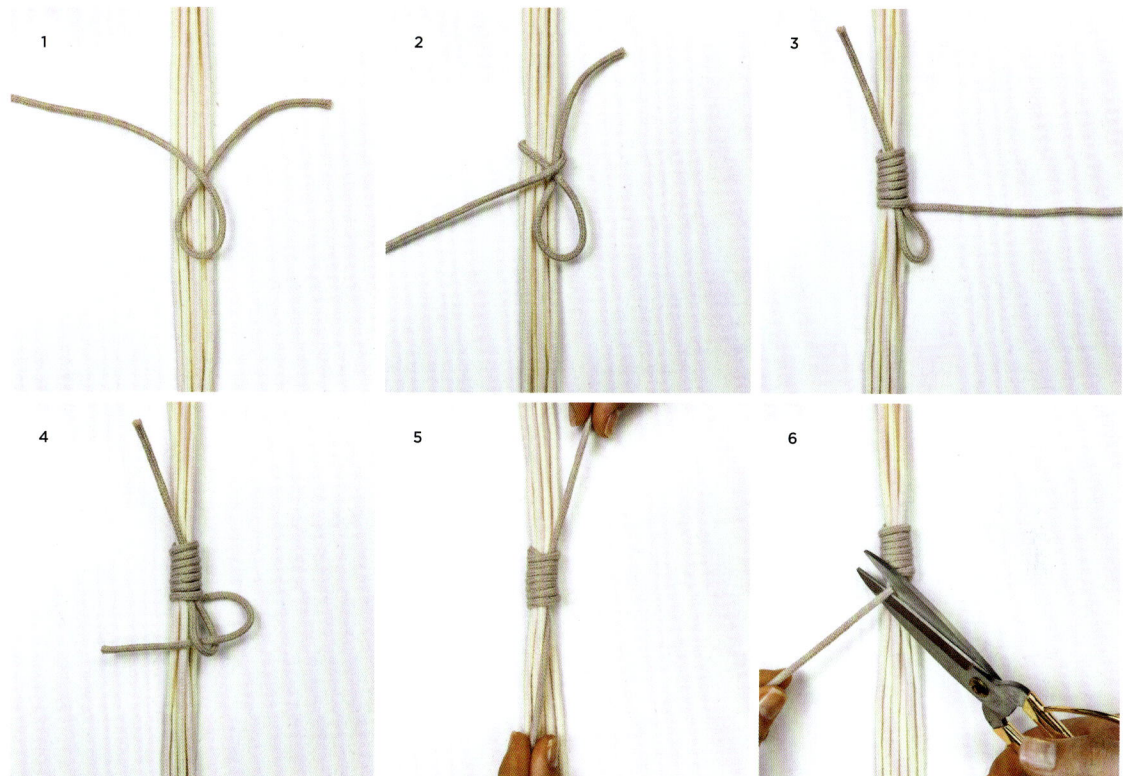

Step 1: Fold one end of the working cord (gray) under itself to create a loop. Place the loop facing down on top of the filler cords (white).

Step 2: Use the long end of the working cord (gray) to wrap the filler cords (white) and the loop.

Step 3: Continue wrapping the working cord five to seven times, making sure each pass is aligned with the previous one. You should end up with a smaller loop at the bottom.

> **TIP:** For a longer gathering knot, initially create a bigger loop in step 1, and wrap it more times around the filler cords and the loop in step 3.

Step 4: Pass the end of the working cord (gray) used for wrapping through the small loop at the bottom.

Step 5: Pull the top end of the working cord (gray) to close the loop and bring it inside the knot. Then, pull the bottom end of the working cord to secure and tighten the knot.

Step 6: For a clean finish, trim the ends of the working cord (gray) and tuck them inside the knot.

Berry Knot

The **berry knot** is one of the most popular decorative knots used in macramé. It will add details and bring depth to your projects. Berry knots are basically made of a square knot sinnet (SKS) with a twist at the end. In this example, I tied the square knot sinnet (SKS) using three square knots (SKs) to create the berry knot. You can change the size of your berry knot by adding more square knots (SKs) to the sinnet. Keep in mind, this knot will need longer cords than the typical square knot (SK).

Macramé Basic Knots

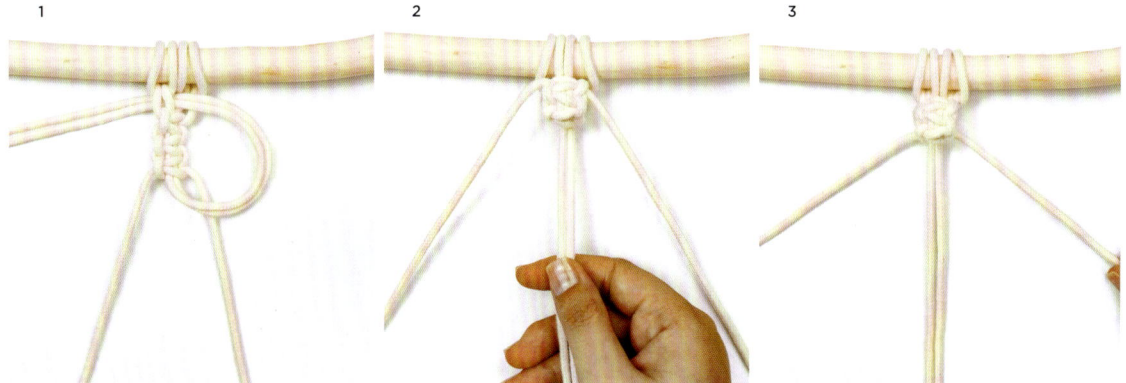

Step 1: Leave a small gap before tying the first SK. Proceed to tie an SKS with three SKs. Bring the ends of both filler cords up front and pass them through the gap between the first and second pair of cords.

Step 2: Pull the filler cords, rolling the SKs of the SKS into a ball shape.

Step 3: Finish the berry knot by tying one more SK below the ball to secure it.

Barrel Knot

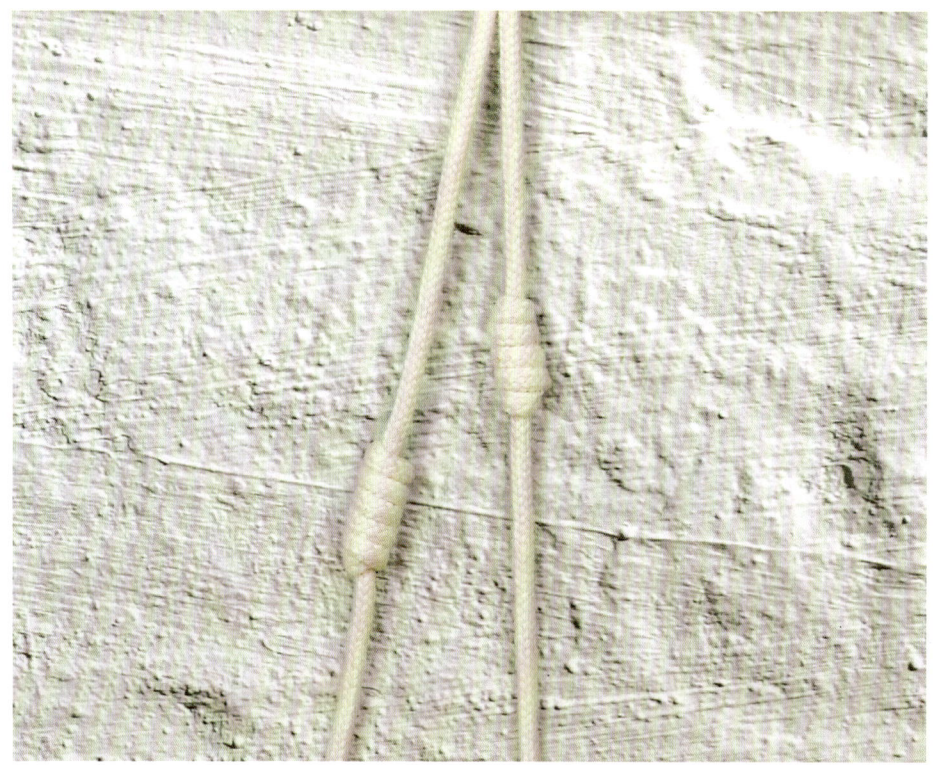

The **barrel knot**, sometimes referred to as the **coil knot**, is a decorative knot that uses a single cord. This knot can also be used to prevent cords from fraying. In this sample, I wrap the cord three times, but please note that you could wrap it more times to get a longer barrel knot.

Macramé Basic Knots

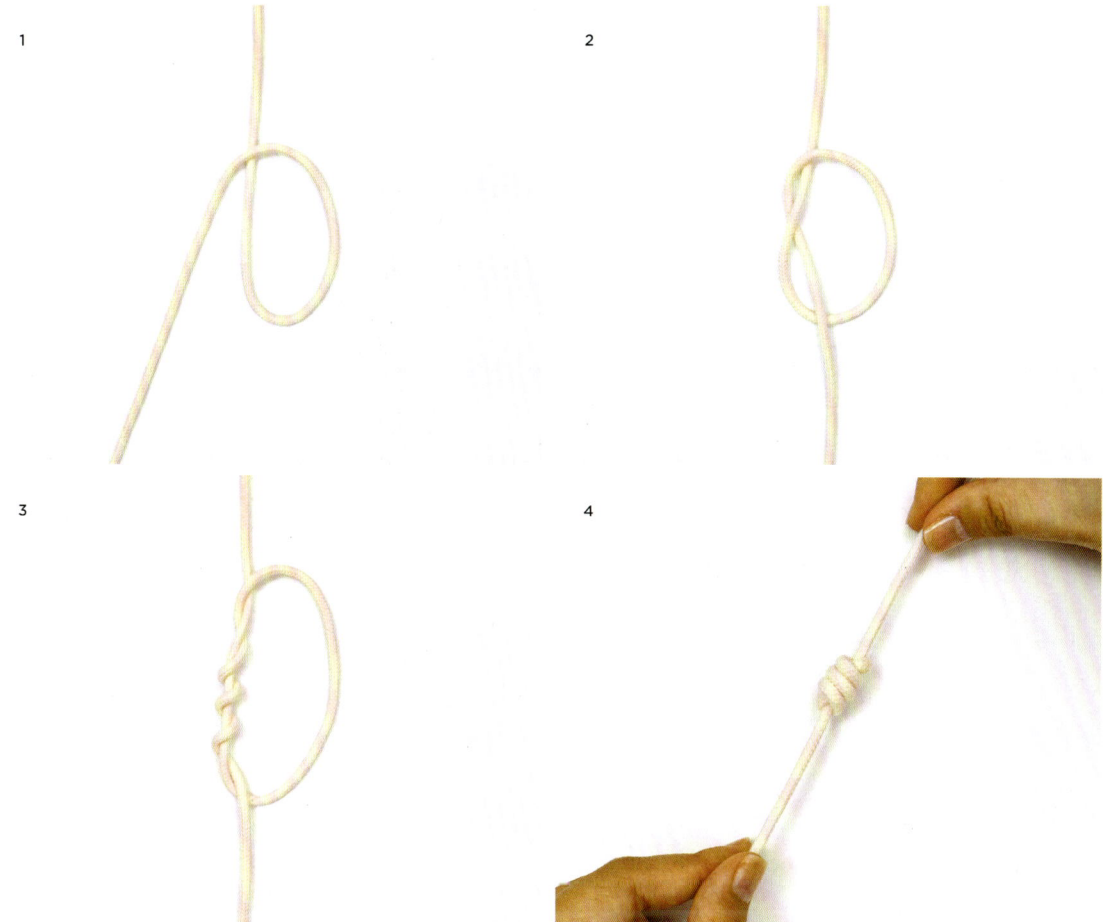

Step 1: Take the end of the cord and bring it up and over itself to create a circular loop.

Step 2: Pass the end of the cord through the loop from behind.

Step 3: Repeat the last step three times (or as many times as you need to achieve the desired length). Do not pull or tighten the cord during this step.

Step 4: Now, to finish the barrel knot, pull the ends of the cord away from the knot to tighten it.

Crown Knot

The **crown knot** is a bit more complex than regular decorative knots. It might look challenging at first, but this beautiful and useful knot is more bark than bite. It will take a few sequences to get the hang of it, but afterward, this knot won't be more difficult to create than any of the knots you've already learned.

The crown knot uses four working cords and can be mounted to a support or not. In this example, I mount the cords to a ring support because this knot is commonly used in projects such as plant hangers, key chains, and bag straps—all of which often incorporate ring elements as supports.

Macramé Basic Knots

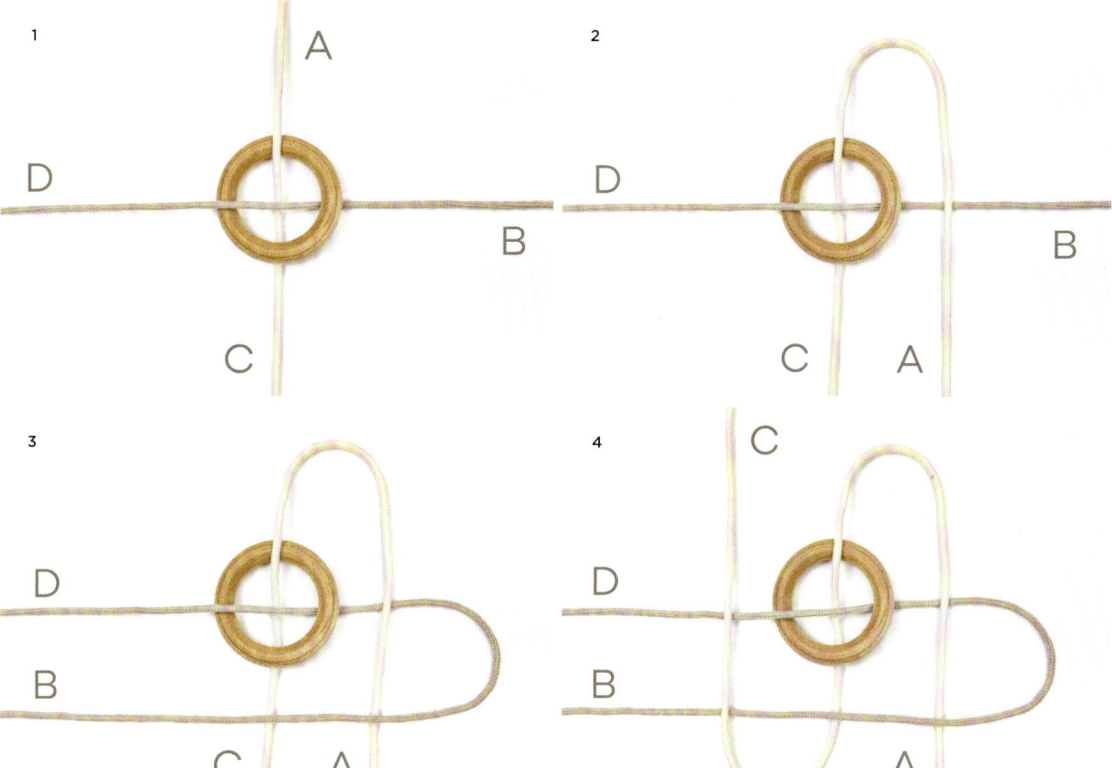

Step 1: To create our four working cords (A, B, C, and D), we first need to pass two long cords through the ring support. Place one of the cords horizontally and the other cord vertically, ensuring the ring is equidistant from the ends of both cords. Make sure to pass the vertical cord under the horizontal cord inside the ring to form a cross.

Step 2: Bring working cord A down and fold it over working cord B. Leave an open loop where the two cords meet.

Step 3: Then take working cord B toward the left, and fold it over both working cords A and C.

Step 4: Next, bring working cord C up, and fold it over working cords B and D.

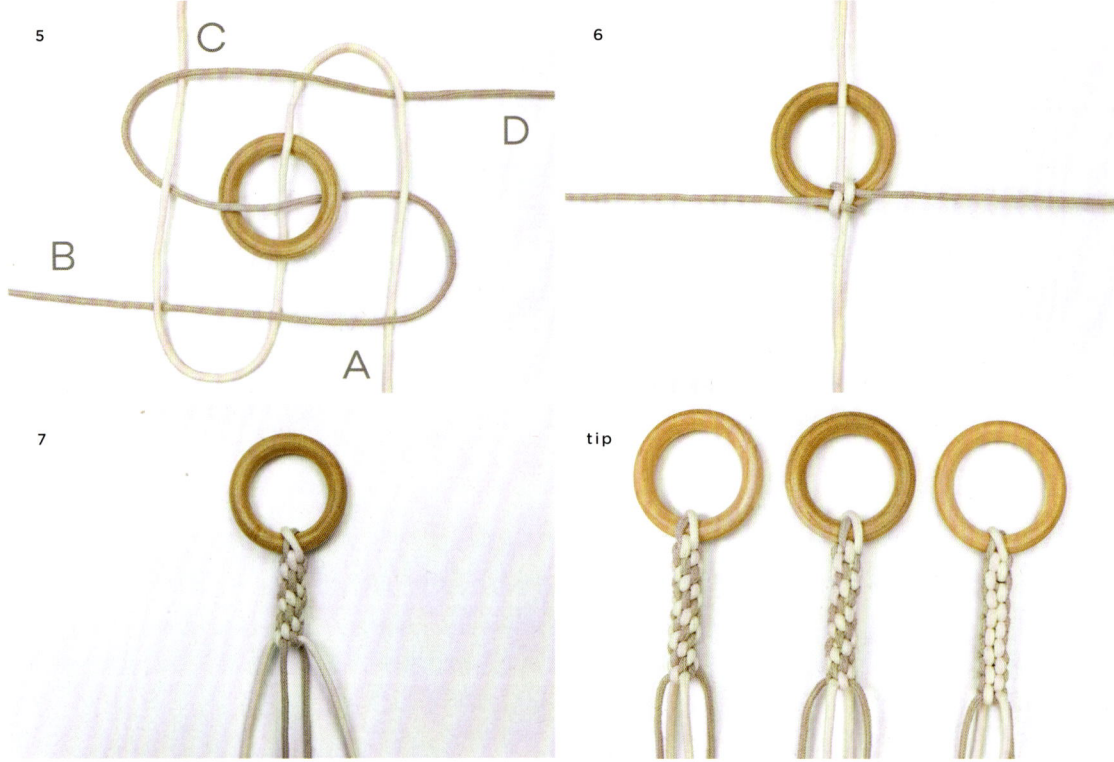

Step 5: Take working cord D and fold it toward the right, over working cord C. Now, pass working cord D front to back, through the loop created in step 2.

Step 6: Tighten the knot slowly by pulling each of the working cords' ends separately. This will complete the first sequence of your crown knot.

Step 7: Add more sequences to your knot by repeating steps 2–6, until you reach the desired length of the design.

TIP: Using two different-color cords at the beginning allows you to create a crown knot with a visible spiral pattern. In the example, after the first sequence, I continue folding the working cords "clockwise" (initially folding working cord A over working cord B) for the rest of the sequences. The result is a spiral pattern that moves down from right to left. (See the picture in step 7)

To create a spiral pattern that moves in the opposite direction (moving down from left to right), fold your working cords "counterclockwise" (initially folding working cord A over working cord D) after the first sequence.

To create a crown knot with a more squared shape and a striped color pattern, alternate folding your working cords clockwise and counterclockwise after the first sequence of the knot.

Josephine Knot

The **Josephine knot** is one of the most delicate decorative knots you will come across. These sophisticated-looking knots can be tied with two single working cords, or with multiple pairs of working cords. The Josephine knot can be found in some home decor projects, but you'll mainly see them as decorative elements of accessories and jewelry artwork. I will demonstrate how to tie the Josephine knot by using two pairs of different-color cords in the following example. Note that each of the pairs of cords are used as individual working cords in this knot.

Macramé Basic Knots

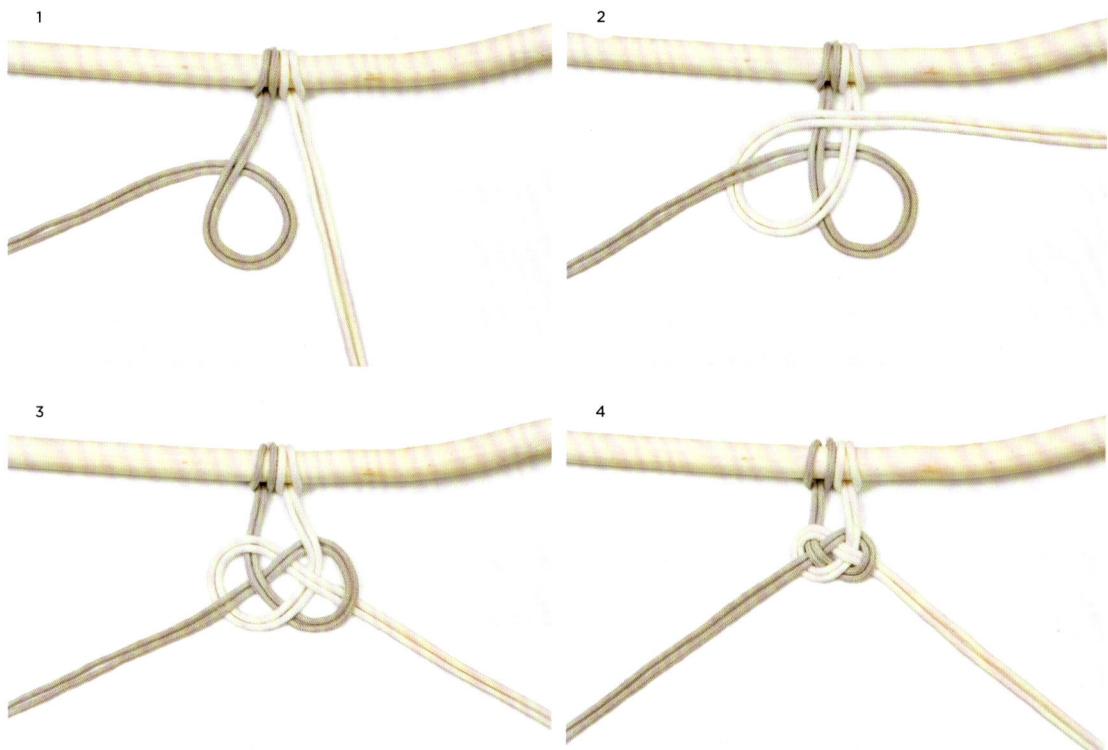

Step 1: Take the ends of the pair of working cords on the left (gray) and bring them up and behind themselves to create a circular loop. The loop should be facing toward the pair of working cords on the right (white). Ensure the cords of each pair of working cords are aligned at all times while tying this knot.

Step 2: Place the white pair of cords over the loop. Bring them toward the left and behind the bottom end of the gray cords. Now, take the white pair of cords to the right, over the top end of gray cords. Now you should have two loops in front of you, one made with each pair of working cords (gray and white).

Step 3: Take the end of the white pair of cords and finish interlocking the loops. To do so, pass the white cords under the top part of the gray loop, over themselves (to complete the white loop), and under the bottom part of the gray loop.

Step 4: Tighten the knot by gently pulling both pairs of cords (gray and white). Remember to keep all cords aligned.

Cross Knot

The **cross knot** is a very generous and elegant decorative knot. Once completed, each side of the knot provides you with a different pattern you can use to decorate your piece, showing a tilted square pattern in the front and a cross section or plus sign at the back. To tie the cross knot, a minimum of two working cords is required.

Macramé Basic Knots

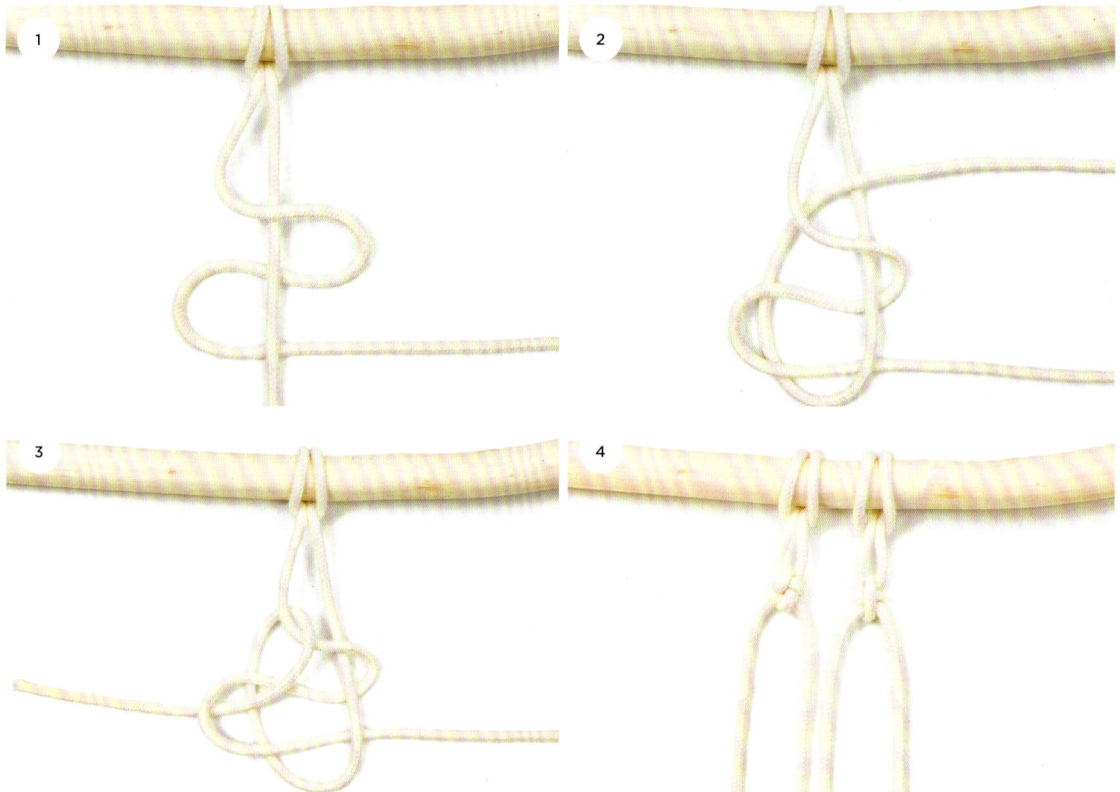

Step 1: While keeping the working cord on the right straight, use the working cord on the left to create a zigzag pattern. First, bring the left cord over the right one, creating a closed loop. Then, use the same cord to create an open loop on the right by passing the cord under the straightened working cord. Finally, pass the left working cord under the right one again to create a second open loop. The second open loop, as shown in the picture, is placed to the left of the straightened cord. Notice how the left working cord goes over, under, and then under the straightened cord again to create the zigzag pattern.

Step 2: Bring the end of the straightened working cord up and to the left. Pass it behind the open loop at the bottom and back to front through the closed loop at the top.

Step 3: Take the cord from step 2 and bring it down toward the left. Pass it through the bottom loop at the right, this time front to back.

Step 4: To tighten the knot, pull all the cords' ends gently in opposite directions. Before tightening the knot completely, make sure it is in its final position.

Chapter 4

15 Patterns & 4 Projects for Novice Artists

The time has come to put into practice all you have learned so far. In the remaining chapters, you are going to explore a wide variety of patterns and knotting techniques. These, in combination with the basic knots explained in the previous chapter, will provide you with all you need to know to attempt your first pieces. I have divided a total of forty-five patterns and twelve projects into three levels of difficulty: novice, intermediate, and advanced. To best navigate this section of the book, first choose a project that fits your level. Learn, review, and practice the patterns and basic knots used to complete it. Then, on the count of, "Ready, set… knot!" just go for it.

Novice Patterns

Macramé: The Power of Knots

Square Knot Net

Nets are some of the most common patterns in macramé, and the square knot net is probably the most prevalent of them all. This pattern is very often incorporated in projects such as bags, wall hangings, and hammocks. You can knot the square knot net using the left-facing or right-facing techniques. However, it is important to keep the same technique throughout the pattern to keep it consistent and smooth. Tie your knots closer to each other for a tighter-looking net, or further from each other for a looser-looking net. This pattern is used frequently in projects throughout this book to show you the versatility of the square knot net. To demonstrate this pattern, I use a vertical setup, mounting four groups of cords (four cords/group) to a dowel.

Knots Used:
Square knot (SK), see page 47
Alternating square knot (ASK), see page 51

Knotting Sequence:
4 x SK
3 x ASK
4 x ASK
3 x ASK

Step 1: Begin by tying a row of 4 SKs, using all the cords.

Step 2: Before you start knotting the second row with ASKs, you need to decide how much space to leave between them. In this demonstration, I leave a space of 2 cm (0.8 in). For a consistent look, be sure to keep the same distance between all rows throughout the pattern. For the second row, skip the first two cords and tie three ASKs, alternating working and filler cords.

Step 3: Continue tying rows of ASKs, alternating the working and filler cords, until you reach the desired length of your pattern.

Switch Knot Net

The **switch knot net** bears a strong resemblance to the square knot net. They are both used for creating the same types of projects, and they use a very similar technique. Nevertheless, the switch knot net, because of the way the cords are twisted to create switch knots, has a lighter look in comparison. For this pattern, I use a vertical setup, mounting four groups of four cords each to a dowel.

Knots Used:
Square Knot (SK), see page 47
Switch Knot (SWK), see page 52

Knotting Sequence:
4 x SK
3 x Alternating SWK
4 x Alternating SWK
3 x Alternating SWK

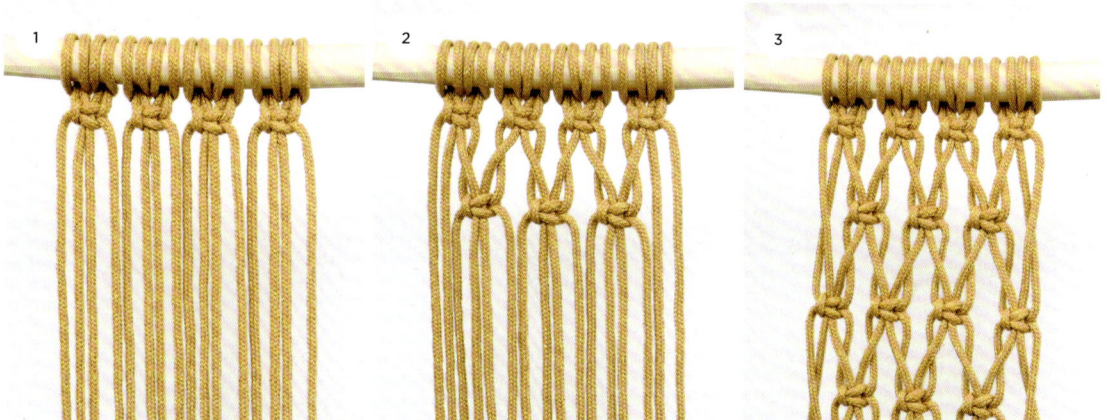

Step 1: Begin tying the first row of SKs, using all the cords: four SKs total.

Step 2: Leave a space of 3 cm (1.2 in) after the row of SKs. Skip the first 2 cords, and tie a row of 3 SWKs. Remember, to create an SWK, you need to switch working and filler cords.

Step 3: Continue alternating rows of SWKs until you reach the desired length for your design.

Macramé: The Power of Knots

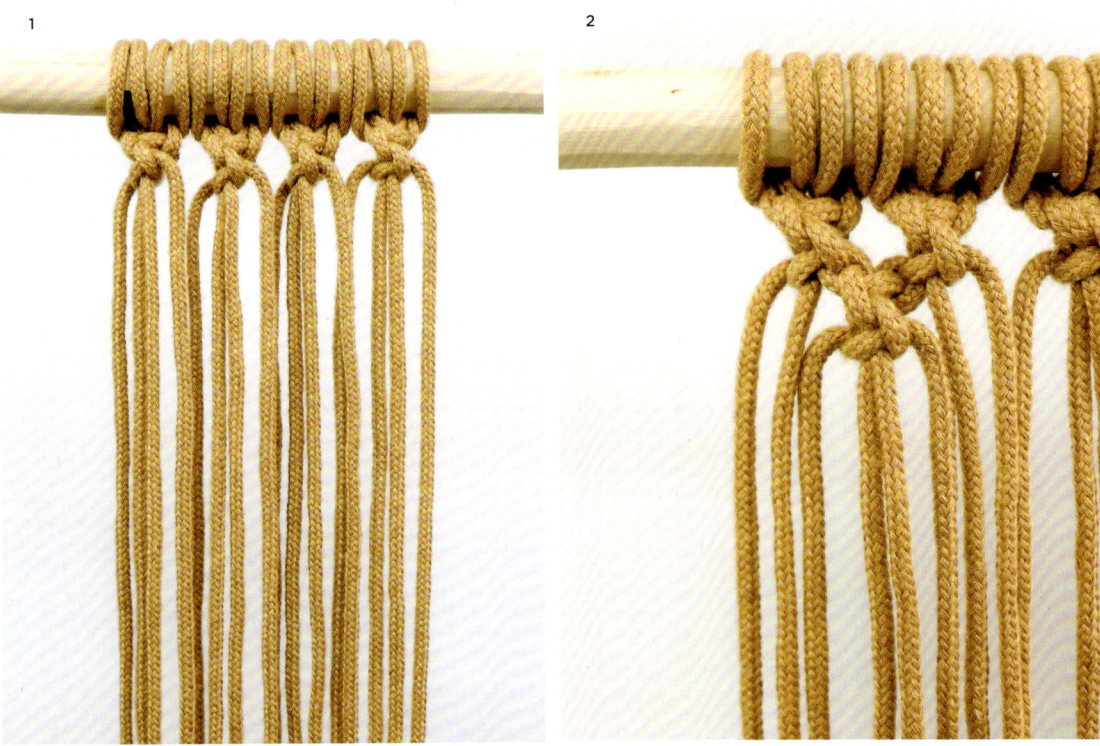

Spiral Knot Net

This pattern is perfect for designs that require a net with a compact look and some depth. As it happens with all net patterns, the best way to approach the **spiral knot net** is with a vertical setup. In the example I'll show you next, I tie three left-facing half square knots (LFHSKs) per spiral knot with four groups of four cords. In reality, you can choose as many left-/right-facing half square knots as you wish for your spiral knots. Just make sure all your spiral knots remain the same from beginning to end.

Knots Used:
Left-facing half square knot (LFHSK), see page 48
Left-twist spiral knot (LSPK), see page 59

Knotting Sequence:
4 x LSPK
3 x Alternating LSPK
4 x Alternating LSPK
3 x Alternating LSPK

Step 1: Start the first row of your pattern by tying three LFHSKs with every one of the four cords to create four LSPKs. Twist the knots to make sure all of the cords are placed in the same position and your LSPKs form a half spiral.

Step 2: Skip the first two cords and tie the first LSPK of the second row. To create this pattern, do not leave any space between rows.

Step 3: Finish the second row by tying two more LSPKs with the next eight cords. Again, ensure the cords are in place and twist the LSPKs if needed before continuing with the next row. Notice how the first and last two cords in this row remain unknotted.

Step 4: Repeat steps 1 and 2 as many times as you please, until you reach the desired length for your design.

Overlay Net

The **overlay net** is basically two square knot nets overlapping each other. This is the pattern of choice for many macramé artists as a way to start wall hanging projects because of its beautiful multilayered triangular shape. To ensure the two square knot net patterns overlap all the way to the end, you need a minimum of five groups of four cords. In this example, seven groups of cords (twenty-eight cords total) are used mounted on a horizontal dowel.

Knots Used:
Square knot (SK), see page 47
Alternating square knot (ASK), see page 51

Knotting Sequence:
7 x SK
3 x ASK (layer 1) / 2 x ASK (layer 2)
2 x ASK (layer 1) / 1 x ASK (layer 2)
1 x ASK (layer 1)

Step 1: To start the pattern, mount each group of cords 5 cm (2 in) apart. Then, tie an SK with each group of cords, completing the first row with seven SKs.

Step 2: Leave an 8-cm (3.1-in) space before you begin tying the first layer of the second row. To create this layer, use the cords from the first, third, fifth, and seventh SKs and tie three ASKs.

> TIP: Be consistent with your spacing between rows. If you use an 8–cm (3.1–in) division at first, make sure to keep it throughout the pattern.

Step 3: To create the second layer of the second row, leave 8 cm (3.1 in) and tie two ASKs, this time using the cords from the second, fourth, and sixth initial SKs. After step 2 (layer one) and step 3 (layer two), you should have five ASKs aligned.

Step 4: Leave another 8 cm (3.1 in) to begin knotting the first layer of the third row. Tie two ASKs using cords from the first, third and fifth ASKs from the second row.

Step 5: Now, after leaving 8 cm (3.1 in) again, tie one single ASK using cords from the second and fourth ASKs from the second row. The third row of knots will be completed once you have three SKs aligned in a row.

Step 6: To finish this pattern and close the triangular shape, tie a single ASK using cords from the first and the third ASKs from the third row.

15 Patterns & 4 Projects for Novice Artists

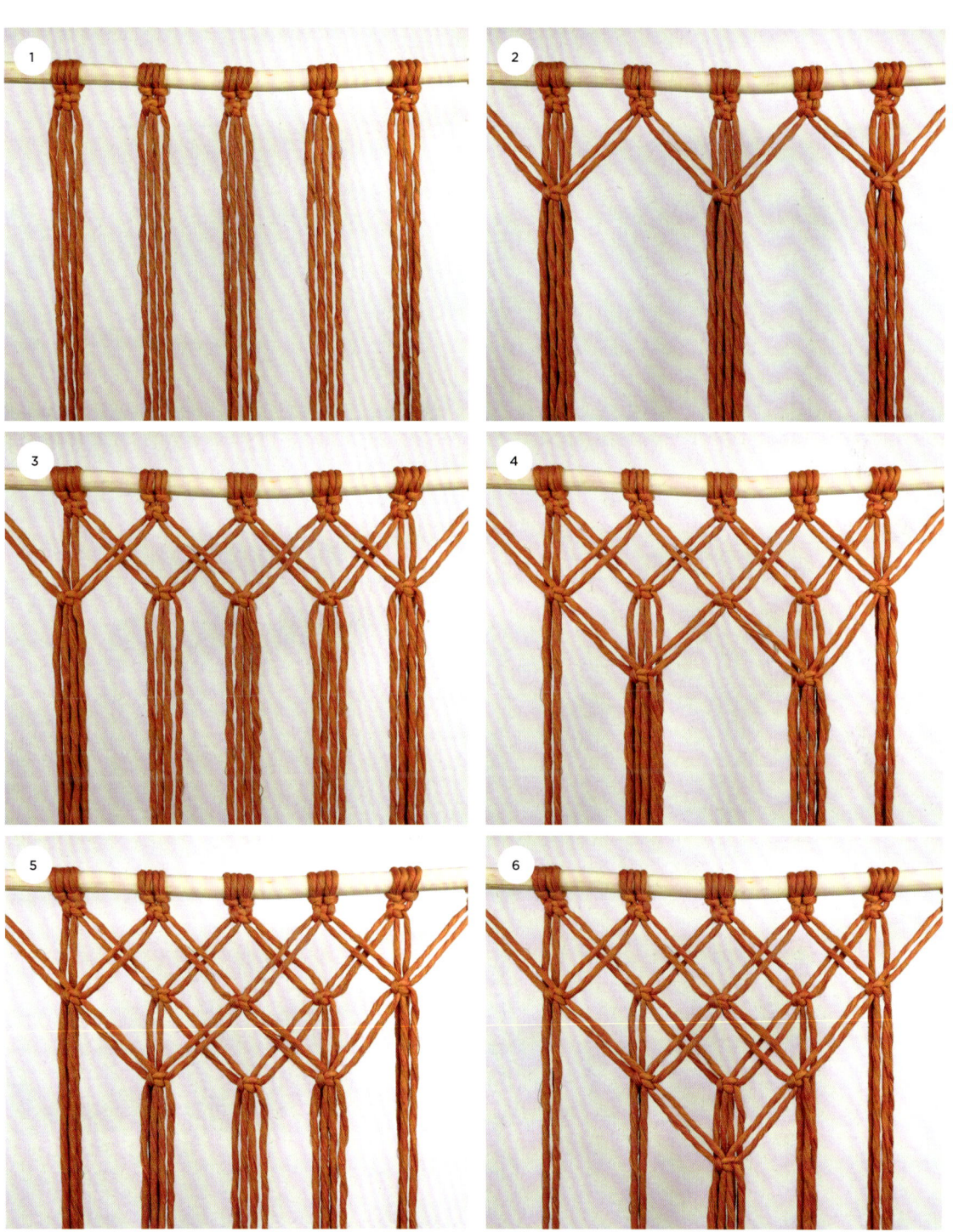

Macramé: The Power of Knots

15 Patterns & 4 Projects for Novice Artists

Triangle Square Knot

As its name indicates, the **triangle square knot** is a pattern used to add full triangle shapes to our designs by knotting square knots. The knots in this pattern alternate from row to row, decreasing the number of knots by one from one row to another. In the example for this pattern, I use twenty cords. Adding more cords at the beginning allows you to create bigger triangles. The best setup to knot this pattern is a vertical one, which is the one used in the demonstration.

Knots Used:
Square knot (SK), see page 47
Alternating square knot (ASK), see page 51

Knotting Sequence:
5 x SK
4 x ASK
3 x ASK
2 x ASK
1 x ASK

Step 1: Begin tying the first row of SKs using all the cords: five SKs total.

Step 2: For the second row, skip the first two cords and tie four ASKs.

Step 3: Then, for the third row, skip the first four cords and tie three ASKs.

Step 4: Next, for row number four, skip the first six cords and tie two ASKs.

Step 5: Finally, in row number five, only one ASK is used to complete the triangle shape. To do so, skip the first eight cords and tie one single ASK. The final eight cords will also remain untouched.

Double Half Hitch Diamond

This pattern is one of those most commonly used to create home decor projects. These include wall hangings, plant hangers, table runners, rugs, and so on. In this book, the **double half hitch diamond** pattern is used in two projects: a belt and a hanging shelf. This simple pattern is the perfect way to add geometric shapes into your designs. As you will see in this section of the book, the double half hitch diamond pattern works as the foundation for many of the various diamond-shaped patterns. Once your macramé skills develop, you will use the double half hitch pattern to create your own variations by combining it with other knots and different patterns. In this example, eight cords are used to demonstrate a medium-size diamond pattern using a vertical setup.

Knots Used:
Diagonal double half hitch, see pages 62–63

Knotting Sequence:
4 x DDHH-right-to-left / 3 x DDHH-left-to-right
3 x DDHH-left-to-right / 4 x DDHH-right-to-left

Step 1: Begin by taking the fifth cord from your left as your filler cord. Cords 1–4 are used as working cords. Then, tie four DDHHs-right-to-left, going down.

Step 2: Now, take the fifth cord from your left as your filler cord again. Cords 6–8 are used as working cords. Then, tie three DDHHs-left-to-right, going down. Note how this line of knots to the right starts just under the first row going to the left, creating the top section of the diamond.

Step 3: To begin knotting the bottom part of the diamond, use the first cord from the left as your filler cord. Cords 2–4 are now used as working cords to tie three DDHHs-left-to-right, going down.

Step 4: To complete and close the pattern, take the eighth cord from the left as your filler cords and cords 4–7 as your working cords. Tie four DDHHs-right-to-left, going down. The last DDHH you'll knot is the one closing the diamond.

15 Patterns & 4 Projects for Novice Artists

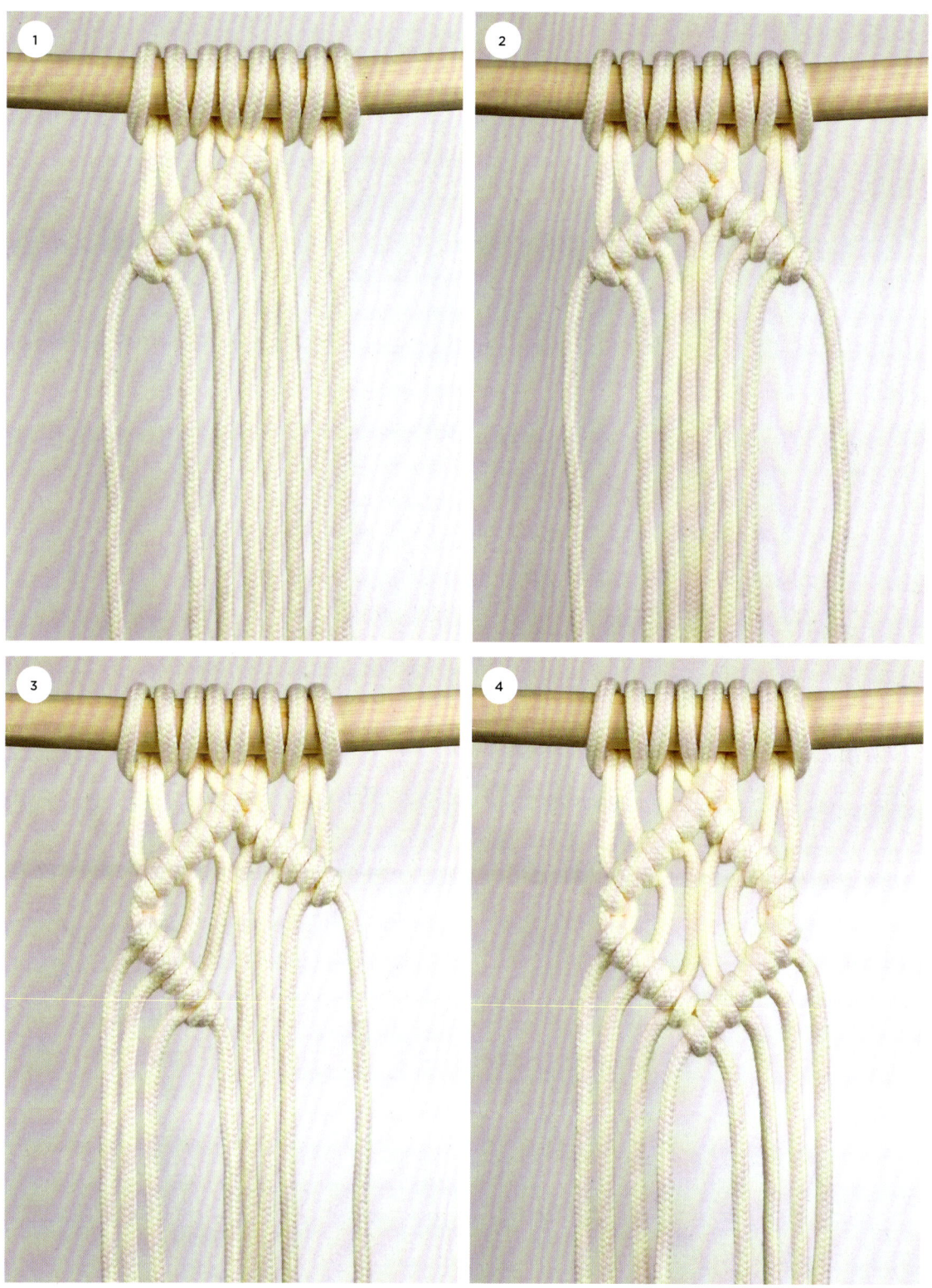

Macramé: The Power of Knots

Double Half Hitch Diamond with Square Knot

The **double half hitch diamond with square knot** is an upgraded version of a double half hitch diamond pattern. In this pattern, the diamond has a square knot (SK) inside. A minimum of six cords is needed, but more cords can be added to create a bigger diamond shape. Adding cords will also increase the size of the square knot (SK) inside, as more filler cords are used to create it. In this demonstration, eight cords are used in a vertical setup. This number of cords is ideal for a medium-size double half hitch with square knot pattern.

Knots Used:
Diagonal double half hitch, see pages 62–63
Square knot (SK), see page 47

Knotting Sequence:
4 x DDHH–right–to–left / 3 x DDHH–left–to–right
1 x SK
3 x DDHH–left–to–right / 4 x DDHH–right–to–left

Step 1: To create the top section of the diamond, follow steps 1 and 2 from the double half hitch diamond pattern (see page 94).

Step 2: The SK inside the diamond is created with cords 2–7 from the left, leaving cords 1 and 8 free. Now, tie an SK using the second and seventh cord as your working cords and cords 3–6 as filler cords.

Step 3: To create the bottom section of the diamond, follow steps 3 and 4 from the double half hitch diamond pattern (see page 94).

Hollow Double Half Hitch Diamond

The **hollow double half hitch diamond** is yet another variation of the double half hitch diamond pattern. This pattern allows you to create see-through hollow designs to be added to your pieces. If you have already mastered the double half hitch diamond, this new version of the pattern will be hassle-free. However, be mindful of the order in which you use your working cords. In the following demonstration, eight cords are used to create a medium-size pattern and work on a vertical setup.

Knots Used:
Diagonal double half hitch, see pages 62–63

Knotting Sequence:
4 x DDHH–right-to-left / 3 x DDHH–left-to-right
3 x DDHH–left-to-right / 4 x DDHH–right-to-left

Step 1: To create the top section of the diamond, follow steps 1 and 2 from the double half hitch diamond pattern (see page 94).

Step 2: Now, take the first cord starting from the left, and use it as your filler cord. Knot three DDHHs–left-to-right, going down, using working cords 4, 3, and 2 respectively. By reversing the order of our working cords with respect to the order in which we use them in the double half hitch diamond, a hollow will be created in the middle of the pattern at the end.

Step 3: Repeat the same technique in step 2 with the rest of the cords to complete the right side of the diamond. On this occasion, the eighth cord will be your filler cord, and cords 7, 6, and 5 your working cords.

Step 4: To complete and close the diamond pattern, continue using the same filler cord as in step 3, now the fifth cord, and tie a single DDHH–right-to-left, going down. Use the fourth cord as your working cord to do so.

15 Patterns & 4 Projects for Novice Artists

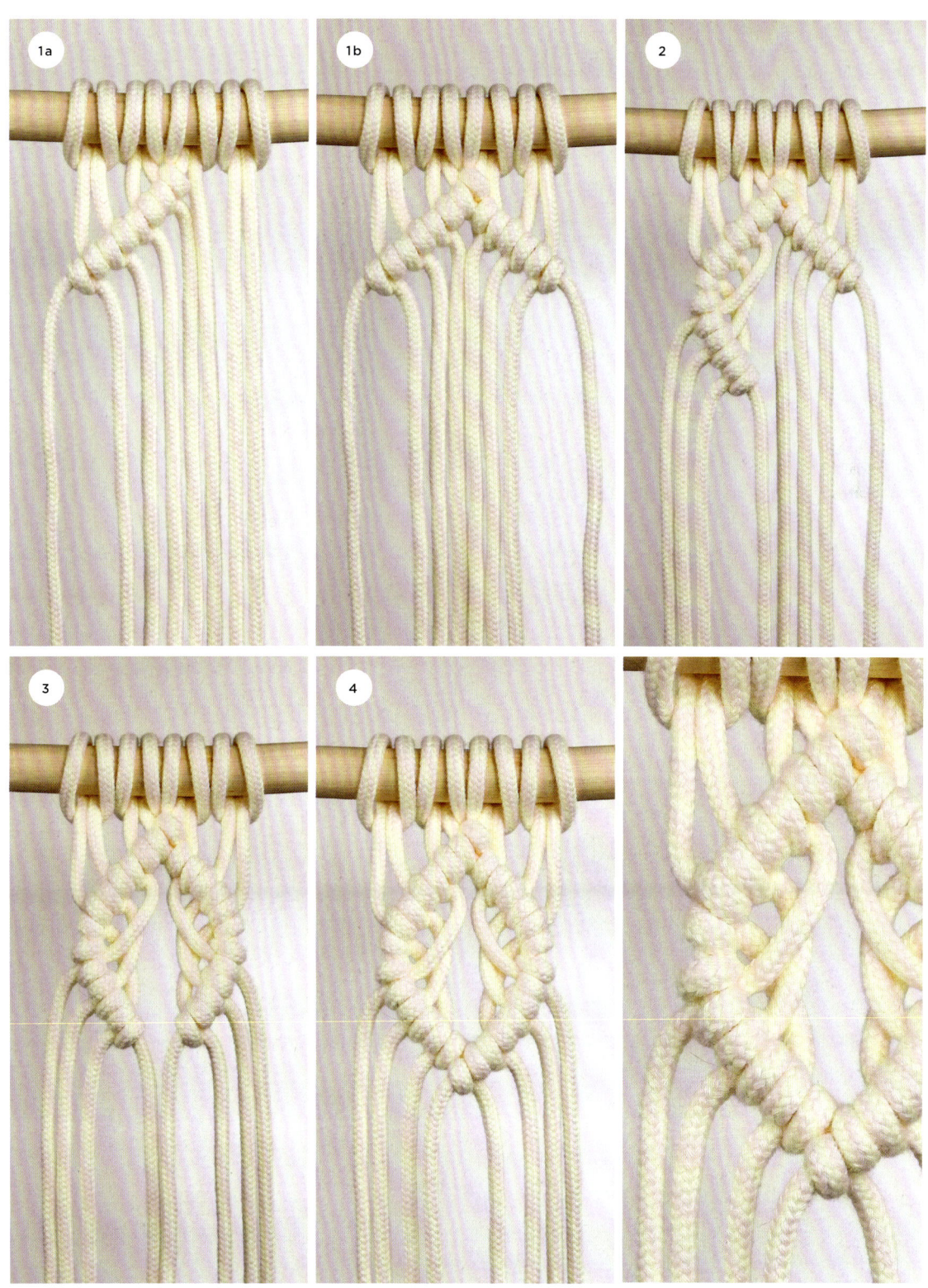

Macramé: The Power of Knots

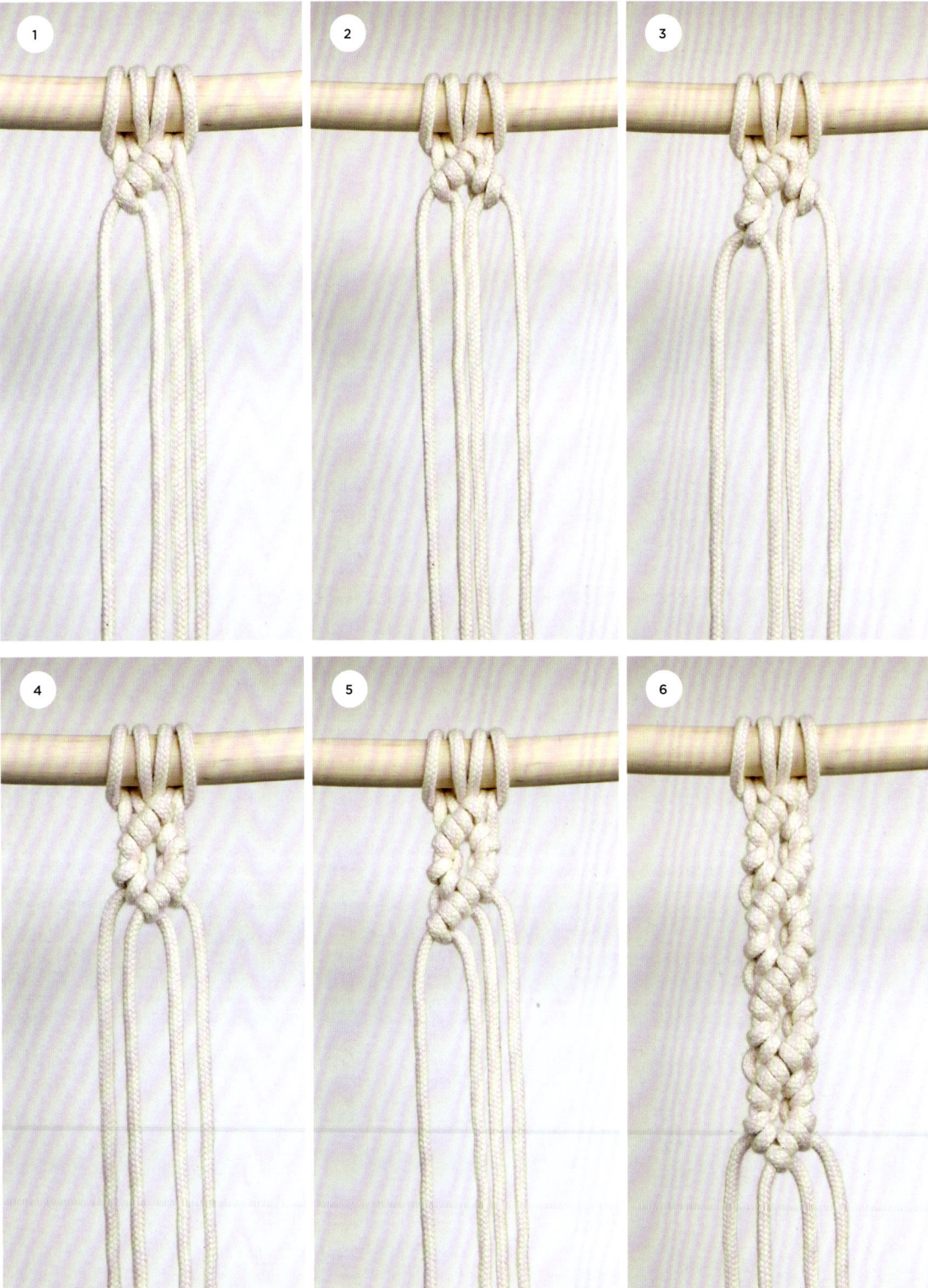

Small Diamond Chain

The **small diamond chain** is a variation of the double half hitch diamond pattern. This time, we only use four cords to create a chain of smaller diamonds. Plant hangers and hanging shelves are some of the most common projects which include this pattern. I recommend using a vertical setup to practice knotting this pattern. You will see this pattern being used in the Eartha Plant Hanger project.

Knots Used:
Diagonal double half hitch, see pages 62–63

Step 1: Starting from the left, take the third cord as your filler cord and tie two DDHHs–right–to–left, going down. Using cords 1 and 2 as working cords.

Step 2: Take the third cord from your left, again as your filler cord, and use the fourth cord as your working cord. Then tie one single DDHH–left–to–right.

Step 3: Use the first cord from the left as your filler cord, and tie a single DDHH– left–to–right, using the second cord as your working cord.

Knotting Sequence:
2 x DDHH–right–to–left / 1 x DDHH–left–to–right
1 x DDHH–left–to–right / 1 x DDHH–right–to–left

Step 4: To complete the first small diamond of the chain, now take the fourth cord as your filler cord and tie two DDHHs, going down, toward the left. Use cords 2 and 3 as working cords.

Step 5: The last DDHH of the first diamond is the first DDHH of the second diamond. This time, only tie an extra DDHH–right–to–left, using the second cord as your filler cord and the first as the working cord.

Step 6: Repeat steps 2–5 until you reach the desired chain length. The last diamond in the chain does not include an extra DDHH–right–to–left.

Square Knot Diamond with Big Square Knot

This **square knot diamond with square knot** (SK) allows you to add diamond shapes to your designs, this time using square knots (SKs) instead of diagonal double half hitches (DDHHs). Using a vertical setup, it is easy to alternate square knots (SKs) to create a perfect pattern for flat decorative pieces. In this demonstration, there are twenty cords. You will put this pattern to use in the Aura Coaster and Tayanna Wall Hanging project.

Knots Used:
Square knot (SK), see page 47
Alternating square knot (ASK), see page 51

Knotting Sequence:
1 x SK
4 x ASK / 4 x ASK
1 x big SK
3 x ASK / 3 x ASK
1 x ASK

Step 1: Start by tying an SK using cords 9–12 from the left.

Step 2: Take the seventh and eighth cords from the left, and the first two cords from the previous SK to knot an ASK underneath it. Create three more ASKs toward the left to complete one side of our diamond.

Step 3: Now take the thirteenth and fourteenth cords and the last two cords from the SK in step 1 to tie an ASK underneath it. Create three more ASKs toward the right to complete the second side of the pattern.

Step 4: To create the big SK inside our diamond, use the fifth and sixteenth as working cords, leaving cords 6–15 as filler cords.

Step 5: The third side of the diamond shape is created by tying three ASKs using cords 3–10. Notice how the ASKs move toward the right, surrounding the big SK in the center.

Step 6: For the fourth side of the diamond shape, use cords 11–18 to tie three ASKs. This time, the ASKs move toward the left, surrounding the big SK.

Step 7: To complete this pattern and close the diamond shape, tie the final ASK using cords 9–12.

15 Patterns & 4 Projects for Novice Artists

Zigzag

A simple, yet resourceful, design commonly used in wall hangings and plant hanger projects. The **zigzag pattern** is basically a series of continuously tied diagonal double half hitch (DDHH) lines which change direction. The best setup to knot this pattern is a vertical one, which is the one you will use, along with eight cords, to demonstrate.

Knots Used:
Diagonal double half hitch (DDHH), see pages 62–63

Knotting Sequence:
7 x DDHH-right-to-left
7 x DDHH-left-to-right

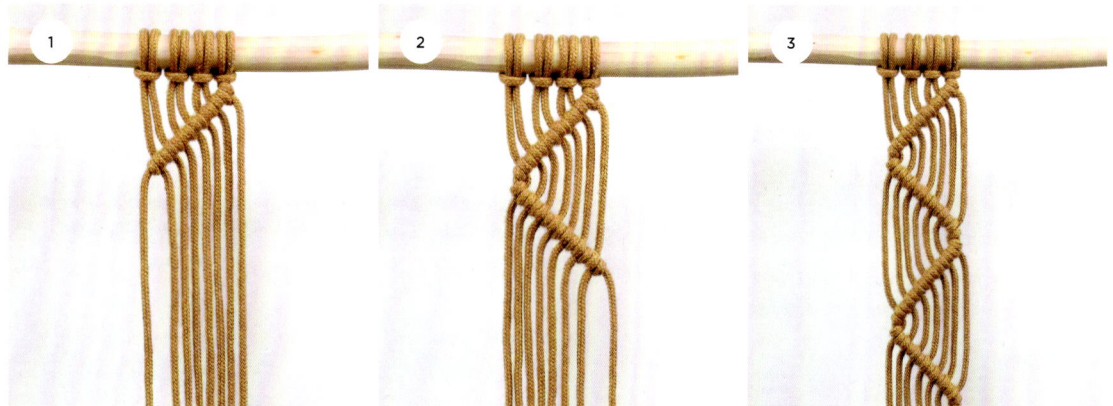

Step 1: Start the zigzag pattern from the right. Take the eighth cord as your filler cord, and tie seven DDHHs-right-to-left, going down, using cords 1–7 as your working cords.

Step 2: Continue using the same filler cord, now the first cord, to tie 7 DDHHs-left-to-right, going down, using cords 2–8 as working cords.

Step 3: Repeat steps 1 and 2 until you reach the desired length of your design. Notice how we use the same filler cord all throughout the pattern.

15 Patterns & 4 Projects for Novice Artists

Arrows

In this geometric pattern, we use diagonal double half hitches (DDHHs) to create **arrow shapes**. It is best to attempt the arrows pattern using a vertical setup. To achieve a striking pattern that is visible in your design, use a minimum of eight cords. For this demonstration, however, and with the aim of showing you how to create a wider pattern, I'll use twelve cords. Arrows are generally added to pieces such as wall hangings, hanging shelves, and bag straps. You will have the chance to practice this pattern in the Tayanna wall hanging project in this book.

Knots Used:
Diagonal double half hitch (DDHH), see pages 62–63

Knotting Sequence:
3 x (5 x DDHH–left-to-right) / 3 x (5 x DDHH–right-to-left)

1 x DDHH–right-to-left
3 x (5 x DDHH–right-to-left) / 3 x (5 x DDHH–left-to-right)

Step 1: Tie three rows of five DDHHs–left-to-right, going down. For each row, the first cord is always your filler cord, and cords 2–6 are working cords.

Step 2: Now, tie three rows of DDHHs–right-to-left, going down. This time, for each row, the twelfth cord is your filler cord, and cords 7–11 are working cords.

Step 3: To connect the sections and create the first arrow, tie one single DDHH–right-to-left using the sixth and seventh cords as your working and filler cord respectively.

Step 4: Repeat step 2, only this time using the sixth cord as your filler cord, and cords 1–5 as working cords.

Step 5: Repeat step 1. This time, use the seventh cord as your filler cord, and cords 8–12 as working cords.

Square Knot Mesh

The **square knot mesh** is a pattern of several square knot sinnets (SKSs) connected by swapping working cords. Compared to the square knot net, this pattern is more compact and structurally stronger. That's why the square knot mesh is ideal for projects such as bags and hammocks, where holding weight is required. In this demonstration, twelve cords are used to create three connecting sinnets in a vertical setup.

Knots Used:
Square knot (SK), see page 47
Square knot sinnet (SKS), see page 50

Knotting Sequence:
4 x SK
4 x [4 x SKS (swapping working cords)]

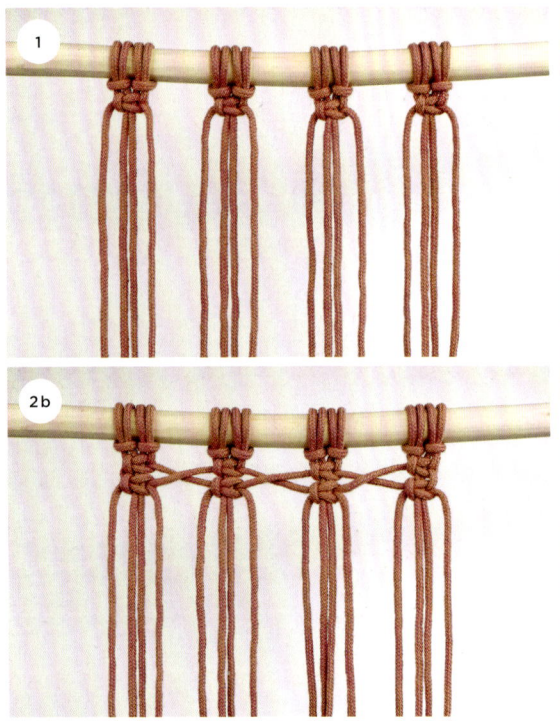
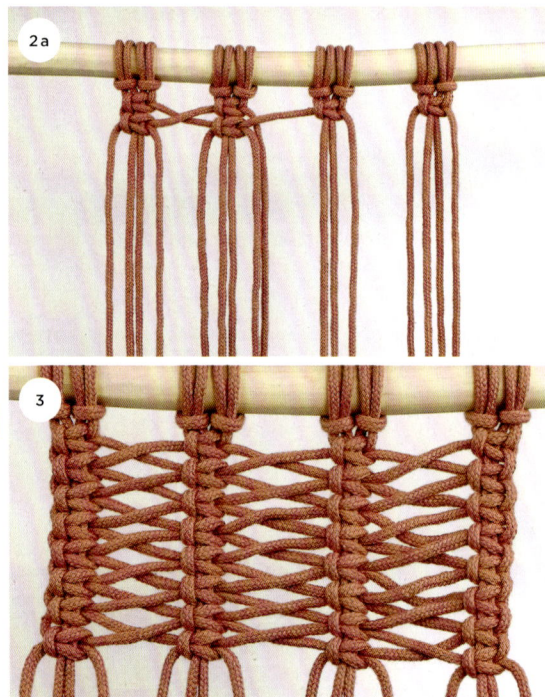

Step 1: Create four SKs using all the cords, and space them out evenly. The spacing of the SKs is up to you. In this example, the distance between knots is 3 cm (1.2 in).

> **TIP:** Keep the SKs closer to each other for tighter and more compact patterns. Space the SKs wider to get looser patterns.

Step 2: In order, tie the next row of SKs, starting from the left, by swapping the last working cord of the SKs with the first working cord of the next. This creates four connected SKSs.

Step 3: Repeat step 2 as many times as needed until you reach the desired length for your mesh.

15 Patterns & 4 Projects for Novice Artists

Tabby Weave

The **tabby weave** pattern, also referred to as the **plain weave**, is the first of two weaving techniques in this book. This pattern is created by passing a horizontal working cord over and under various filler cords, preferably using a horizontal setup. It is necessary to use a row of knots to hold and block the weaving working cord. A row of horizontal double half hitches (HDHHs) is used in this demonstration.

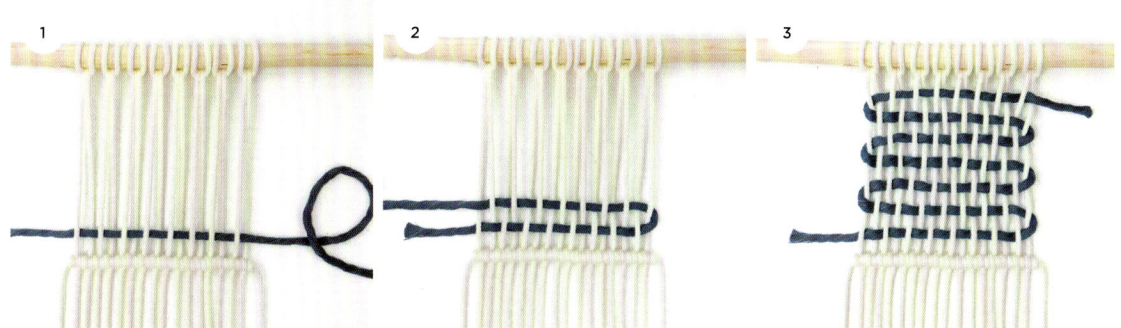

Step 1: Take your working cord (blue), and pass it through your filler cords (white) from left to right. Alternate going under and over the filler cords. Make sure most of the working cord is now to the right of your design.

Step 2: Bend the working cord (blue) around the last of your filler cords and, using the same technique, pass it through the rest of filler cords, this time from right to left.

Step 3: Repeat steps 1 and 2 until you reach the desired length for your design.

TIP: In this demonstration, the working cord is threaded under and over the filler cords one by one. Alternatively, you can pair or group your filler cords. You can see this in the Mandala Mirror project in this book, where filler cords are threaded in groups of four (see page 221).

Macramé: The Power of Knots

TIP: Fluffy fringes are a great addition to wall hanging designs because they add depth and texture. Use, for instance, four brushed working cords to tie a single rya knot inside a double half hitch diamond pattern and trim excess for an enhanced look.

Rya Knot Weaving Technique

This weaving technique has a very clear and particular use: adding fringes to your pieces. The **rya knot weaving technique** can be performed in either horizontal or vertical setups. For this example, a horizontal setup and a row of horizontal double half hitches (HDHHs) are used to block and hold several working cords in place. This unique way of weaving creates fascinating looks and textures in our designs, as you can see in the Tayanna Wall Hanging and Cressida Hanging Shelf projects illustrated in this book.

Step 1: Fold the first working cord (brown) in half over and around the first two filler cords (white) from the left. Pass both ends of the working cord between the filler cords, and pull them down to secure the knot over the row of HDHHs.

Step 2: Repeat step 1 to create a row of rya knots.

Step 3: To create the next row of fringes, skip the first vertical filler cord (white) and alternate rya knots.

Step 4: Repeat steps 1–3 to add as many rows of fringe as needed in your design.

Novice Projects

15 Patterns & 4 Projects for Novice Artists

Noelle Jar Cover

The Noelle Jar Cover is a beautiful and simple project to begin putting your knotting skills into action. This design only uses one pattern and a few basic knots to cover a jar with a small opening. The project is ideal to transform a plain household item like a jar into an eye-catching decorative piece that will complement both indoor and outdoor spaces. This decorative piece is commonly used as a flower display, or candle holder. I love the way this design looks when a tea light or candle is placed inside a transparent or translucent jar—an alluring way to add a light source to any room inside your home or to a patio area.

To create the Noelle Jar Cover in this project, you need a 20-cm (7.9-in) tall jar with a neck diameter of around 10 cm (3.9 in). For jars of different heights and neck openings, you will need to adjust the number and length of the cords you work with.

♦ ♦ ♦

Finished project specs: length 17 cm (6.7 in) x width 11 cm (4.3 in)
Approximate completion time: 30 minutes

Tools and Materials

Scissors
Measuring tape
Brush
Approximately 19.6 m (63.6 ft) natural color 2 mm cotton string
Jar

Knots and Patterns

Knots Used:
Reverse lark's head knot (RLHK), see page 43
Square knot sinnet (SKS), see page 50
Square knot (SK), see page 47
Alternating square knot (ASK), see page 51

Pattern Used:
Triangle square knot, see page 93

Preparation

Horizontal setup (only in step 1–3)
Vertical setup

Cut the following:
1 anchor cord, 1.2 m (3.9 ft) long
23 mounting cords, each 80 cm (2.6 ft) long

Macramé: The Power of Knots

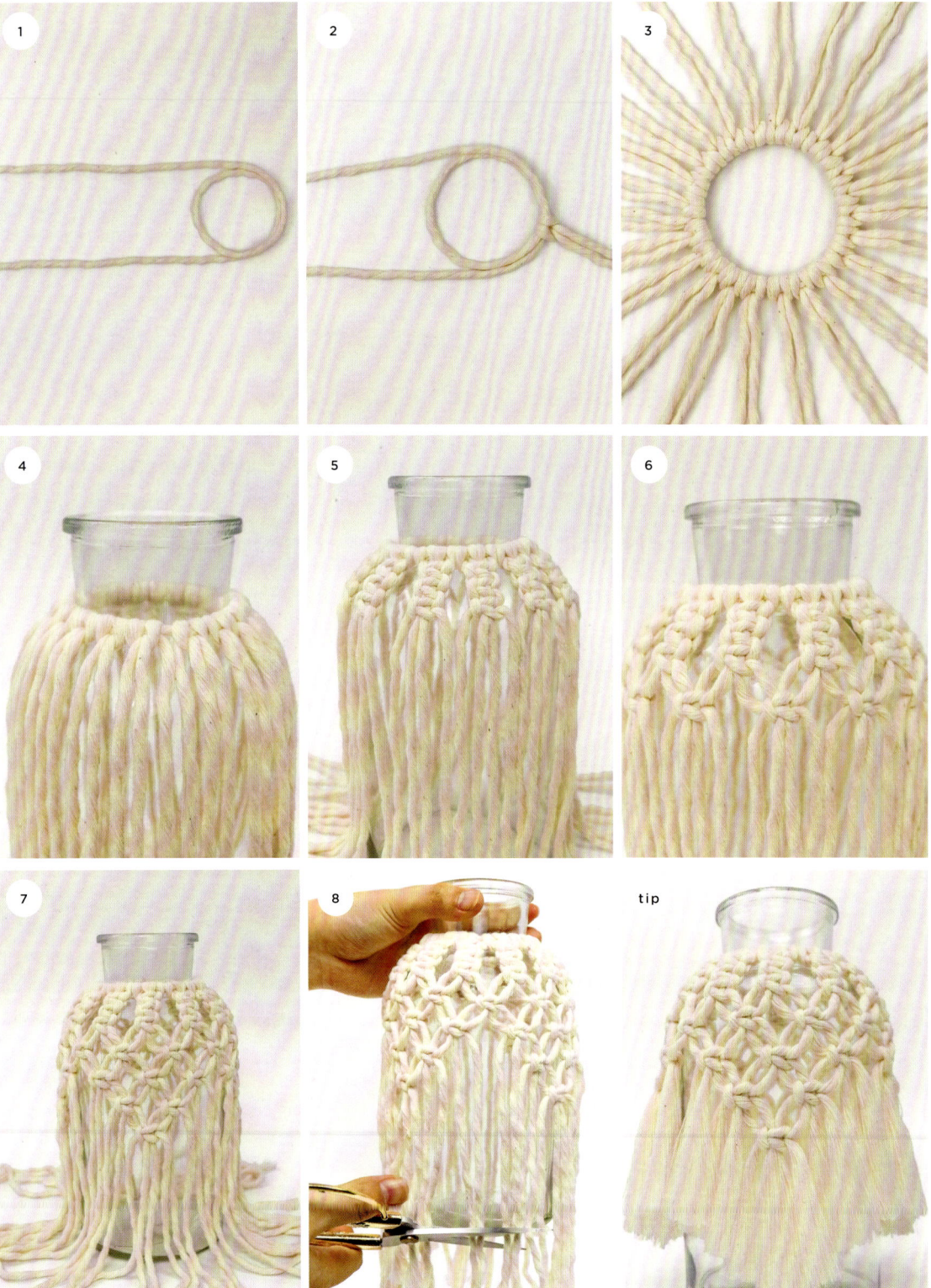

Instructions

Step 1: Using a horizontal setup, fold the 1.2-m (3.9-ft) cord to create a circumference 11 cm (4.3 in) in diameter. The length between the circumference and the ends of the cord should be equal. This creates the anchor for our pattern, and we will use it to mount the rest of the cords.

> TIP: For jars with bigger or smaller neck openings, make sure the distance from the circumference to both ends of the anchor cord is equal to the length of the mounting cords folded in half. I recommend cutting all mounting cords first and then cutting your anchor cord.

Step 2: Fold one 80-cm (2.6-ft) cord in half and mount it to the circumference with an RLHK.

Step 3: Repeat step 2 with the rest of the mounting cords. There should now be forty-eight cords, including the two ends of our anchor cord.

Step 4: Pass the neck of the jar through the circumference created in step 3. This is the vertical setup we'll be using for the remaining steps on this project.

Step 5: Create twelve SKSs around the circumference. It is very important to ensure both ends of the anchor cord are included in the same sinnet. First, take both ends of the anchor cord and use the next two cords to create the first sinnet. Each sinnet has three SKs.

Step 6: Move 1 cm (0.4 in) down from the SKSs and create a row of alternating SKs.

Step 7: Continue by making four triangle square knot patterns using all of the cords, twelve cords per triangle. Leave 1 cm (0.4 in) between rows to create a loose pattern. This gives our design a light and relaxed look.

Step 8: To finish this piece, cut the fringe equal to the length of the jar.

> TIP: To achieve a fluffy fringe, brush and trim all the cords. If you are using a different type of rope, you may have to untwist the cords before brushing.

Boheme Belt

If you grew up in the '90s like I did, the Boheme Belt project will probably send you down memory lane. I remember using this style of belt during summer days with long linen dresses and wide-legged denim jeans. This stylish accessory will be a great addition to your wardrobe and the perfect finish to a boho-style outfit. The Boheme Belt combines beautifully with skirts and both mini and long dresses, as well as jeans, defining the silhouette of these clothing items and enhancing a retro look.

To complete this project, you will need a belt buckle. O-ring or D-ring belt buckles work best with this design. The one used for this piece is a wooden O-ring-style buckle with a diameter of 6 cm (2.4 in).

✦ ✦ ✦

Finished project specs: length 1 m (3.2 ft) x width 5 cm (2 in)
Approximate completion time: 2 hours

Tools and Materials

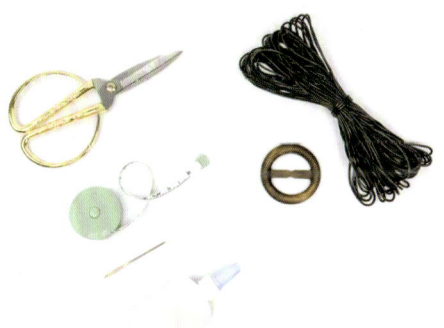

Knots and Patterns
Knots Used:
Lark's head knot (LHK), see page 42
Diagonal double half hitch (DDHH), see pages 62–63
Square knot (SK), see page 47
Patterns Used:
Double half hitch diamond, see page 94
Double half hitch diamond with square knot, see page 97
Preparation
Vertical setup
Cut the following:
1 cord, 5 m (16.4 ft) long
2 cords, each 6 m (19.6 ft) long
2 cords, each 7 m (22.9 ft) long

Scissors
Measuring tape
Tapestry needle
Glue
Approximately 36 m (118.1 ft) black 2 mm waxed rope
6-cm (2.4-in) diameter belt buckle

Macramé: The Power of Knots

1

2

3
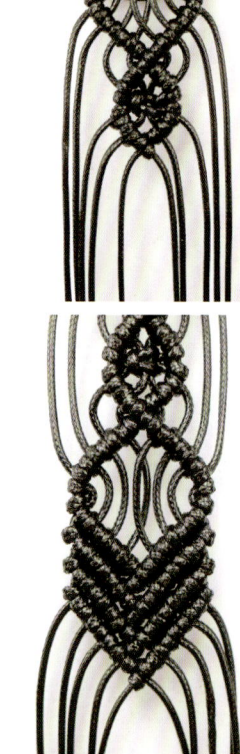

4

5

6

7

TIP: Working with waxed rope is a bit more challenging than cotton. This rope is harder and tends to stick to your fingers while knotting. I recommend using gloves to make the belt and gently pulling cords after tying each knot.

TIP: After tucking the cords, add a small dab of glue to secure the ends.

Instructions

Step 1: Fold the cords in half and mount them to your belt buckle with LHKs. Follow this sequence: 6 m (19.6 ft)–7 m (22.9 ft)–5 m (16.4 ft)–7 m (22.9 ft)–6 m (19.6 ft).

Step 2: Start by creating a double half hitch diamond pattern using all the cords. Use the fifth and sixth cords as your filler cords and the rest as working cords.

Step 3: Continue by knotting a small double half hitch diamond with square knot pattern using cords 3–8, leaving the first and last two cords untied. The fifth and sixth cords continue being your filler cords. The SK inside the diamond is tied using cords 4–7. To close the diamond shape in this step, take the fifth and sixth cords as your filler and working cords, respectively, to knot the last DDHH.

Step 4: Repeat steps 2 and 3 until you reach the desired length. I repeated these steps ten times for this project. Be sure to complete this sequence of patterns with a double half hitch diamond (step 2).

Step 5: Now tie four DDHHs toward the right, going down. Use the first cord as your filler cord and cords 2–5 as working cords. Then, tie five DDHHs toward the left, going down. Use the tenth cord as your filler cord this time, and cords 5–9 as your working cords.

Step 6: Repeat step 5 twice.

Step 7: To complete your belt, trim the cords 2 cm (0.8 in) from the DDHHs. Then use a tapestry needle to tuck the end of the cords into the back of the belt.

15 Patterns & 4 Projects for Novice Artists

Aura Coaster

The Aura Coaster is a small ornamental piece excellent for adding warmth. Tiny in size, compared to more traditional macramé artwork, this decorative element has the power to transform the ambience of any area into an elegant, stylish, and cozy space. These coasters are ideal to place hot or cold beverages on top of, as they are flat and super absorbent. If you like scented candles, the aura coaster is also an ideal decorative plate you can place under them.

♦ ♦ ♦

Finished project specs: length 17 cm (6.7 in) x width 12 cm (4.7 in)
Approximate completion time: 45 minutes

Tools and Materials

Scissors
Measuring tape
Glue
Brush
Approximately 7.4 m (24.2 ft) natural color 3 mm 4-ply twisted rope
A dowel/horizontal support, 30 cm (11.8 in) long, at least 1 cm (0.4 in) diameter

Knots and Patterns

Knots Used:

Lark's head knot (LHK), see page 41
Horizontal double half hitch (HDHH), see page 65
Diagonal double half hitch (DDHH), see pages 62–63
Square knot (SK), see page 47
Alternating square knot (ASK), see page 51

Pattern Used:

Square knot diamond with big square knot, see page 102

Preparation

Horizontal setup
Firmly tape or secure the dowel/ horizontal support to ease knotting.

Cut the following:

2 cords, each 30 cm (11.8 in) long
2 cords, each 80 cm (2.6 ft) long
2 cords, each 90 cm (2.9 ft) long
2 cords, each 100 cm (3.3 ft) long
2 cords, each 110 cm (3.6 ft) long
2 cords, each 120 cm (3.9 ft) long

Macramé: The Power of Knots

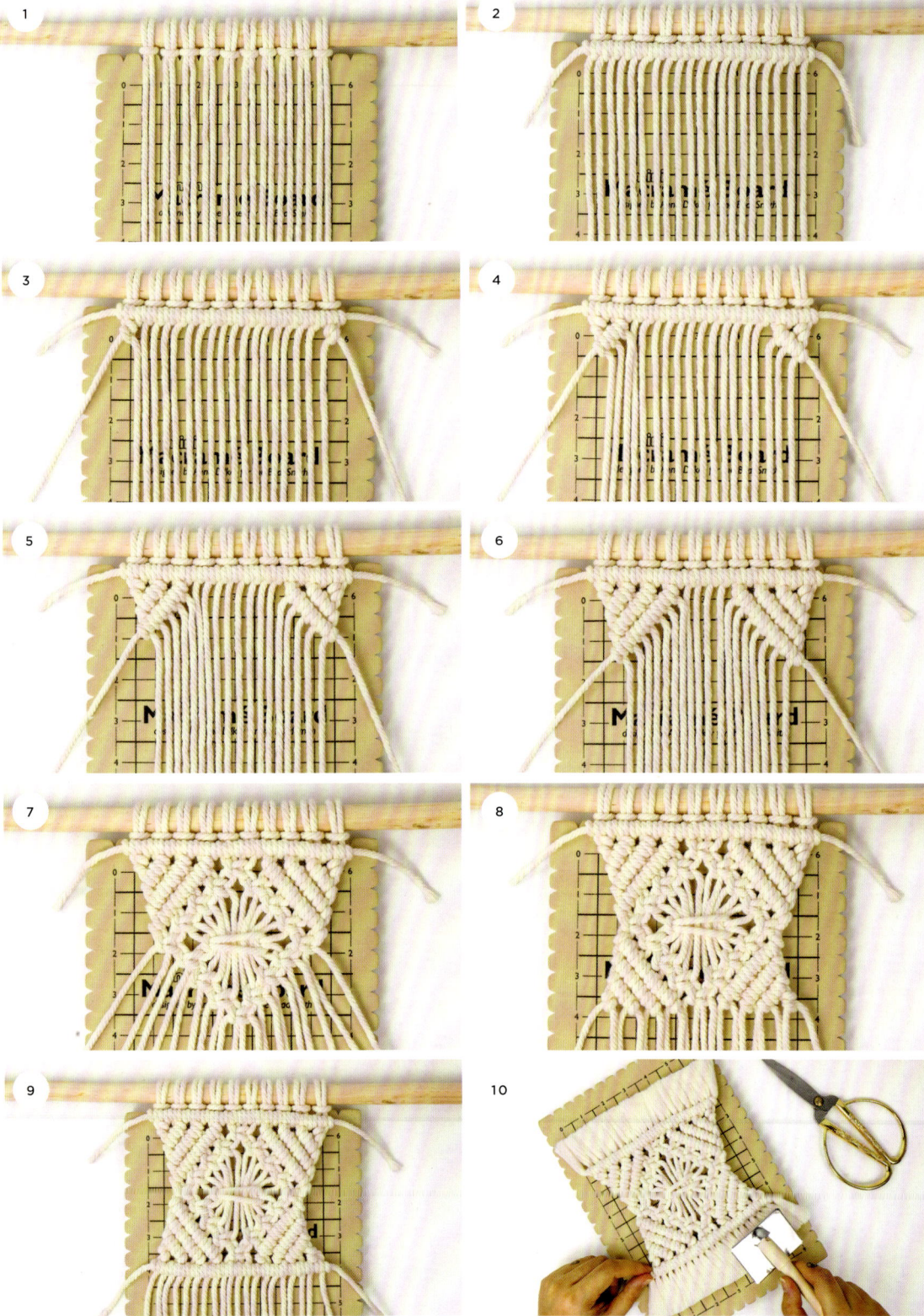

Instructions

Step 1: Fold the cords in half and mount them to your dowel/horizontal support with LHKs. Follow this sequence: 120 cm (3.9 ft)–110 cm (3.6 ft)–100 cm (3.3 ft)–90 cm (2.9 ft)–80 cm (2.6 ft)–80 cm (2.6 ft)–90 cm (2.9 ft)–100 cm (3.3 ft)–110 cm (3.6 ft)–120 cm (3.9 ft).

Step 2: Take one 30-cm (11.8-in) long cord to work as your filler cord. Place it over all the cords and tie a row of ten HDHHs from right to left, under the LHKs.

> **TIP:** Add a small dab of glue on both ends of the HDHH row to secure it.

Step 3: Starting from the left, take the second cord as your filler cord and the first cord as your working cord to knot a single DDHH. Repeat this technique in reverse on the right side of your piece in reverse.

Step 4: Starting from the left, take the fourth cord as your filler cord and cords 1–3 as your working cords. Tie three DDHHs toward the left, going down. Repeat this technique on the right side of your piece in reverse.

Step 5: Take the sixth cord from the left as your filler cord and cords 1–5 as your working cords. Tie five DDHHs toward the left, going down. Repeat this technique on the right side of your piece in reverse.

Step 6: Now take the eighth cord from the left as your filler cord and cords 1–7 as your working cords. Tie seven DDHHs toward the left, going down. Repeat this technique on the right side of your piece in reverse.

Step 7: Use all the cords to create a square knot diamond with the big square knot pattern. To tie the big SK in the center, use cords 5 and 16 as your working cords.

Step 8: To mirror the top part of our design, tie four rows of DDHHs on both sides. The first DDHHs rows start with seven knots going down, following the direction of the ASKs. The number of knots per DDHH row decreases by two after each row. Use the first and last cords as your filler cords for every row on the left and right side of your design respectively.

Step 9: Repeat step 2.

Step 10: Remove the dowel/horizontal support and cut the loops of the LHKs to create a fringe. Trim the ends of both sides of your design at the same length. Untwist the cords and then brush them to create fluffy fringes.

15 Patterns & 4 Projects for Novice Artists

Eartha Plant Hanger

Plants are a fantastic way to improve indoor spaces, giving them an earthy and natural look. Plants enhance the overall appearance of a room, and they can also help you become healthier and happier. A perfect addition to your home or workspace, plant hangers allow you to display your favorite greenery without having to worry about pets messing with them or children's safety. If you are a plant lover like me, the Eartha Plant Hanger project is right up your alley. This elegant plant hanger is perfect for novices, even though it involves a few different knots. This is the project you want to do before moving up to projects on an intermediate level.

In this project, two colors are used to practice mixing color cords in your designs. Feel free to use any color combination to fit your style. This plant hanger is intended for pots of 15 cm (5.9 in) in diameter and 10 cm (3.9 in) height. If you plan to use a different size pot, you'll have to adjust the number of knots and amount of spacing between them in the pot holder section of the project.

✦ ✦ ✦

Finished project specs: Length 90 cm (2.9 ft)
Approximate completion time: 1 hour

Tools and Materials

Scissors
Measuring tape
Tape or tapestry needle, glue
Approximately 7.6 m (24.9 ft) white 3 mm cotton braided rope
Approximately 8 m (26.2 ft) green 3 mm cotton braided rope
A wooden ring, 6 cm (2.4 in) in diameter
4 large hole wooden beads, 2 cm (0.8 in) in diameter

Knots and Patterns
Knots Used:
Crown knot, see page 76
Diagonal double half hitch (DDHH), see pages 62–63
Square knot (SK), see page 47
Alternating square knot (ASK), see page 51
Lark's head knot (LHK), see page 41
Gathering knot, see page 70
Barrel knot, see page 74
Pattern Used:
Small diamond chain, see page 101
Preparation
Vertical setup
Cut the following:
4 white cords, each 3.6 m (11.8 ft) long
4 green cords, each 3.6 m (11.8 ft) long
4 white cords, each 1 m (3.3 ft) long
4 green cords, each 1 m (3.3 ft) long
1 green cord, 80 cm (2.6 ft) long

Macramé: The Power of Knots

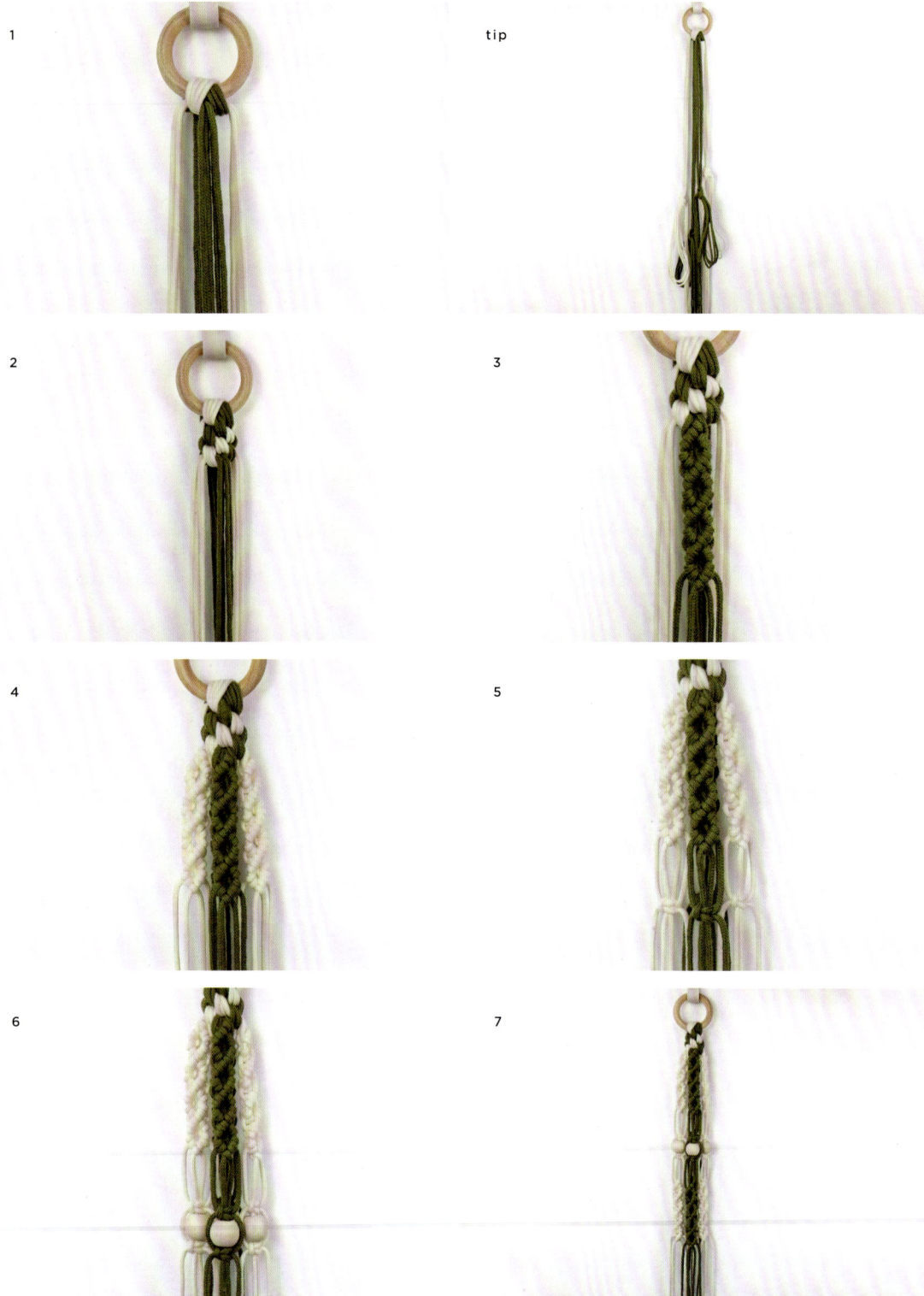

Instructions

Step 1: Group the cords by color (four white cords and four green cords). Then, mount them to the wooden ring using a crown knot.

> **TIP:** To maneuver the cords with ease, tie both ends of each group of cords with an overhand knot (see page 38).

Step 2: Tie five crown knots using the clockwise technique to create the top section of the plant hanger. After this section, we are going to divide our cords in four groups with four cords in each group.

> **TIP:** If you followed the tip in step 1, you should now untie the overhand knots to release all cords and continue with the next step.

Step 3: Take one group of cords and tie a small diamond chain with four diamonds in it.

Step 4: Repeat step 3 with the rest of the groups.

Step 5: Take one chain, move down 3 cm (1.2 in), and tie one single SK. Do the same with the remaining three chains.

Step 6: For a more natural look, add wooden beads as the decorative elements. Add one bead to each individual chain. To do this, take the filler cords of one chain and pass them through the bead. The working cords are used to hold the bead from the outside. Lock the bead in place by tying another SK underneath the bead. Now, do the same with the three remaining chains.

> **TIP:** To pass the filler cords through the bead's hole easily, tape the ends of the cords together, or use a tapestry needle.

Step 7: Move another 3 cm (1.2 in) down after the SKs and tie another four small diamond chains. With this step, the body section of the plant hanger is completed.

Step 8: Start the bottom section of the project, the pot holder, by splitting the cords of one chain into two pairs of cords and adding a new cord to each pair. To attach the new cords, first move down 5 cm (2 in) and mount 1-m (3.3-ft) long cords folded in half using LHKs.

Step 9: Now tie an SK, using the newly added cords, 3 cm (1.2 in) down from the LHKs.

Step 10: Repeat step 8 and 9 with the remaining three chains.

Step 11: Now, it is time to start connecting the chains. To connect the first two chains, use the right pair of untouched cords of the left chain and the left pair of untouched cords of the right chain to tie an SK 3 cm (1.2 in) from the LHKs. Make sure all SKs are aligned.

Step 12: Connect all chains to each other using the technique explained in step 11.

Step 13: Move down 3 cm (1.2 in) and tie a row of ASKs using all the cords.

> **TIP:** If you are using a larger or smaller pot, you may need to adjust the spacing between the two rows of SKs, making it longer or shorter respectively.

Step 14: To close the pot holder section of the plant hanger, move 5 cm (2 in) down and use the 80-cm (2.6-ft) separate piece of cord to create a gathering knot around all the cords.

> **TIP:** Add a small dab of glue to secure the end of the gathering knot.

Step 15: To decorate the tail of your plant hanger, randomly tie barrel knots in as many cords as you want. To finish this project, trim the cords to your desired length.

SUGGESTION: If you are using twisted or single-strand cords to make this project, you can make fluffy fringes by untwisting and brushing the cords in the tail.

15 Patterns & 4 Projects for Novice Artists

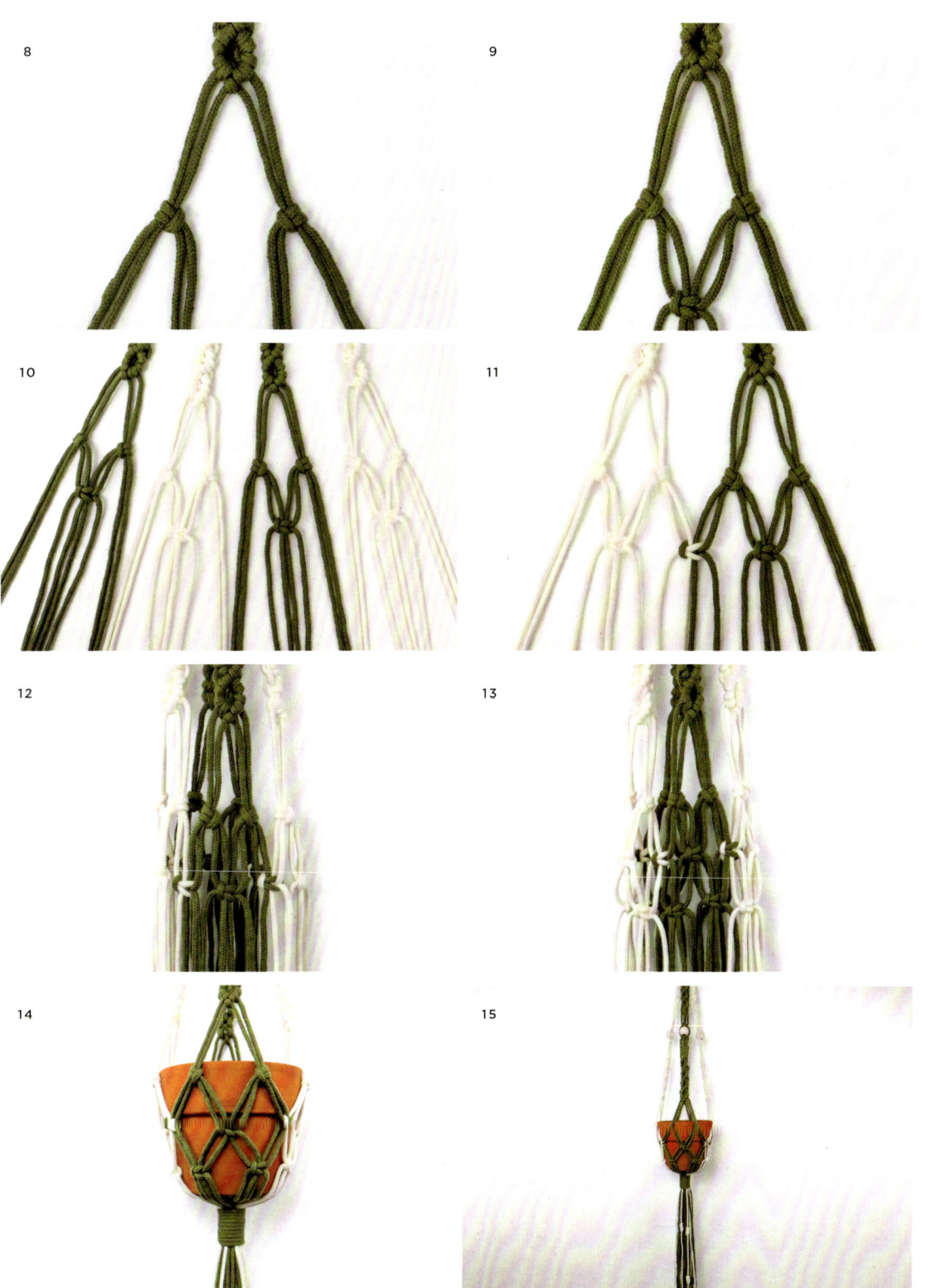

CHAPTER 5

15 Patterns & 4 Projects for Intermediate Artists

Intermediate Patterns

Double Half Hitch Diamond Mesh

The **double half hitch diamond mesh**, despite its long name, is a very simple filling pattern used predominantly in flat and hanging pieces. It is created by connecting a series of diamond chains with square knots (SKs). For this demonstration, you need to arrange thirty-two cords in a vertical setup.

Knots Used:
Diagonal double half hitch (DDHH), see pages 62–63
Square knot (SK), see page 47

Pattern Used:
Double half hitch diamond with square knot,
  see page 97

Knotting Sequence:
4 x (4 x DDHH–right-to-left / 3 x DDHH–left-to-right)
4 x SK
4 x (3 x DDHH–left-to-right / 4 x DDHH–right-to-left)
4 x SK

Step 1: Make four double half hitch diamonds with square knot patterns. Use eight cords for each diamond.

Step 2: Then, tie three SKs between diamonds using cords 6–11, 14–19, and 22–27. There are four filler cords in each of the SKs.

Step 3: Repeat steps 1 and 2 as many times as you please, until you reach the desired length for your design.

15 Patterns & 4 Projects for Intermediate Artists

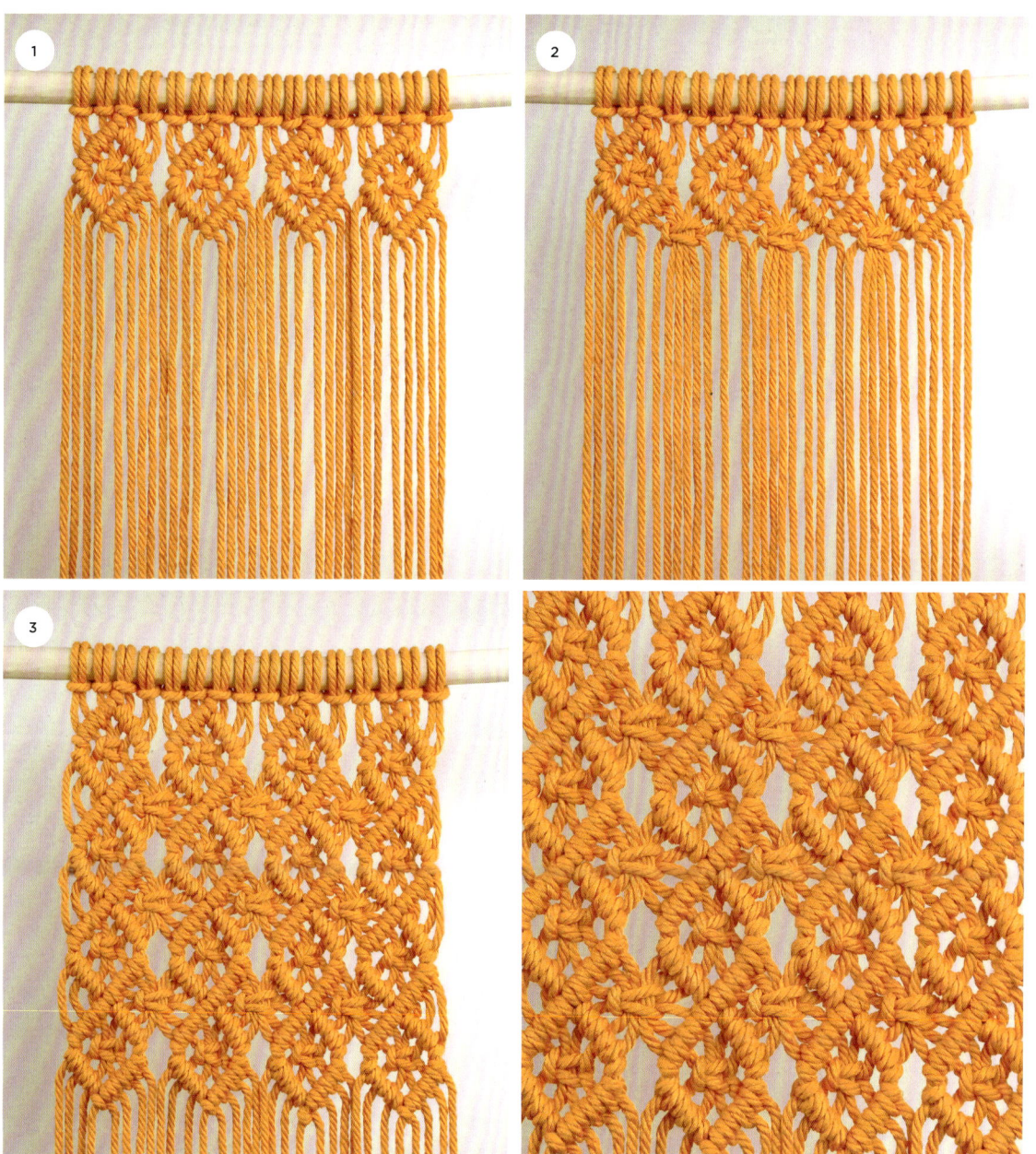

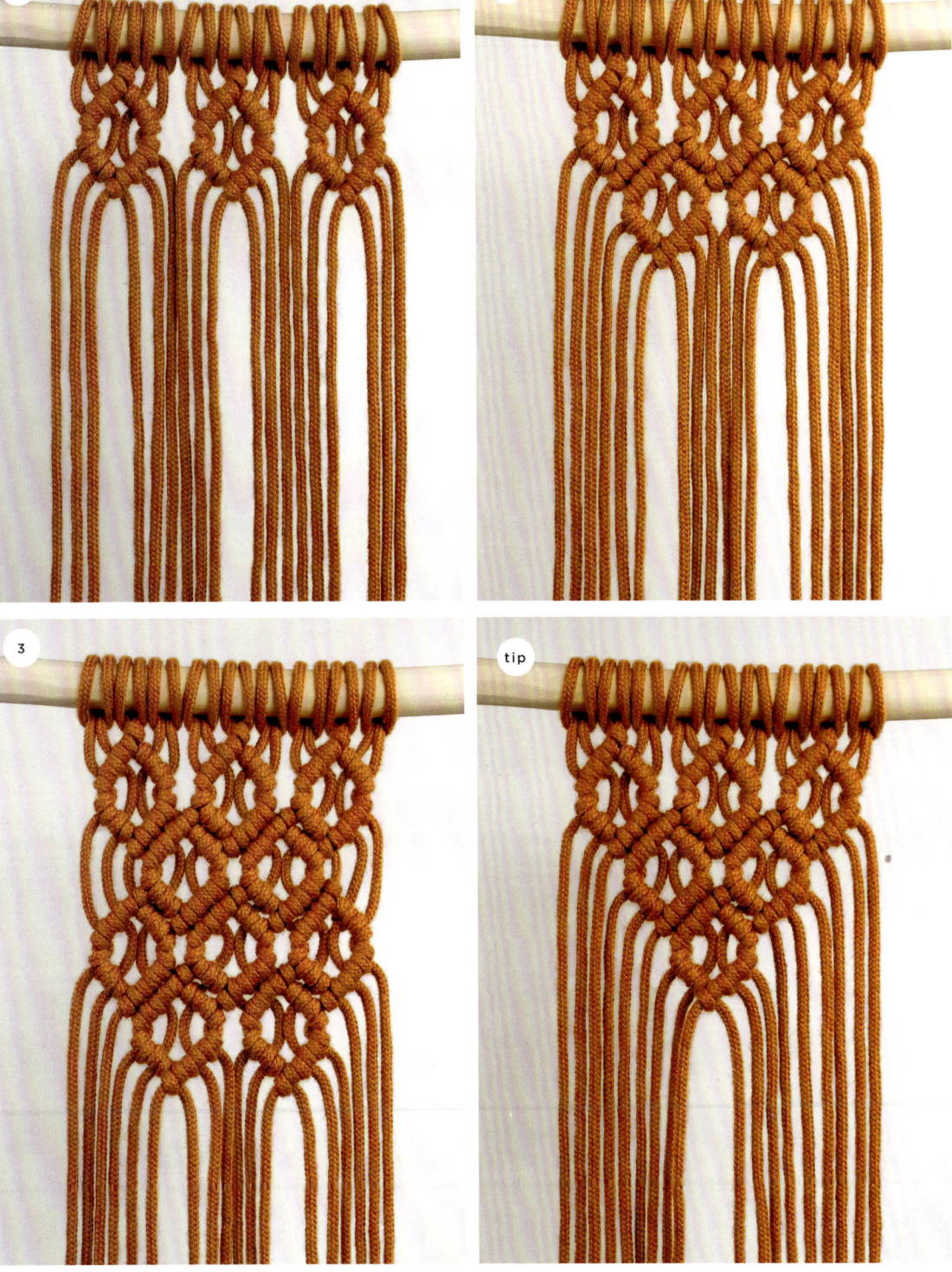

Alternating Double Half Hitch Diamond Mesh

A very appealing pattern commonly used in wall hangings and many other decorative pieces. The **alternating double half hitch diamond mesh** is ideal to add a structured and organized feeling to your artwork. This pattern is created by alternating diamonds to create a mesh. You can see this pattern being used in the Cressida Hanging Shelf project. I use a vertical setup to demonstrate the pattern, and mount nine cords to a wooden dowel.

Knots Used:
Diagonal double half hitch (DDHH), see pages 62–63

Pattern Used:
Double half hitch diamond, see page 94

Knotting Sequence:
3 x (3 x DDHH–right-to-left / 2 x DDHH–left-to-right)
3 x (2 x DDHH–left-to-right / 3 x DDHH–right-to-left)
2 x (3 x DDHH–right-to-left / 2 x DDHH–left-to-right)
2 x (2 x DDHH–left-to-right / 3 x DDHH–right-to-left)

Step 1: Make a row of three double half hitch diamonds, using six cords per diamond.

Step 2: Alternate the pattern by making two double half hitch diamonds underneath. Each diamond in this step uses three cords from one diamond and the following three cords from the next one.

Step 3: Repeat steps 1 and 2 until you reach the desired length of your mesh.

TIP: You can use this technique of placing double half hitch diamonds to create a mesh, to form other geometric shapes such as triangles and diamonds. As an example, I show you here how to create an inverted triangle shape by simply reducing the number of diamonds row by row.

Diagonal Double Half Hitch Triangle

The **diagonal double half hitch triangle** is a stunning pattern that works perfectly in elegant mandala pieces as well as mirrors and dream catchers. It is created by knotting layers of diagonal double half hitches (DDHHs) in a triangular shape. In the demonstration, I use a horizontal setup and eight cords mounted to a wooden ring. The more cords you add to this pattern, the bigger the triangular shape will be.

Knots Used:
Diagonal double half hitch (DDHH), see pages 62–63

Knotting Sequence:
1 x DDHH–left-to-right / 2 x DDHH–right-to-left
3 x DDHH–left-to-right / 4 x DDHH–right-to-left
5 x DDHH–left-to-right / 6 x DDHH–right-to-left
7 x DDHH–left-to-right / 8 x DDHH– right-to-left

Step 1: Using cord 7 as your filler cord and cord 8 as your working cord, tie one DDHH–left-to-right.

Step 2: Next, take cord 10 as your filler cord, and cords 8 and 9 as working cords, to tie two DDHHs–right-to-left, going down. This completes the first layer of the pattern and creates a small triangle shape.

Step 3: Now tie three DDHHs–left-to-right, going down, using cord 5 as your filler cord and cords 6–8 as working cords.

Step 4: To finish the second layer of the pattern, take the twelfth cord as your filler cord and cords 8–11 as working cords. Now tie four DDHHs–right-to-left, going down.

Step 5: Using the same technique, tie another two layers of triangles. Notice how, with every line of DDHHs, one more knot is added to the sequence.

Step 6: Repeat steps 1–5 to make as many triangles as you need to complete the ring.

15 Patterns & 4 Projects for Intermediate Artists

TIP: If you wish for a wider pattern, mount extra cords to your anchor cord in this step.

Spiral Double Half Hitch

An incredibly fluid and dynamic design, the **spiral double half hitch** is a simple pattern that naturally curves by tying multiple lines of horizontal double half hitches (HDHHs). I personally love using this pattern to create the top sections of plant hangers. By using different lengths of the spiral double half hitch pattern in three or four different plant hangers, and playing with the type of plants you use, you can get creative and fill the spaces of any corners around your house. I use six cords and a wooden ring arranged in a vertical setup for this demonstration.

Knots Used:
Lark's head knot (LHK), see page 41
Horizontal double half hitch (HDHH), see page 65

Knotting Sequence:
4 x LHK
11 x HDHH
11 x HDHH

Step 1: Fold all six cords in half, and mount one to the wooden ring with a LHK.

Step 2: Use the second cord as your anchor cord to mount the remaining five cords using LHKs.

Step 3: Take the first cord as your filler cord now, and using cords 2–12 as working cords, tie eleven HDHHs–left-to-right underneath the LHKs line. From now on, the anchor cord is used as a working cord. This step completes the first line of HDHHs.

Step 4: Leave a small gap in the end of the row before finishing the next row of eleven HDHHs to your pattern. This loosens the pattern and allows it to naturally curve.

Step 5: Keep repeating step 4 until you reach the desired length for your design.

Increasing Diamond with Square Knot

The **increasing diamond with square knot** pattern is basically an open diamond shape with a square knot (SK) in the middle, where its top and bottom are contained by small lines of diagonal double half hitches (DDHHs). It is important that the top and bottom lines of diagonal double half hitches (DDHHs) are equal to or smaller than the actual sides of the diamond. In this demonstration, you need to use eight cords in a vertical setup. You will be able to practice this pattern in the Avery Pillow project.

Knots Used:
Square knot (SK), see page 47
Diagonal double half hitch (DDHH), see pages 62–63

Knotting Sequence:
3 x DDHH–right–to–left / 2 x DDHH–left–to–right
3 x DDHH–right–to–left / 3 x DDHH–left–to–right
1 x SK
3 x DDHH–left–to–right / 3 x DDHH–right–to–left
2 x DDHH–left–to–right / 3 x DDHH–right–to–left

Step 1: Start by tying three DDHHs–right–to–left, going down. Use the fifth cord as your filler cord and cords 2–4 as working cords.

Step 2: Next, take the fifth cord as your filler cord once again, and now tie two DDHHs–left–to–right, going down, using cords 6 and 7 as your working cords.

Step 3: Continue with two new lines of DDHHs under the previous ones: one line of three DDHHs–right–to–left, and another of three DDHHs –left–to–right, both going down. For the first line, use the fourth cord as your filler cord, and cords 1–3 as your working cords. Do the same for the second line, this time using the fifth cord as your filler cord, and cords 6–8 as working cords.

Step 4: Tie one single SK in the middle of the design with cords 3–6.

Step 5: Take the first cord as your filler cord and cords 2–4 as working cords to tie 3 DDHHs–left–to–right, going down. Then take the eighth cord as your filler cord and cords 5–7 as working cords, and tie 3 DDHHs–right–to–left, going down.

Step 6: Now take the second cord as your filler cord, and tie two DDHHs–left–to–right, going down, using cords 3 and 4 as working cords.

Step 7: To close and complete the pattern, use the seventh cord as your filler cord, and cords 4–6 as working cords, to tie the last 3 DDHHs–right–to–left, going down.

15 Patterns & 4 Projects for Intermediate Artists

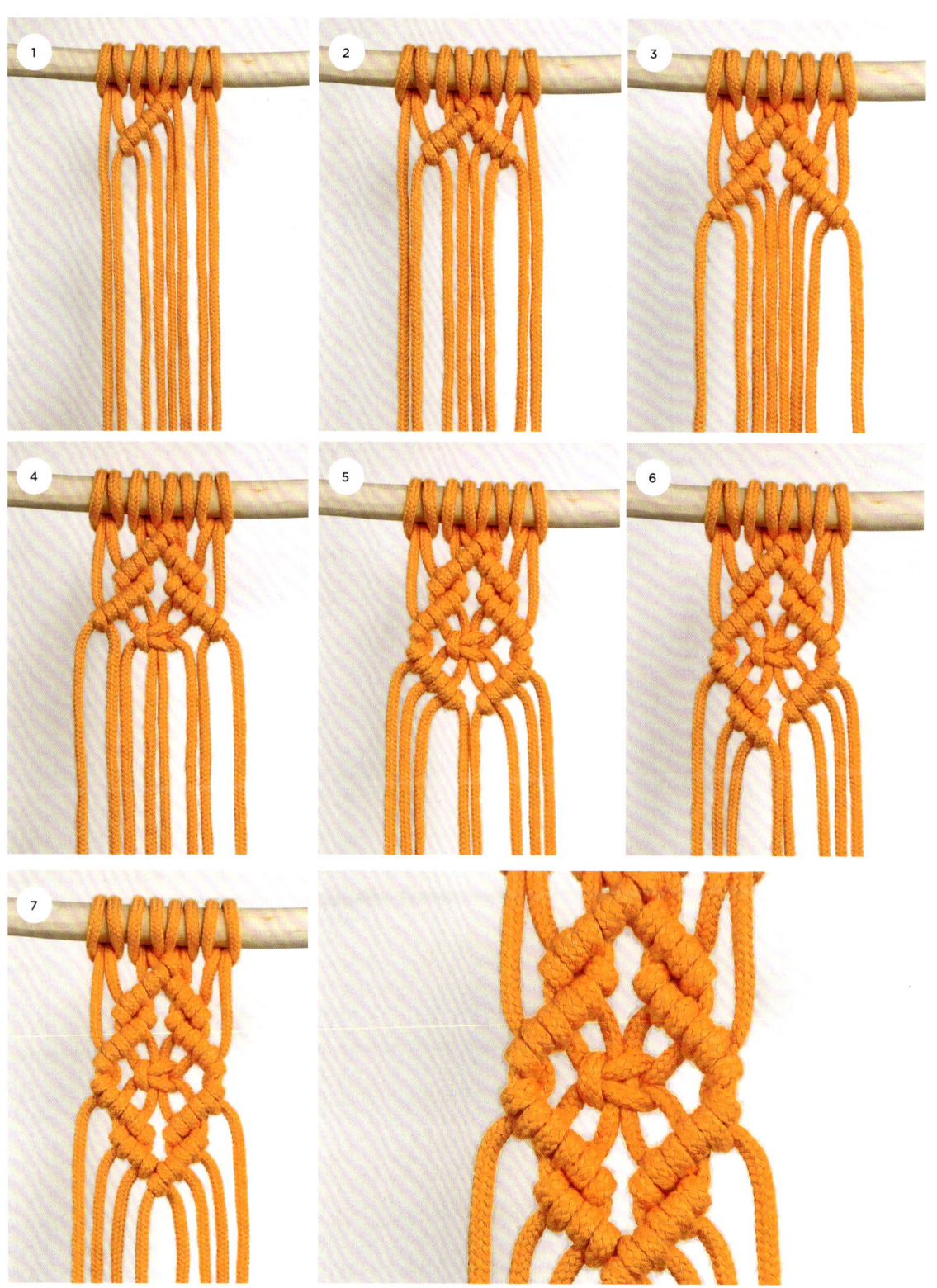

Macramé: The Power of Knots

140

Overlap Horizontal Zigzags

The **overlap horizontal zigzags** is a pattern created by overlapping two individually knotted horizontal zigzag patterns facing opposite directions. The horizontal zigzag pattern uses only one basic knot, the horizontal double half hitch (HDHH). Rows of horizontal double half hitches (HDHHs) are placed one after the other toward one direction. Changing the direction of the rows gives the pattern the zigzag effect. Plant hangers and hanging shelves are some of the most common projects where this pattern is included. In the following example, you need sixteen cords in a vertical setup, changing direction every seven rows. In order to achieve neat horizontal zigzag patterns, ensure your knotting is consistent so your rows are perfectly aligned.

Knots Used:
Horizontal double half hitch (HDHH), see page 65

Knotting Sequence:
7 x (7 x HDHH-left-to-right)
7 x (7 x HDHH-right-to-left)

Step 1: To begin your overlap horizontal zigzags pattern, start by mounting eight cords to your dowel. The first four cords are used to create an individual horizontal zigzag pattern that initially moves toward the right. The second four cords are used to create the second horizontal zigzag pattern which, opposite to the first one, moves toward the left at the beginning.

> **TIP:** To bring color to your design, you can use different-colored cords for each of the individually knotted horizontal zigzag patterns.

Step 2: Start the first horizontal zigzag pattern, the one moving toward the right initially, by taking the first cord from the left as your filler cord, and using cords 2-8 as working cords to tie seven HDHHs-left-to-right.

Step 3: Repeat step 2 six more times.

Step 4: To change the direction of the pattern, use the eighth cord now as your filler cord, and cords 1-7 as working cords, to tie seven rows of seven HDHHs-right-to-left.

Step 5: Repeat steps 2-4 as many times as you need until you reach the desired length of your design. This completes the first horizontal zigzag pattern of your overlap horizontal zigzags pattern.

Step 6: The second horizontal zigzag pattern of your design uses cords 9-16. To create it, use the technique explained in steps 2-5 in reverse. Notice how, this time, the second horizontal zigzag pattern initially moves toward the left.

Step 7: To complete the overlap horizontal zigzags pattern, simply braid the two horizontal zigzag patterns together.

Fishbone

Fishbone patterns are a creative way to add square knot sinnets (SKSs) to projects such as wall hangings, plant hangers, and pretty much all flat decorative pieces. They are created by including new working cords while knotting the sinnets. It is possible, as you will see in this demonstration, to alternate fishbone patterns to create a net. For this example, I mount twelve cords to a wooden dowel in a vertical setup, and connect three fishbones together. You can find a practical example of this pattern in the Maya Basket project of the book.

Knots Used:
Square knot (SK), see page 47
Square knot sinnet (SKS), see page 50

Knotting Sequence:
2 x SKS
1 x alternating SKS

Step 1: Begin the fishbone pattern by tying two SKs. Use cords 5–8 for one knot, and 17–20 for the other.

Step 2: Continue the sinnets by tying another two SKs. Use the same filler cords, but this time add a new set of working cords: cords 4 and 9 for the first, and cords 16 and 21 for the second.

Step 3: Using the same technique, continue tying SKs, adding new sets of working cords each time until there are no cords left. You should have now tied five SKs in each sinnet and completed the first two fishbone patterns.

Step 4: The third sinnet is an alternating fishbone, and is used to connect the previous patterns. Take two working cords from step 1 (one from each SK) and two working cords from step 2 (one from each SK) as filler and working cords, respectively, and use them to knot the first SK of the third sinnet.

Step 5: Using the same technique, tie another 4 SKs by adding a new set of working cords.

15 Patterns & 4 Projects for Intermediate Artists

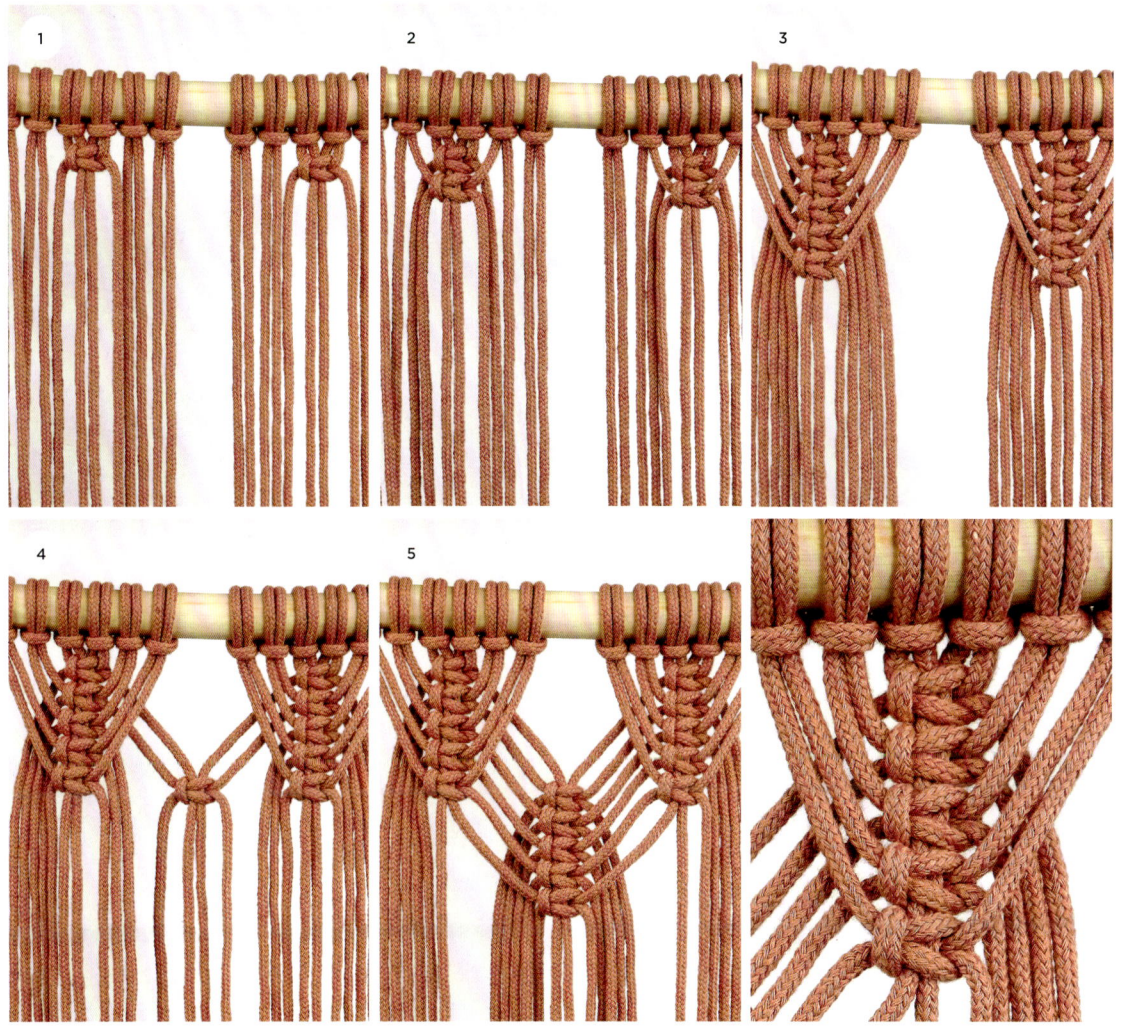

Macramé: The Power of Knots

TIP: Cut the extra working cord at double the length of the previous working cord.

15 Patterns & 4 Projects for Intermediate Artists

Circular

The **circular pattern** gets away from the lines and corners that most other macramé patterns offer to designs. A not-so-common geometric shape that perfectly fits flat macramé artwork. This pattern was brought to fame thanks to its most popular piece, the circular coaster. The circular pattern is created by tying an uninterrupted line of knots following a spiral shape, adding extra working cords along the way. I use one anchor cord and four mounting cords to demonstrate this technique in a horizontal setup, and include it in the Heather Table Mat project.

Knots Used:
Reverse lark's head knot (RLHK), see page 43
Horizontal double half hitch (HDHH), see page 65

Step 1: Fold the anchor cord to create a circumference. Make sure the length of one of the cord ends leaving the circumference is equal to half the length of the mounting cords. The other end of the cord should be longer as it is used as a filler cord in the next steps.

Step 2: Fold four cords in half and mount them to the circumference using RLHKs.

Step 3: Pull both ends of the anchor cord while holding the rest of the cords. This closes and tightens the circumference.

Step 4: Take the longer cord as your filler cord now, and using the rest of the cords as working cords, begin to tie HDHHs, following a spiral shape.

Step 5: Keep tying HDHHs until a gap between the filler cord and the next working cord appears. This is when the first extra working cord needs to be added. To do so, fold one extra working cord in half and mount it to the filler cord with a RLHK.

Step 6: Pull the RLHK tightly and slide it into place next to the last HDHH previously knotted.

Step 7: Continue knotting HDHHs and adding more cords when gaps appear again until you reach the desired size of your pattern.

Infinity

In the **infinity pattern**, you use diagonal double half hitches (DDHHs) to create an infinity symbol. This ancient character represents infinity, immortality, and eternal return. It's a very creative and delicate way to add some mystical elements to any design. You need ten cords arranged in a vertical setup in this demonstration.

Knots Used:
Diagonal double half hitch (DDHH), see pages 62–63

Knotting Sequence:
5 x DDHH
9 x DDHH
5 x DDHH

Step 1: Begin the infinity pattern with five DDHHs–right-to-left, going down. Use cord 10 as your filler cord, and cords 5–9 as working cords. Finish this step by bending the line of knots gently to create a curve.

Step 2: Then, under the first line of knots, tie nine DDHHs –right-to-left, going down. Use cord 10 as your filler cord, and cords 1–9 as working cords. Leave some space between the first and second lines, and gently curve the knots of the second line.

Step 3: To complete the infinity pattern, continue with five DDHHs–right-to-left, going down. Use cord 6 as your filler cord, and cords 1–5 as working cords. Leave some space between lines and remember to curve the last line of DDHHs.

> **TIP:** If you wish to create a left–to–right–looking infinity pattern, use the technique explained in steps 1-3, in reverse. To do so, you should start counting your cords from the right, and tying your DDHHs left–to–right.

15 Patterns & 4 Projects for Intermediate Artists

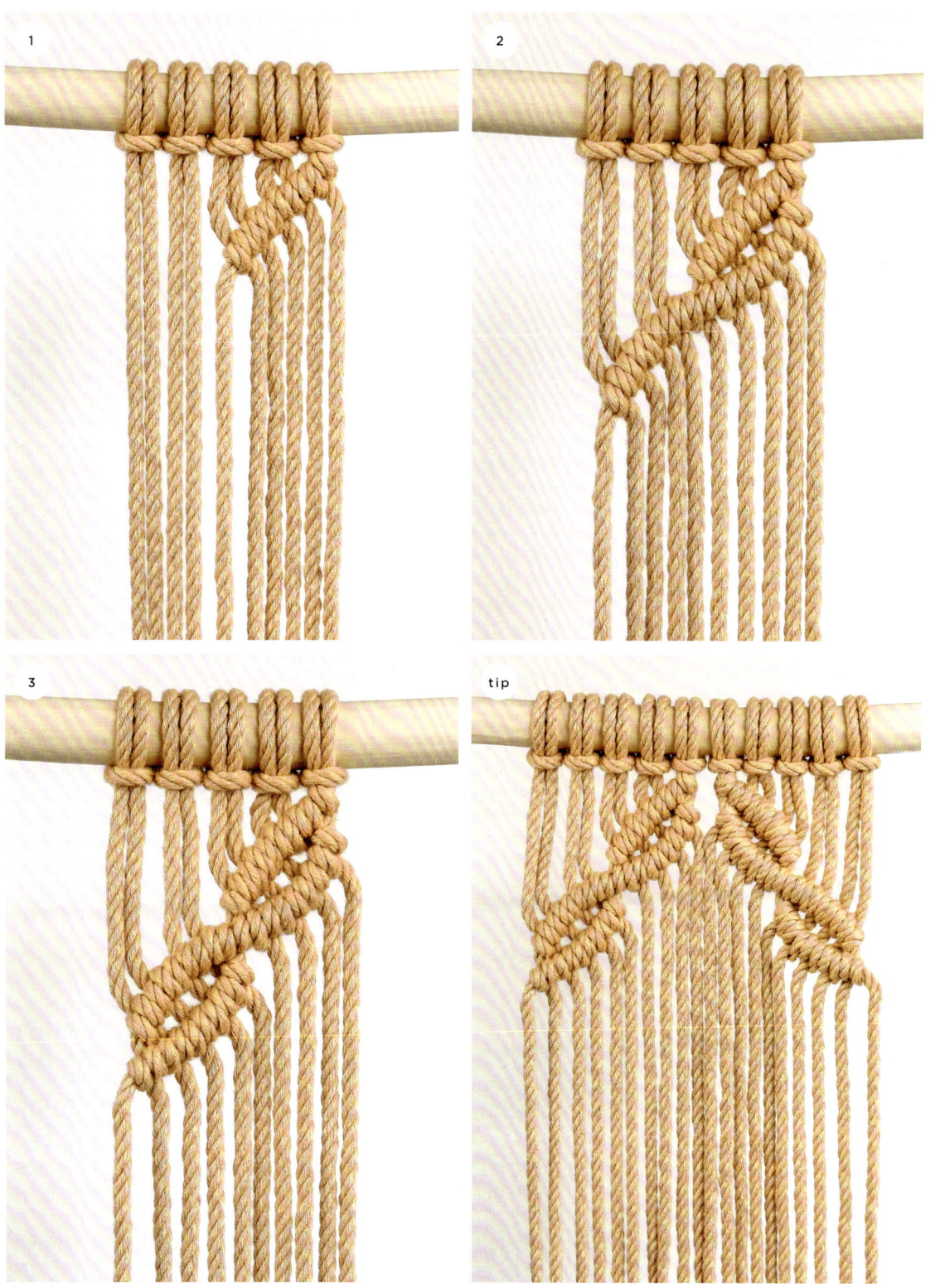

Macramé: The Power of Knots

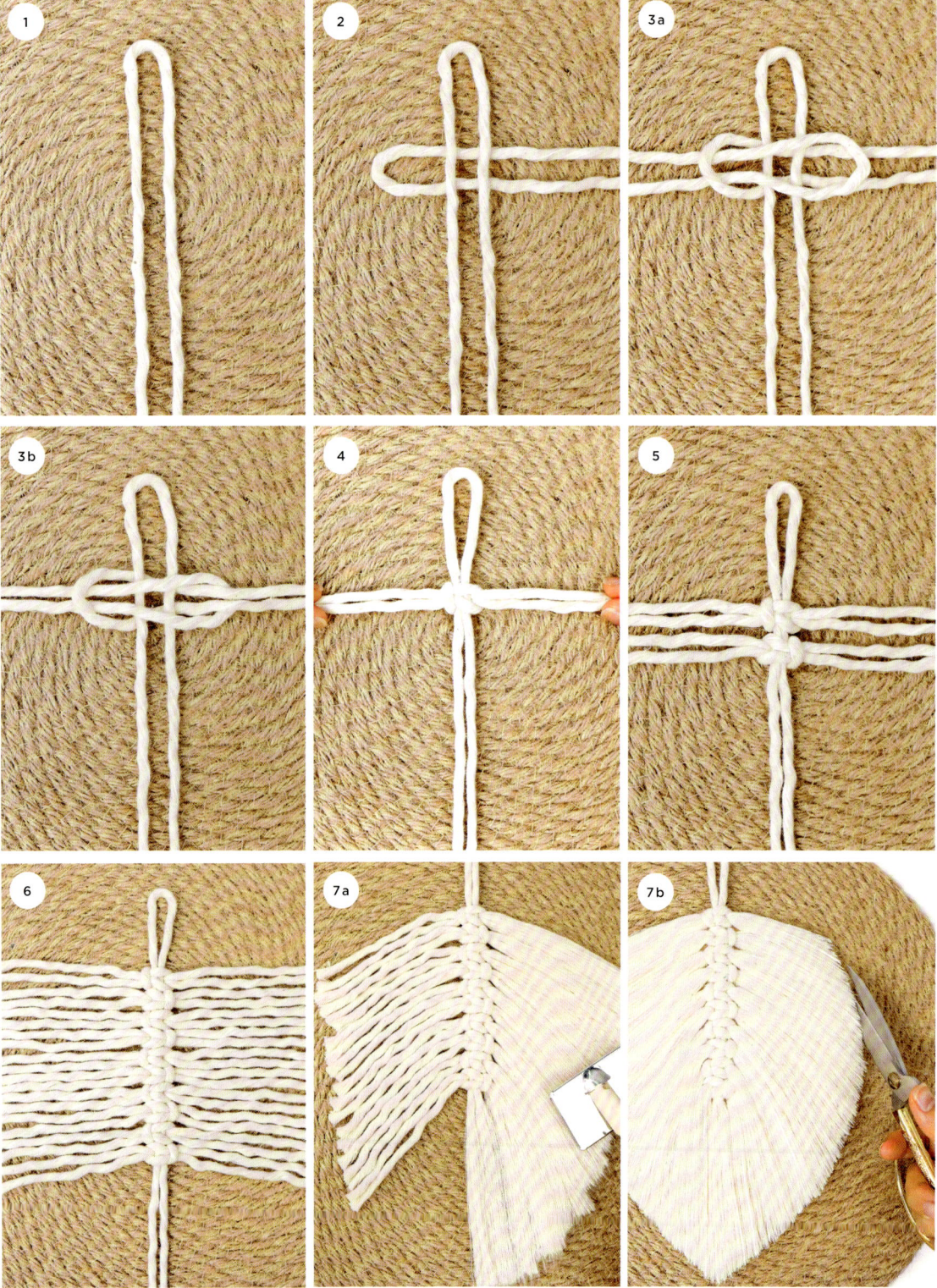

Feather

Feathers are a trendy way to style any macramé project. These powerful patterns can be included in home decor designs such as dream catchers, or can be used on their own as jewelry or accessories projects. Some of my favorite designs are key chains and earrings, as they look fabulous as part of a boho summer look. They are quick-to-make gifts, as well as an ideal way to take care of your scrap cords. I use a long cord and multiple shorter cords to demonstrate this pattern in a horizontal setup.

Step 1: Start by folding the long cord in half and placing it vertically on your horizontal setup. This piece will be the spine of the feather.

Step 2: Take one of the shorter cords, fold it in half, and place it horizontally under the longer cord 3 cm–5 cm (1.2 in–2 in) down. Make sure the loop of the shorter cord is to the left of the long cord.

Step 3: Take another short cord, fold it in half and place it horizontally over the long cord on top of the previous short cord. The loop this time should be facing right. Then pass the ends of each horizontal cord through each other's loops.

Step 4: Pull the ends of both cords to tighten the knot. This creates a left-facing square knot (LFSK).

Step 5: For the second knot, use the same technique in reverse to create a right-facing square knot (RFSK).

Step 6: Keep adding knots until you reach the desired length of your feather. You should stop once the length of your shorter cords matches the length of the spine cord that is left untied.

Step 7: Hold the pattern by the spine and brush all the cords. Then, flip the design and brush it again to ensure every cord has been untangled. Finish by trimming the fringes for a nice feather shape.

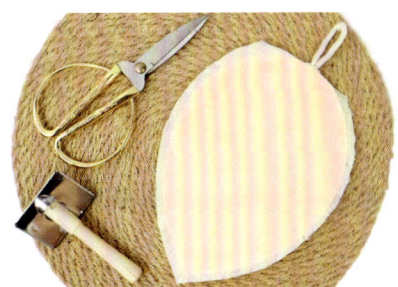

TIP: To keep your feather flat and straight while hanging, you can attach a piece of felt or paper, the same shape as the feather, at the back of the design to support it. I also recommend using hairspray or stiffening spray to add extra strength.

Honeycomb

The **honeycomb pattern** is a mesmerizing geometric macramé design often included in curtains, wall hangings, and backdrops. It is formed by simply combining square knots (SKs) and square knot sinnets (SKSs) to create hexagon shapes. To follow this demonstration, you need thirty-six cords in a vertical setup.

Knots Used:
Square knot (SK), see page 47
Alternating square knot (ASK), see page 51
Square knot sinnet (SKS), see page 50

Knotting Sequence:
4 x SK
8 x ASK
5 x ASK
5 x SKS
8 x ASK
4 x ASK
4 x SKS
8 x ASK
5 x ASK

Step 1: The first row of knots is created by tying four SKs using cords 5–8, 13–16, 21–24, and 29–32. There should be four cords left untied in between each SK.

Step 2: For the second row, skip the first two cords and tie eight ASKs underneath the first row.

Step 3: Now, for the third row of ASKs, use cords 1–4, 9–12, 17–20, 25–28, and 33–36 to tie five ASKs.

Step 4: Add two extra SKs underneath each of the ASKs from the previous step to create five SKSs.

Step 5: Use the same cords and techniques as in steps 1 and 2. First, follow directions from step 2, and then from step 1, to close the first row of hexagons of our pattern.

Step 6: Next, tie four SKSs, one sinnet underneath each hexagon. Every SKS is formed by tying two SKs.

Step 7: Use the same cords and techniques as in steps 2 and 3 to complete the second row of hexagons. Notice how this row has three full hexagons in the middle, and two half hexagons, one on each side of the design.

Step 8: Use this technique to complete as many hexagon rows as you need to reach the desired length of your design.

15 Patterns & 4 Projects for Intermediate Artists

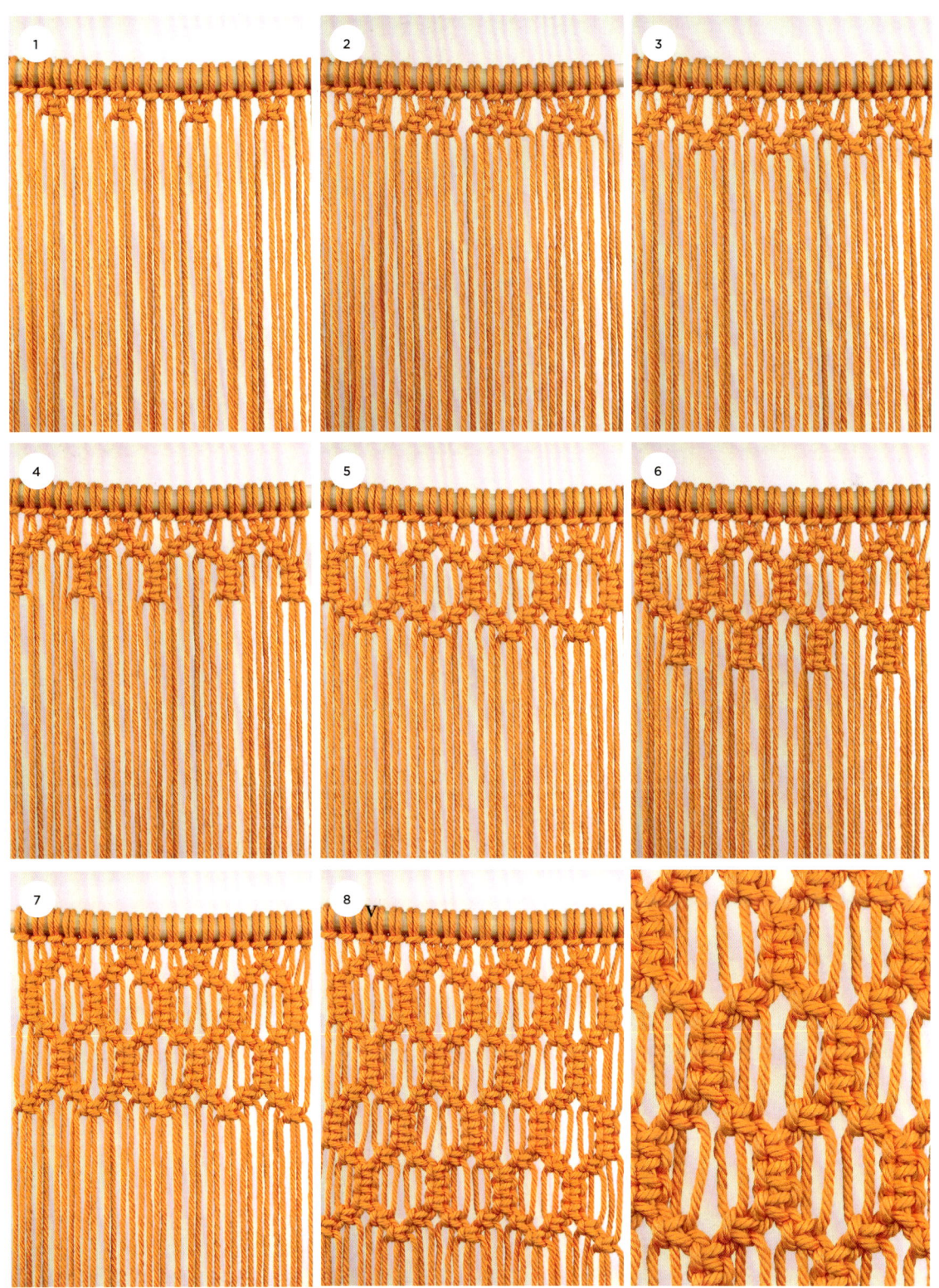

Tassels

These are one of the most added-on decorative elements you will use in your macramé artwork. **Tassels** work perfectly in pretty much all types of projects, from wall hangings to fiber jewelry, to key chains, even to curtain tiebacks. These pretty ornaments are not just an amazing way to enhance your designs, they're also a great way to get rid of those annoying leftover string scraps we all have lying around. In this demonstration, I show you two different ways you can make tassels: a separated tassel in a horizontal setup, and an attached tassel using a vertical setup.

15 Patterns & 4 Projects for Intermediate Artists

Separated Tassel

Knots Used:
Alternating half hitch (AHH), see page 57
Gathering knot, see page 70
Overhand knot, see page 38

Preparation:
7 white cords, each 30 cm (15.7 in) long
2 sage cords, each 40 cm (15.7 in) long

Step 1: Gather all the white cords and lay them horizontally.

Step 2: Take one of the sage cords and tie it to the white cords securely in the middle with twenty AHHs.

Step 3: Now take the other sage cord and make a gathering knot 1 cm (0.4 in) from the top around all the white cords.

Step 4: Trim the ends of your tassel at the desired length.

Attached Tassel

Knots Used:
Overhand knot, see page 38
Gathering knot, see page 70

Preparation:
6 twisted cords, each 40 cm (15.7 in) long

Step 1: Start the attached tassel by untwisting the five cords until you end up with individual strands.

Step 2: Hold the cords on one end tightly, and use a comb or brush to untangle the strands. Then, do the same by holding the cords from the opposite end and brushing them out in reverse.

Step 3: Fold all the brushed-out cords in half and place them at the end of your chain/pattern. Ensure these are placed midway between the cords of your design.

Step 4: Use one cord of your chain/pattern as a working cord, and using the rest as filler cords, tie one overhand knot securely underneath the brushed-out cords.

Step 5: Untwist and brush all the remaining cords of your chain/pattern using a comb or brush.

Step 6: Next, untwist the last cord and take a single strand to make a gathering knot 1 cm (0.4 in) from the top around all the cords.

Step 7: Trim the ends of your tassel at the desired length.

15 Patterns & 4 Projects for Intermediate Artists

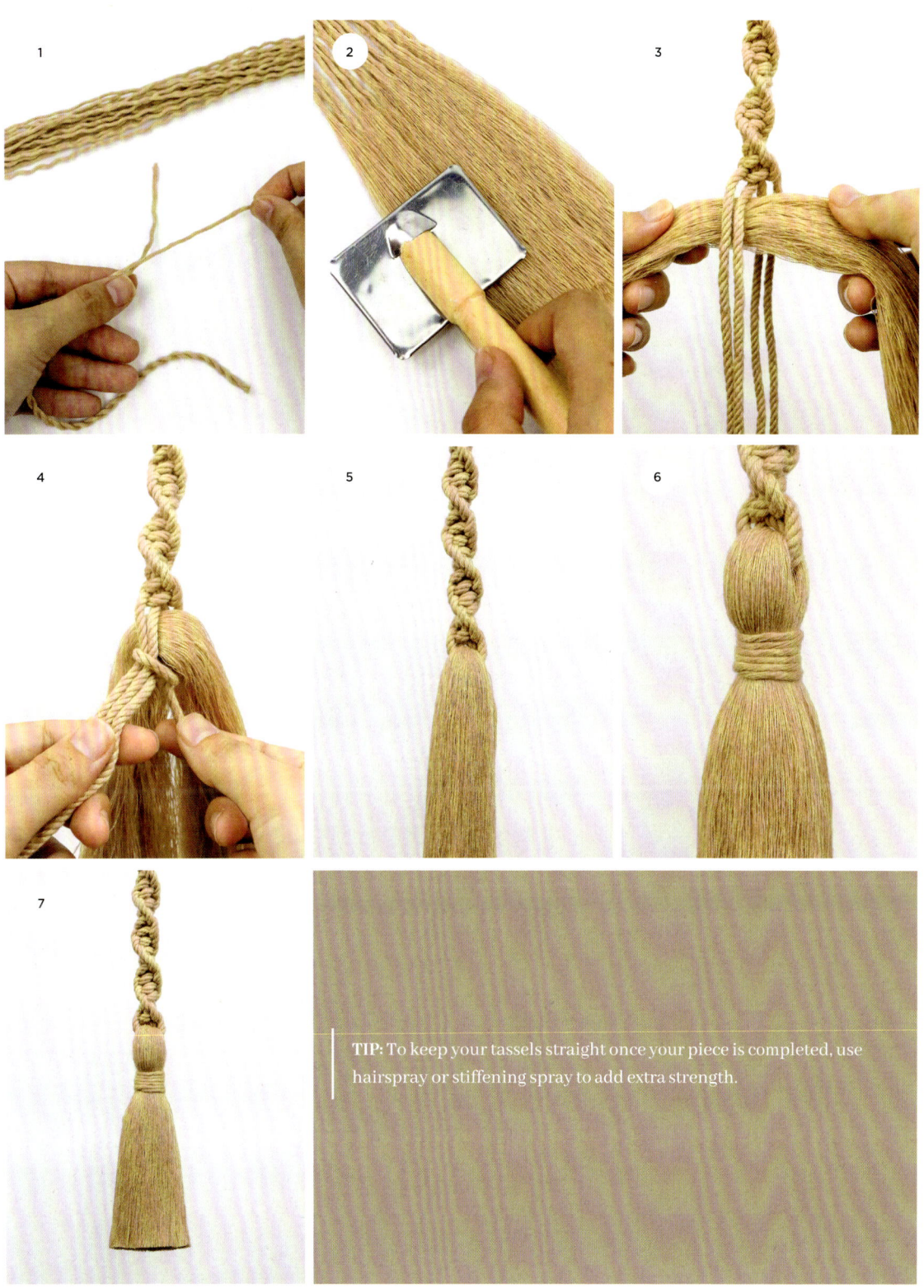

TIP: To keep your tassels straight once your piece is completed, use hairspray or stiffening spray to add extra strength.

Macramé: The Power of Knots

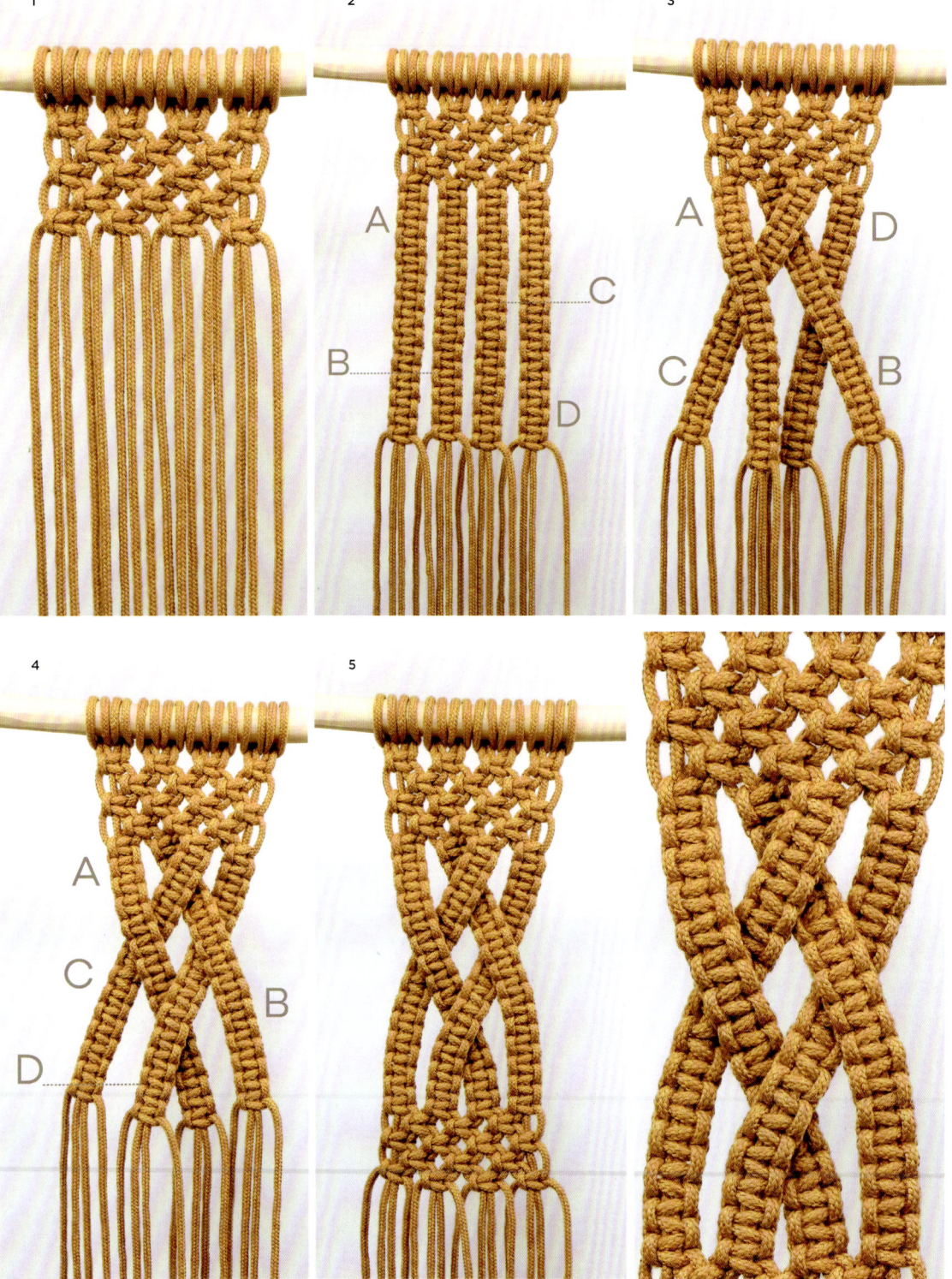

15 Patterns & 4 Projects for Intermediate Artists

Braided Square Knot Sinnets

Combining braiding and knotting techniques in macramé artwork is an ingenious way macramé artists add visually captivating details and texture to designs. The **braided square knot sinnets** pattern is an example of that. This charming pattern does wonders if added to any flat macramé piece. I personally adore how this pattern brings macramé bags to life. To attempt this demonstration, you need to arrange sixteen cords in a vertical setup.

Knots Used:
Square knot (SK), see page 47
Alternating square knot (ASK), see page 51
Square knot sinnet (SKS), see page 50

Pattern Used:
Square knot net, see page 86

Step 1: Start the pattern by creating a square knot net using all cords available.

Step 2: Tie four SKSs. Use the last row of ASKs as your starting point for your sinnets. Tie fifteen SKs in each sinnet. Now we have four sinnets: A, B, C, and D from left to right.

Step 3: Next, take sinnet C and pass it over sinnet B and under sinnet A toward the left. Then, take sinnet B and pass it over sinnet D toward the right.

Step 4: Now, pass sinnet D over sinnet A toward the left.

Step 5: Keeping all sinnets in place, repeat step 1 to complete the pattern.

Semi-Circle

The **semi-circle** is a very versatile pattern found in all types of macramé projects. Thanks to the technique used to create this pattern, adding extra cords regularly to widen the design, you can get creative and add color to your projects. Simply use different-colored cords every time you add them to the semi-circle pattern. Your cords should be at least 1.2 m (3.9 ft) long. I suggest arranging your cords in a vertical setup for this demonstration, but feel free to try a horizontal setup, especially with a small design.

Knots Used:
Lark's head knot (LHK), see page 41
Horizontal double half hitch (HDHH), see page 65
Reverse lark's head knot (RLHK), see page 43

Step 1: Start your semi-circle pattern by folding two cords in half and mounting them to a dowel with LHKs. Then, use the second cord as your filler cord, and cords 3 and 4 as working cords, to tie two HDHHs–left-to-right, underneath the second LHK from the left.

Step 2: Using the same filler cord as in step 1, you have to knot a continuous LHK to mount the remaining filler cord to the dowel. First, bring the filler cord over the dowel front to back. Then, pass its end through the loop created between the cord and the dowel.

Step 3: Continue with the same filler cord, and now bring it under and over the dowel toward the front. After that, pass its end through the loop created between the cord and the dowel. Finally, pull down the end of the cord to tighten the knot.

Step 4: Next, fold an extra cord in half and mount it to the dowel with an LHK on the right side of the design.

Step 5: Now take cord 5 as your filler cord, and cords 1–4 as working cords. Tie four HDHHs–right-to-left underneath the first line of HDHHs. Make sure this line follows the curvature of the previous line of knots.

Step 6: After every line of HDHHs, from this step onwards, an extra cord needs to be added at the end of the line. You do this by folding a cord in half, and mounting it to the filler cord with an RLHK.

Step 7: Keep using the same filler cord to tie another continuous LHK. Follow the technique explained in steps 2 and 3.

Step 8: Next, fold an extra cord in half and mount it to the dowel with an LHK on the left side of the design.

Step 9: Now take cord 2 as your filler cord, and cords 3–10 as working cords. Tie eight HDHHs–left-to-right underneath the second line of HDHHs. Make sure this line follows the curvature of the previous line of knots.

Step 10: Repeat step 6.

Step 11: Repeat steps 2 and 3.

Step 12: Keep adding lines of HDHHs using the technique explained in this pattern until you reach the desired size of your semi-circle.

15 Patterns & 4 Projects for Intermediate Artists

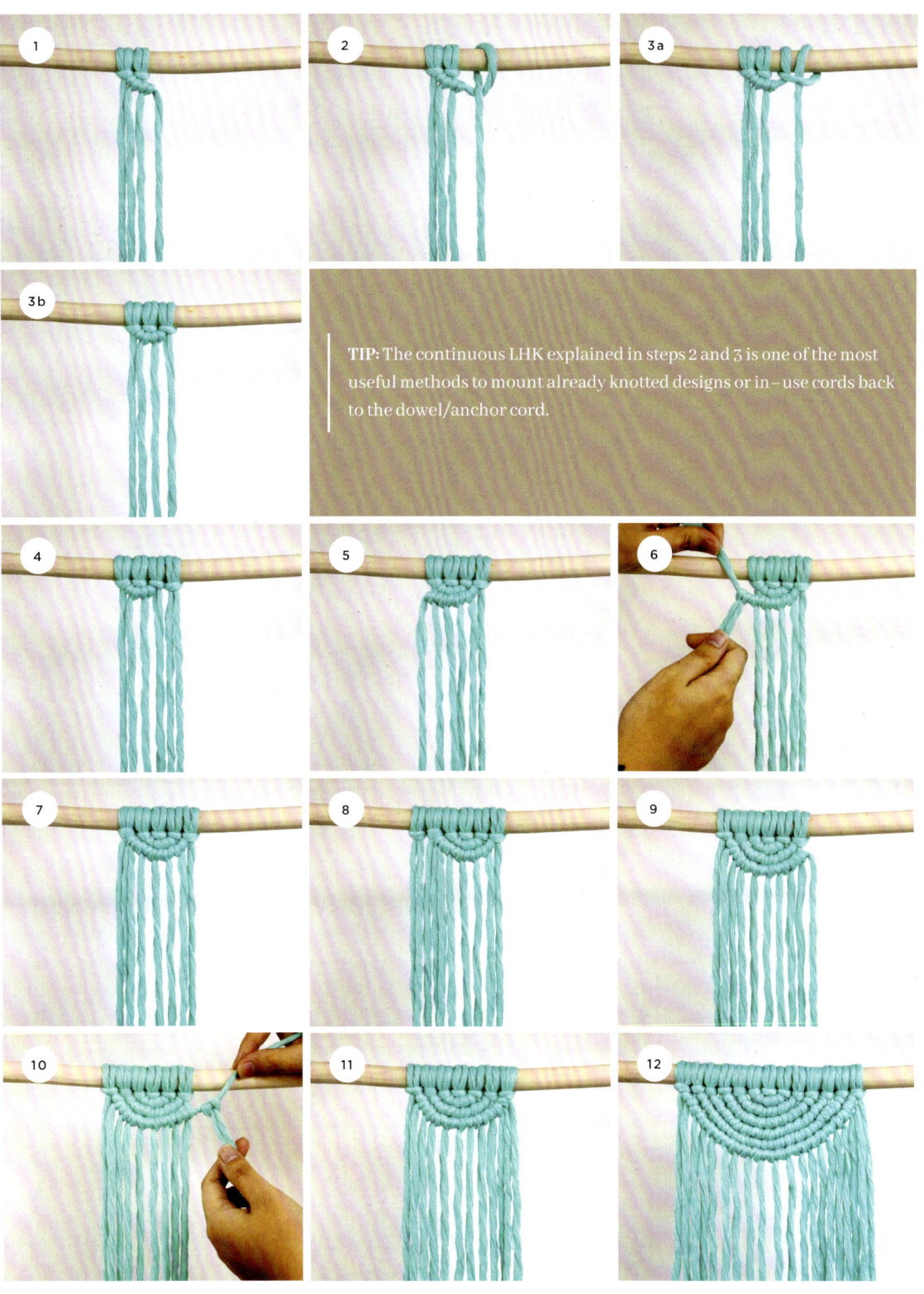

TIP: The continuous LHK explained in steps 2 and 3 is one of the most useful methods to mount already knotted designs or in-use cords back to the dowel/anchor cord.

Macramé: The Power of Knots

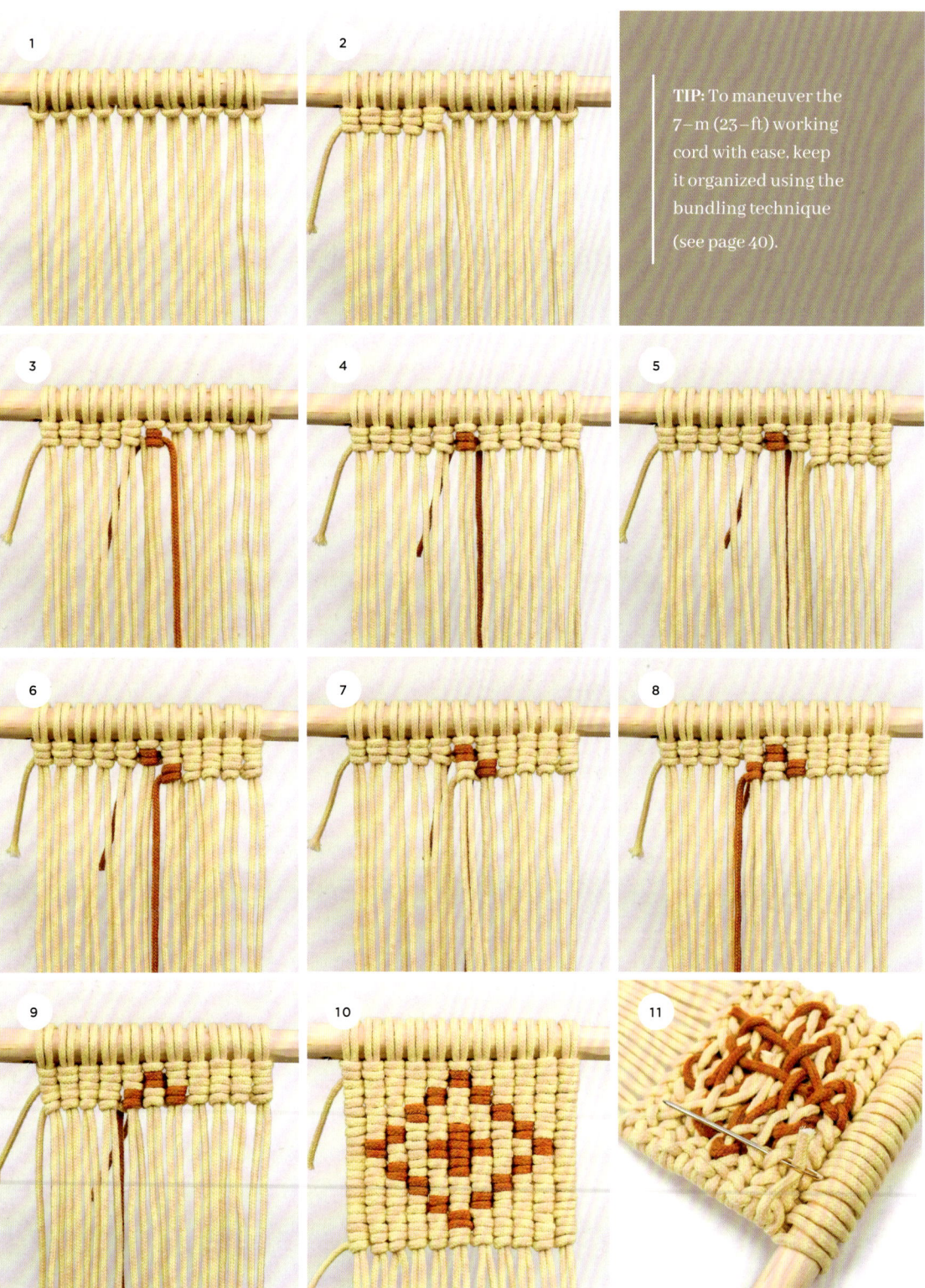

TIP: To maneuver the 7–m (23–ft) working cord with ease, keep it organized using the bundling technique (see page 40).

Vertical Double Half Hitch Pixel

This one is a simple pattern in terms of knotting knowledge for people who want to explore their creative side. To create designs using the **vertical double half hitch pixel** pattern, only one type of knot is required, the vertical double half hitch (VDHH). You should look at this pattern as a canvas where different-colored working cords are added to create "pixels" of contrasting color. What design goes into your canvas is completely up to you. You only need to transfer your idea to a canvas grid, and then use this as the blueprint of your pattern. In this demonstration, I use this technique to create a simple diamond shape. The best way to approach this pattern is by arranging your cords in a vertical setup.

Knots Used:
Lark's head knot (LHK), see page 41
Vertical double half hitch (VDHH), see page 67

Preparation:
11 yellow filler cords, each 60 cm (2 ft) long
1 yellow working cord, 7 m (23 ft) long
1 brown working cord, 2.5 m (8.2 ft) long

Step 1: Start by folding the eleven yellow filler cords, 60 cm (2 ft) long, in half and mounting them to a wooden dowel with LHKs.

Step 2: Begin the first row by tying a line of VDHHs toward the right. To do so, take the 7-m (23-ft) yellow working cord and use it to tie five VDHHs-left-to-right. Make sure to use two filler cords per VDHH throughout the design.

Step 3: Begin by adding the contrasting color pixels to your design. Take the 2.5-m (8.2-ft) brown working cord, and tie one VDHH-left-to-right, continuing the line of VHDDs.

Step 4: Bring the long end of the brown working cord back and continue tying five VHDDs-left-to-right using the yellow working cord. This step completes the first row of the pattern.

Step 5: Begin the second row by tying a line of VDHHs toward the left using the yellow working cord to tie four VHDDs-right-to-left.

Step 6: Next, bring the yellow working cord to the back and use the blue working cord to tie one VDHH-right-to-left.

Step 7: Switch to the yellow working cord and tie one VDHH-right-to-left.

Step 8: Repeat step 6.

Step 9: Repeat step 5 to complete the second row.

Step 10: Continue switching your different-colored working cords and changing the direction of the knots row by row until you create a diamond shape.

Step 11: Finalize your piece by tucking all the ends of your working cords into the back of your design with a tapestry needle.

Intermediate Projects

15 Patterns & 4 Projects for Intermediate Artists

Maya Basket

This project will transform your living space, enhancing and adding style to one of the most common household items, the basket. In the Maya Basket project, you use macramé techniques previously learned in this book to decorate a sea grass basket. The Maya Basket helps you organize your home while adding a boho and rustic feel to it. This stunning and functional macramé project is perfect for bedrooms, laundry rooms, and living rooms. As different patterns and several macramé basic knots are used to create the project, it is the perfect transition between the novice and intermediate level.

The decorative macramé pieces that I show you here are used to cover both sides of a basket with the following dimensions: height 40 cm (15.7 in) x length 55 cm (21.6 in) x width 35 cm (13.8 in). If you wish to use a different basket, make sure to adapt your design accordingly.

Finished project specs: length 60 cm (23.6 in) x width 24 cm (9.4 in) each decorative macramé piece
Approximate completion time: 2 hours

Tools and Materials

Scissors
Measuring tape
Glue gun
Brush
Tapestry needle
Approximately 117 m (384 ft) natural color 3 mm cotton string
Approximately 7 m (23 ft) 2 mm jute cord

Knots and Patterns
Knots Used:
Lark's head knot (LHK), see page 41
Diagonal double half hitch (DDHH), see pages 62–63
Square knot sinnet (SKS), see page 50
Crown knot, see page 76
Gathering knot, see page 70
Overhand knot, see page 38

Patterns Used:
Diagonal double half hitch triangle, see page 134
Fishbone, see page 142

Preparation
Vertical setup
Cut the following for two decorative macramé pieces.
Anchor cords:
2 anchor cords, 80 cm (31.5 in) long
Mounting cords:
24 cords, each 80 cm (31.5 in) long
24 cords, each 90 cm (35.4 in) long
24 cords, each 100 cm (39.4 in) long
24 cords, each 110 cm (43.3 in) long
Tassels:
60 cords, each 40 cm (15.7 in) long
10 jute cords, each 30 cm (11.8 in) long
10 jute cords, each 40 cm (15.7 in) long

Macramé: The Power of Knots

Instructions

Step 1: Fold the mounting cords in half, and using LHKs, mount them to an 80-cm (31.5-in) anchor cord. Follow this sequence: 80-cm (31.5 in)–90 cm (35.4 in)–100 cm (39.4 in)–110 cm (43.3 in)–110 cm (43.3 in)–100 cm (39.4 in)–90 cm (35.4 in)–80 cm (31.5 in). Repeat the sequence six times.

Step 2: Make six diagonal double half hitch triangle patterns using all the cords. One sequence of mounted cords from step 1 equals one triangle pattern.

Step 3: Connect the first and second triangles using a fishbone pattern. The fishbone pattern is created by tying a six SKs sinnet.

Step 4: Now, take cord 9 as your filler cord and cords 10–16 as working cords to tie seven DDHHs–left-to-right, going down.

Step 5: To close the fishbone pattern, tie eight DDHHs–right-to-left, going down, this time using cord 24 as your filler cord, and cords 16–23 as working cords.

Step 6: Connect the rest of the triangles using fishbone patterns with the technique explained in steps 3–5.

Step 7: Before adding the tassels to the design, trim all the cords at 5 cm (2 in).

Step 8: To make one tassel, use six cords, 40 cm (15.7 in) long, to tie a crown knot. Then, flip it over and tie another crown knot in the back.

Step 9: Thread a 30-cm (11.8-in) long jute cord through the tapestry needle and tie the ends with an overhand knot. Then use the tapestry needle to push the jute cord through the crown knots.

Step 10: Pull all the cords away from the tapestry needle and use a 40-cm (15.7-in) long jute cord to tie a gathering knot around the cords. Cut the jute cord to remove the tapestry needle. The jute cords will later be used to attach the tassel to the design.

Step 11: Cut the cords 6 cm (2.4 in) from the gathering knot. To make your tassel fluffy, brush the cords and trim the ends.

Step 12: Make four more tassels using the technique explained in steps 8–11.

Step 13: Use the jute cords to attach the tassels to the design. Add one tassel to the end of each fishbone pattern, using overhand knots at the back of the design. Our first decorative macramé piece is now complete.

Step 14: To create the second decorative macramé piece needed to complete this project, repeat steps 1–13.

Step 15: Use the glue gun to adhere one of the macramé pieces to each side of the basket. Cut the ends of your anchor cords so they match the length of the rest of the fringes.

> **TIP:** If you plan to use the basket regularly and think it might get dirty over time, you can use thread instead of glue to sew the macramé pieces to the basket. This will allow you to remove them easily and wash them when needed. Make sure the color of your sewing thread is the same as your cords.

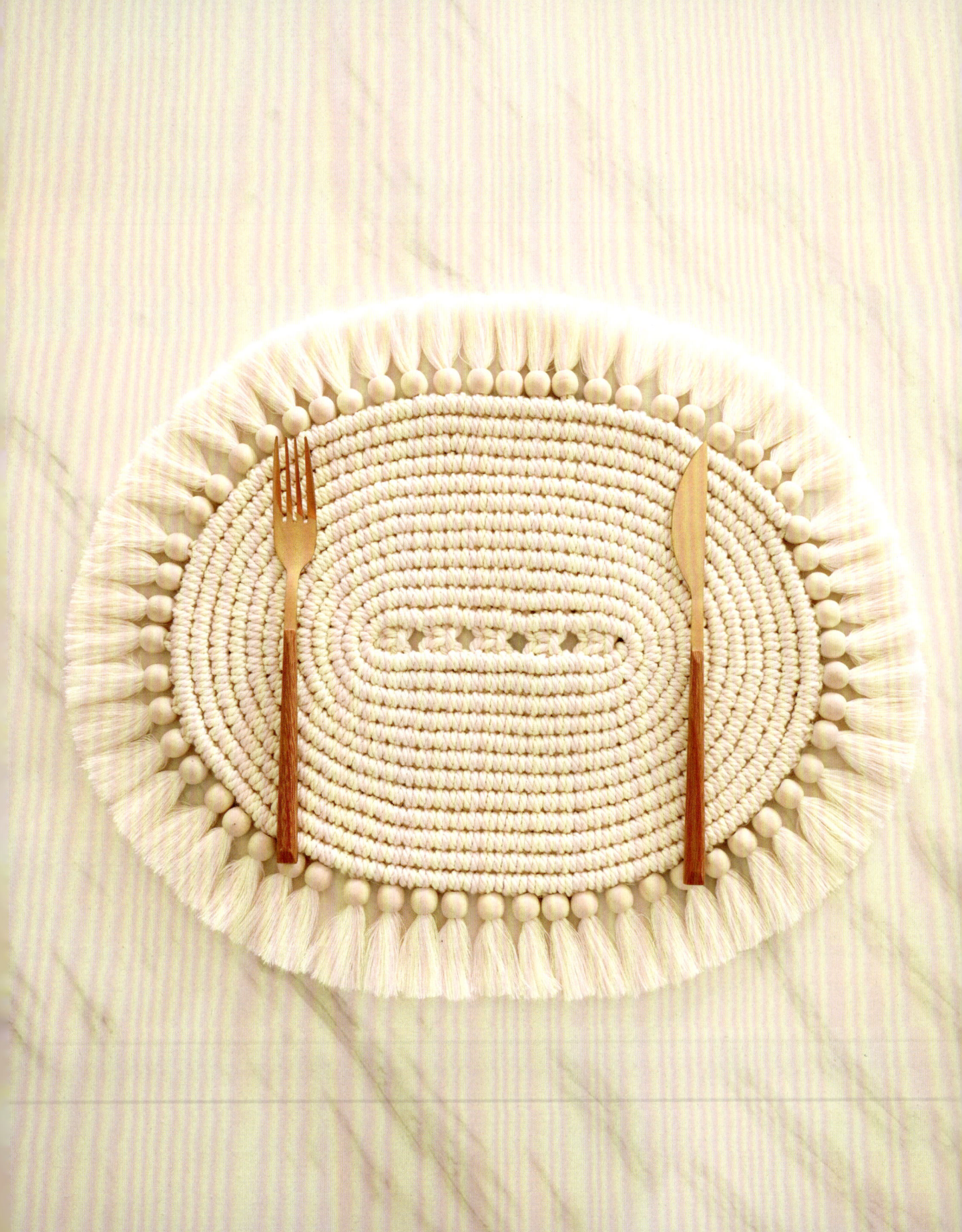

ns & 4 Projects for Intermediate Artists

Heather Table Mat

The Heather Table Mat is a macramé decoration project that will put your knotting skills to the test. Since it uses mainly horizontal double half hitches (HDHHs), keeping the right tension in the cords is key to achieving a perfectly flat and neat surface. This eye-catching piece is the ideal centerpiece for any table around your house, or the perfect addition to spaces with a rustic or minimalistic vibe. Use the Heather Table Mat to brighten up your kitchen, coffee table, nightstand, or dining table, or to wow your guests during a special celebration. This versatile piece also works beautifully under flower or candle displays, and it is a great way to reveal your macramé skills to anyone visiting your home.

♦ ♦ ♦

Finished project specs: length 45 cm (17.7 in) x width 35 cm (13.8 in)

Approximate completion time: 4 hours

Tools and Materials

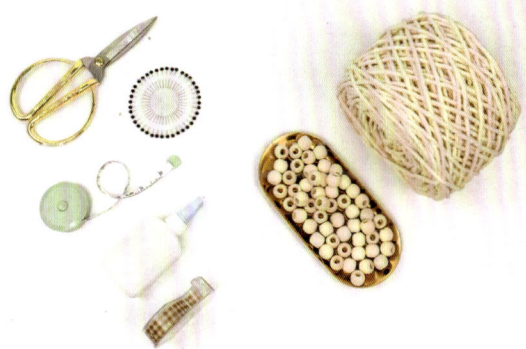

Scissors
Measuring tape
Pins
Glue
Tape
Brush
Approximately 85 m (279 ft) natural color 4 mm 4-ply twisted rope

60 large-hole round wooden beads, 15 mm (0.6 in) diameter

Knots and Patterns

Knots Used:
Vertical double half hitch (VDHH), see page 67
Square knot (SK), see page 47
Horizontal double half hitch (HDHH), see page 65
Reverse lark's head knot (RLHK), see page 43

Patterns Used:
Circular, see page 145

Preparation

Horizontal setup

Cut the following:
1 filler cord, 8 m (26.2 ft) long
20 working cords, each 1.8 m (5.9 ft) long
Extra cords are to be cut whenever needed at double the length of the previous working cord, following instructions below.
37 extra working cords, each approximately 0.6 m–1.8 m (2 ft–5.9 ft) long.

Instructions

Step 1: Take the 8-m (26.2-ft) filler cord and secure it to the horizontal setup using a pin. Pin the filler cord 0.9 m (2.9 ft) from the top end of the cord, leaving the remaining 7.1 m (23.3 ft) under the pin. This is our starting knotting point.

Step 2: Take a 1.8-m (5.9-ft) working cord and mount it to the filler cord with a single VDHH at the knotting point. Make sure both ends of the mounting cord are equidistant to the VDHH.

Step 3: Take the remaining 19 working cords, and mount them to the filler cord with VDHHs using the same technique as in step 2.

Step 4: Rotate the design 90 degrees counterclockwise. The short and long parts of the filler cord should now be placed to the left and right of the line of VDHHs respectively. Now tie five SKs using all the mounting cords under the line of VDHHs.

Step 5: Cut one extra working cord, double the length of the previous working cord on the left, and mount it to the long part of the filler cord with a RLHK. Slide the RLHK next to the line of VDHHs.

> **TIP:** To maneuver the filler cord with ease, keep it organized while working on your piece with bundling technique (see page 40).

Step 6: Take the long part of the filler cord and tie HDHHs around the SKs following a spiral shape using the circular pattern technique. The long part of the filler cord is used as the filler cord for the entire design. The short part is to be used as a working cord.

Step 7: Keep tying HDHHs until a gap between the filler cord and the next working cord appears. This is when the extra working cord needs to be added. Remember to cut the extra working cords at double the length of the previous working cord.

> **TIP:** Keep the tension of your knots stable throughout the design in order to achieve a perfectly flat surface. Be especially careful when tying your HDHHs, and make sure they are not too tight. Otherwise the pattern could naturally curl up due to the high tension between knots.

Step 8: Stop tying HDHHs once the length of the filler cord is around 10 cm (3.9 in).

Step 9: Pair the filler cord and the next working cord to add the first wooden bead to your piece. Then, add beads around the entire design using the remaining working cords. Use two cords per bead.

> **TIP:** Tape or glue the end of the cords to easily pass them through the wooden beads.

Step 10: Cut the ends of all cords around the piece 4 cm (1.6 in) from the beads. Then, untwist all the cords, and use a brush to create fluffy fringes. Finish by trimming the fringes for a clean and stylish look.

15 Patterns & 4 Projects for Intermediate Artists

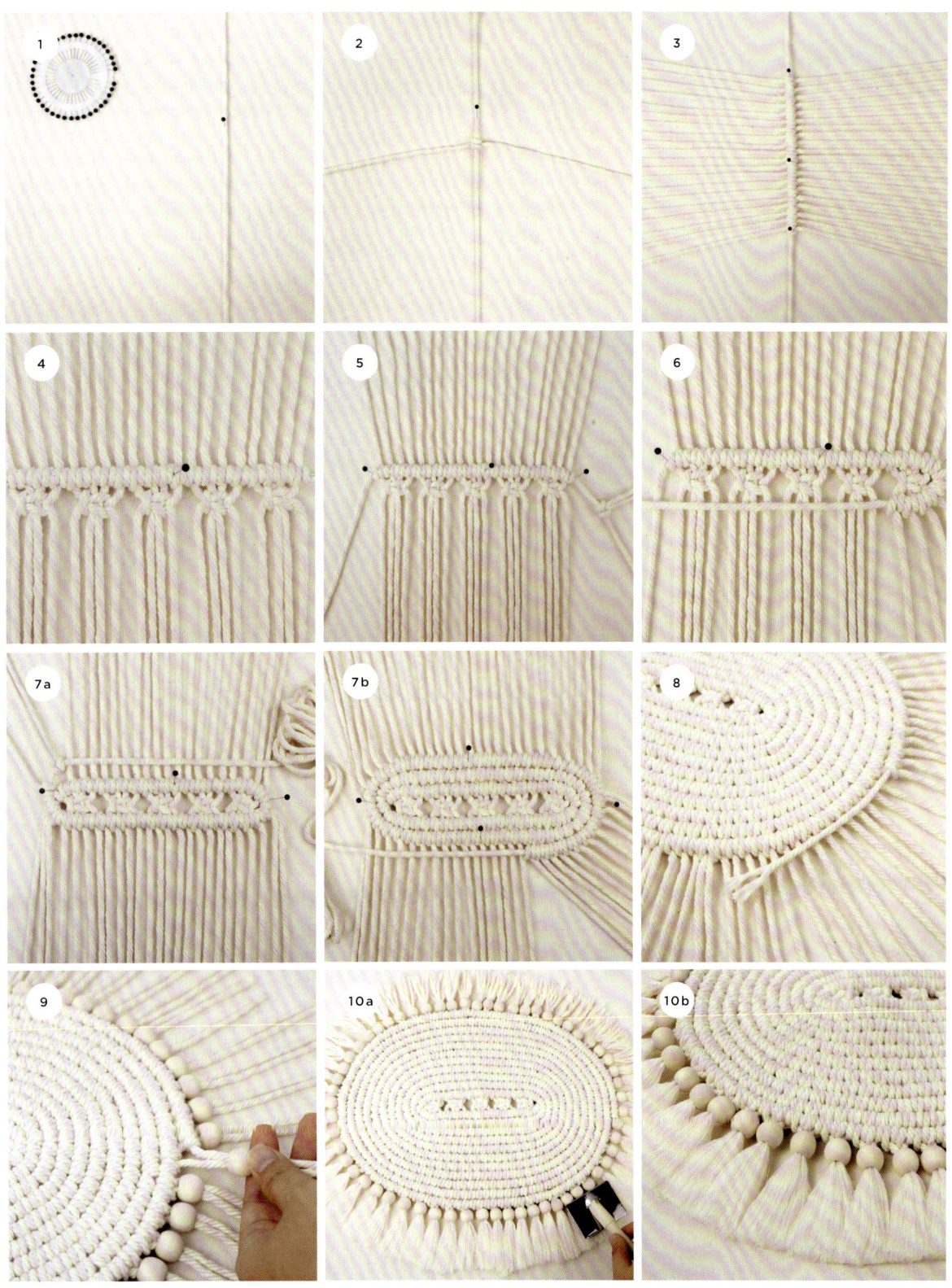

15 Patterns & 4 Projects for Intermediate Artists

Avery Pillow

A mesmerizing macramé piece, the Avery Pillow project is excellent for enhancing with a bohemian vibe any living space around the house. Use as a statement piece on your couch or coffee chair, or in your bedroom or office. The Avery Pillow consists of three beautiful overlapping tiers of macramé patterns, adorned with fluffy fringes which add an earthy and natural touch to the design. It is a wonderful way to add some texture to what could be otherwise a flat and plain piece of home decor. I have chosen a natural color cord for this piece, for a more minimalist look. However, feel free to use different colors for each tier. Be creative and play around with them until you find a palette of colors that fits your style.

◆ ◆ ◆

Finished project specs: length 40 cm (15.7 in) x width 40 cm (15.7 in)
Approximate completion time: 4 hours

Tools and Materials

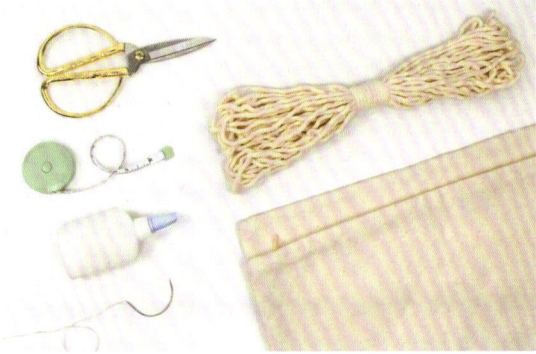

Scissors
Measuring tape
Brush
Glue/sewing needle
Approximately 98 m (322 ft) natural color 2 mm single-strand string
1 pillow cover, 40 cm (15.7 in) x 40 cm (15.7 in)

Knots and Patterns
Knots Used:
Lark's head knot (LHK), see page 41
Diagonal double half hitch (DDHH), see pages 62–63
Square knot (SK), see page 47
Cross knot, see page 82
Overhand knot, see page 38
Patterns Used:
Increasing diamond with square knot, see page 138

Preparation
Vertical setup
Cut the following:
3 anchor cords, each 60 cm (23.6 in) long
120 mounting cords, each 80 cm (31.5 in) long

Macramé: The Power of Knots

SUGGESTION: Before gluing or sewing the tiers to the pillow cover, place the tiers on top of the cover and move them around until you are satisfied with their position.

Instructions

Step 1: To begin knotting the first tier, fold forty mounting cords in half. Then, use LHKs to mount them to an anchor cord.

Step 2: Make ten increasing diamond with square knot patterns using all the cords available. Use eight cords per diamond pattern.

Step 3: Tie cross knots in order to connect all the diamond patterns. Use the first two available outer cords, one from each diamond, to tie a total of nine cross knots. Notice how the first and last cords remain unknotted.

Step 4: Next, take the third cord from each diamond pattern as your filler cord, and cords 1 and 2 as your working cords, to tie two DDHHs–right-to-left, going down.

Step 5: Continue by tying two DDHHs–left-to-right, going down. This time use the sixth cord from each diamond pattern as your filler cord, and cords 7 and 8 as your working cords.

Step 6: Connect the lines of DDHHs between diamond patterns with one DDHH–right-to-left.

Step 7: Arrange the cords in groups of four. Then, use one random cord as your working cord, to wrap the other three filler cords with an overhand knot—twenty overhand knots total.

Step 8: Now skip the first two cords, move down 1 cm (0.4 in), and use the same technique as in step 7 to create a row of 19 alternating overhand knots.

Step 9: To complete the tier, create fringes by cutting all cords evenly at 4 cm (1.6 in). Brush and trim all the fringes until you get the fluffy look you desire.

Step 10: Repeat steps 1–9 twice to create the other two tiers.

Step 11: Divide the pillow cover into three parts. Then glue or sew the three tiers to the pillow cover. For a smooth and flowing effect, make sure the tiers overlap.

15 Patterns & 4 Projects for Intermediate Artists

Cressida Hanging Shelf

This elegant macramé project will bring a calm and homey feel to any room of the house. Inspired by blooming sunflower fields, the Cressida Hanging Shelf is a superb way to add texture, personality, and color to empty walls in bedrooms, living and working spaces, nurseries, or even bathrooms. With its endless possibilities, how and where to use this project is entirely up to you—from adding decorative elements like plants or candles to living spaces, to holding functional items such as hand towels or soap dispensers in bathrooms. This is a beautiful wall art piece that can infuse a sense of comfort and harmony into any space around your house.

♦ ♦ ♦

Finished project specs: length 70 cm (27.5 in) x width 40 cm (15.7 in)
Approximate completion time: 3 hours

Tools and Materials

Scissors
Measuring tape
S-hooks
Brush
Tape
Approximately 50 m (164 ft) 4 mm brown color 4-ply twisted rope
Approximately 67 m (220 ft) 4 mm mustard color 4-ply twisted rope
A wooden dowel, 40 cm (15.7 in) long
A wooden board, length 40 cm (15.7 in) x width 10 cm (3.9 in), with four holes, 1 cm (0.4 in) in diameter, one in each corner

Knots and Patterns

Knots Used:
Lark's head knot (LHK), see page 41
Diagonal double half hitch (DDHH), see pages 62–63
Left-twist spiral knot (LSPK), see page 59
Left-facing half hitch (LFHH), see page 55
Overhand knot, see page 38

Patterns Used:
Hollow double half hitch diamond, see page 96
Alternating double half hitch diamond mesh, see page 133
Running weaving diamond chain, see page 186
Double half hitch diamond, see page 94
Rya knot weaving technique, see page 109

Preparation
Vertical setup

Cut the following:
15 brown cords, each 2.4 m (7.9 ft) long
44 brown cords, each 0.3 m (1 ft) long
12 mustard cords, each 3 m (9.8 ft) long
28 mustard cords, each 1.1 m (3.6 ft) long

Macramé: The Power of Knots

TIP: Tape both ends of a tassel to easily pass it through the diamond.

Instructions

Step 1: Use two S-hooks to join the wooden dowel to your vertical setup. Then, fold the fifteen brown cords, 2.4 m (7.9 ft) long, in half, and mount them to the wooden dowel with LHKs.

Step 2: Make an alternating double half hitch diamond mesh with all the cords, reducing the number of diamonds in every row by one to create a triangle shape. Use six cords to create each of the hollow double half hitch diamonds in the pattern.

Step 3: Continue by folding in half eight mustard cords, 3 m (9.8 ft) long. Then, mount four mustard cords to the wooden dowel on each side of the design with LHKs.

Step 4: Use the mustard cords on each side of the design to create two running diamond chains. To do so, use the running weaving diamond chain pattern technique to tie five diamonds in each chain, not including the weaving inside the diamonds.

Step 5: Connect the two running diamond chains with a single double half hitch diamond using four cords from each chain.

Step 6: Fold twenty-eight mustard cords, 1.1 m (3.6 ft) long, in half. Mount two mustard cords with LHKs to the outer working cord, going from the dowel to the first diamond of the chain. Continue mounting mustard cords to the outer working cord of the chain, using LHKs to add three cords between diamonds. Add fourteen mustard cords to each chain.

Step 7: It's time to add the tassels to our design. Each tassel is made by untwisting and brushing four brown cords, 0.3 m (1 ft) long. Using the rya knot weaving technique, add a total of eleven tassels inside the diamonds of both chains. Then, brush and trim the ends of the tassels to give them an even finish.

Step 8: To create the chains used to hold the wooden board of our shelf, another four mustard cords, 3 m (9.8 ft) long, need to be mounted to the wooden dowel, two cords on each side of our design. Fold the cords and mount them to each side of the dowel using LHKs, following this sequence of lengths: the first cord [2.4 m (7.9 ft)–0.6 m (2 ft)] and the second cord [0.6 m (2 ft)–2.4 m (7.9 ft)] after mounting.

Step 9: Use the 0.6 m (2 ft) cords as your filler cords, and the 2.4 m (7.9 ft) cords as your working cords, to tie sixty LSPKs on each side of the design.

Step 10: Now, divide the cords of both chains of LSPKs, pairing one short filler cord with one long working cord. Then, tie two sets of twenty-five LFHHs with each pair of cords to create an inverted Y-shape at the end of each chain.

Step 11: Pass the remainder of the cords through the holes of the wooden board, two cords per hole. Secure the wooden board by tying four individual overhand knots with each pair of cords. Then, cut the ends of the cords right after the knots.

Step 12: Cut all the cords (brown and mustard) at the back of the wooden board in a V-shape.

CHAPTER 6

15 Patterns & 4 Projects for Advanced Artists

Advanced Patterns

Decreasing Arrows

The **decreasing arrows pattern** uses diagonal double half hitch (DDHH) knots to create the arrow shapes of the design. These geometric arrangements are formed by decreasing the number of knots we use in each row. For this example, you need to use sixteen cords in a vertical setup. You will have the chance to practice this pattern in the Tayanna Wall Hanging project in this book.

Knots Used:
Diagonal double half hitch (DDHH), see pages 62–63

Knotting Sequence:
7 x DDHH–left-to-right / 8 x DDHH–right-to-left
6 x DDHH–left-to-right / 7 x DDHH–right-to-left
5 x DDHH–left-to-right / 6 x DDHH–right-to-left
5 x DDHH–right-to-left / 5 x DDHH–left-to-right
7 x DDHH–right-to-left / 6 x DDHH–left-to-right
8 x DDHH–right-to-left / 7 x DDHH–left-to-right

Step 1: Begin the pattern by tying seven DDHHs–left-to-right, going down. Use the first cord as your filler cord and cords 2–8 as working cords. Then, tie eight DDHHs–right-to-left, going down, using cord 16 as your filler cord, and cords 8–15 as working cords.

Step 2: Skip the first cord on the left, and tie six DDHHs–left-to-right, going down. Use the second cord as your filler cord, and cords 3–8 as working cords. Then, skip the last cords of the design and tie seven DDHHs–right-to-left, going down. Use cord 15 as your filler cord, and cords 8–14 as working cords.

Step 3: Now, skip the first two cords on the left and tie five DDHHs–left-to-right, going down. Use cord 3 as your filler cord and cords 4–8 as working cords. Then, after skipping the last two cords, tie six DDHHs–right-to-left, using cord 14 as your filler cord, and cords 8–13 as working cords. This completes the first decreasing arrow of our pattern.

Step 4: Use the technique explained in the previous steps in reverse, knotting DDHHs right-to-left first and then left-to-right, to create an inverse arrow. Notice how this time the number of knots increases row by row. Because the last DDHH tied in step 3 is used to connect the arrows, only five DDHHs–right-to-left, going down, are needed at the beginning of the inverse arrow.

15 Patterns & 4 Projects for Advanced Artists

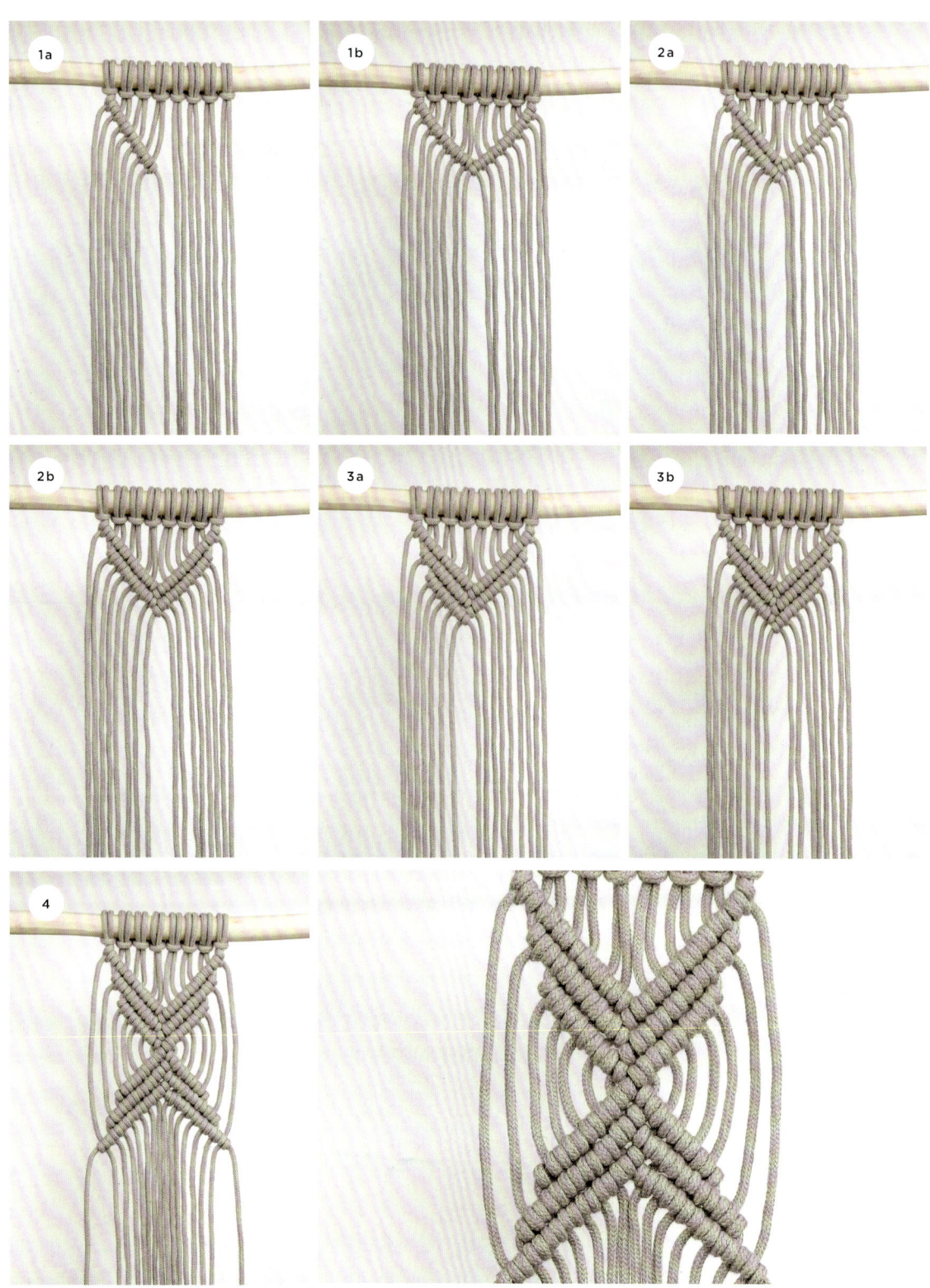

Continuous Double Diamond Chain

This gorgeous design is perfect to elevate your macramé skills if you are already familiar with diamond patterns. The **continuous double diamond chain** is the ideal pattern to add more predominant diamond shapes to your artwork. It uses two double lines of diagonal double half hitches (DDHHs) that intertwine to create these geometric shapes so favored by macramé artists. To follow this demonstration, you need twenty cords arranged in a vertical setup.

Knots Used:
Diagonal double half hitch (DDHH), see pages 62–63

Knotting Sequence:
4 x DDHH–left-to-right
3 x DDHH–left-to-right
9 x DDHH–right-to-left
8 x DDHH–right-to-left
2 x (3 x DDHH–left-to-right)
2 x (3 x DDHH–left-to-right)
2 x (8 x DDHH–right-to-left)
2 x (3 x DDHH–left-to-right)

Step 1: Begin your pattern by tying four DDHHs–left-to-right, going down. Use the first cord as your filler cord, and cords 2–5 as working cords.

Step 2: Now take the first cord as your filler cord, and using cords 2–4 as working cords, tie three DDHHs–left-to-right, going down under the previous line of DDHHs.

Step 3: Next, take the tenth cord as your filler cord, and tie nine DDHHs–right-to-left, going down. Use cords 1–9 as working cords.

Step 4: Now take the tenth cord as your filler cord, and tie eight DDHHs–right-to-left, going down under the previous line of DDHHs. Use cords 2–9 as your working cords.

Step 5: Continue the pattern by tying three DDHHs–left-to-right, going down. Use the seventh cord as your filler cord, and cords 8–10 as working cords.

Step 6: Tie another line of three DDHHs–left-to-right, going down under the line of DDHHs in the previous step. Use cord 6 as your filler cord, and cords 7–9 as working cords.

Step 7: Next, take the second cord as your filler cord, and using cords 3–5 as working cords, tie three DDHHs–left-to-right, going down.

Step 8: Repeat step 2.

Step 9: Then, take the cord 9 as your filler cord, and tie eight DDHHs–right-to-left, going down. Use cords 1–8 as your working cords.

Step 10: Repeat step 4.

Step 11: Repeat steps 5 and 6.

Step 12: To add additional diamonds to the pattern, keep repeating steps 7–11 until you reach the desired length of your chain.

15 Patterns & 4 Projects for Advanced Artists

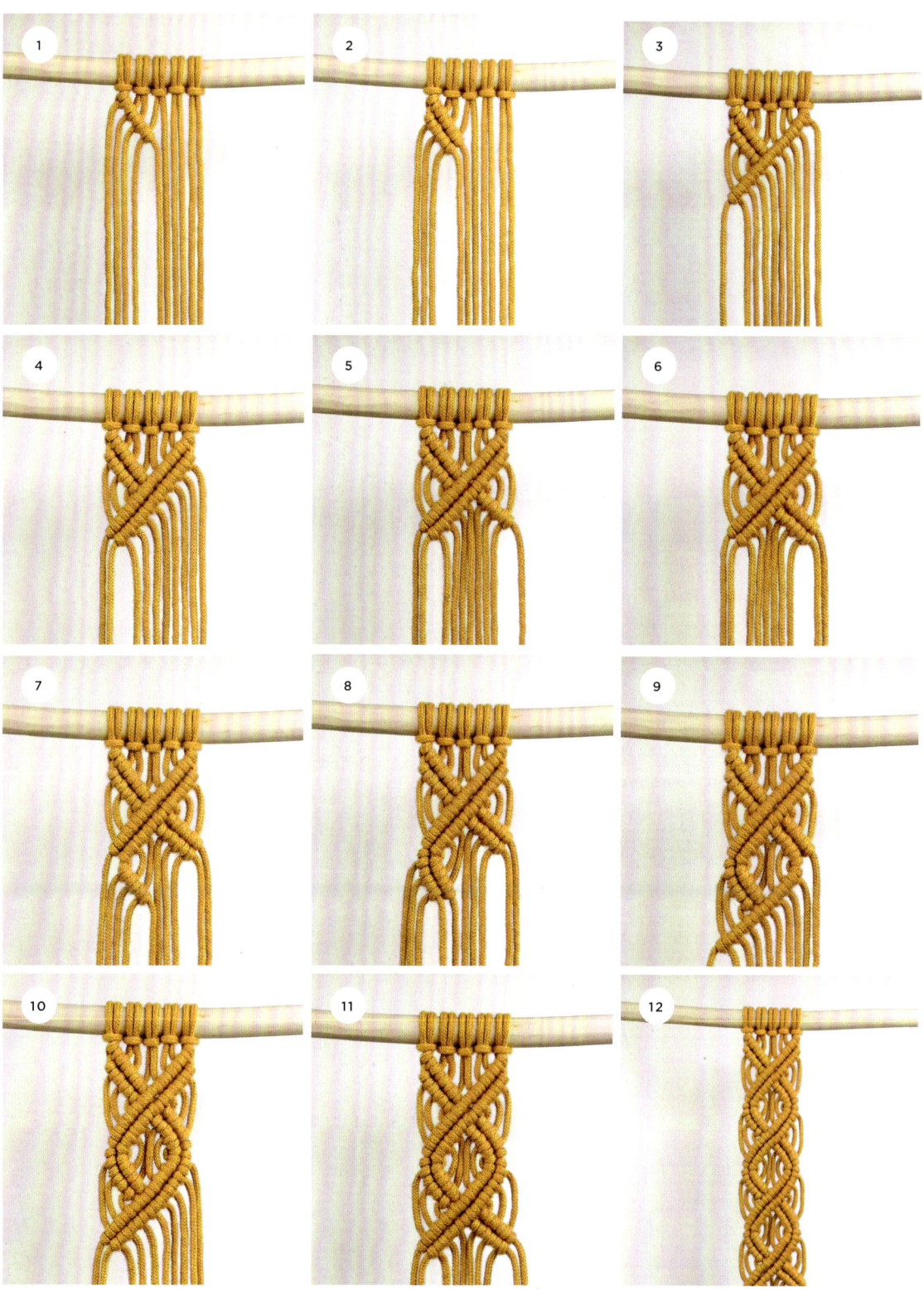

Macramé: The Power of Knots

TIP: If you wish to instead create a Vine Leaf Chain pattern with left-facing leaves, use the technique explained here in reverse.

Vine Leaf Chain

This pattern is a beautiful way to introduce natural elements to your design. The **vine leaf chain pattern** is commonly added to symmetrical wall hangings. The way this pattern is knotted creates a 3D effect ideal to incorporate some depth into your piece. You need six cords arranged in a vertical setup to attempt the vine leaf chain pattern.

Knots Used:
Diagonal double half hitch (DDHH), see pages 62–63

Knotting Sequence:
5 x DDHH–right–to–left
3 x (4 x DDHH–left–to–right)
3 x (4 x DDHH–right–to–left)
5 x DDHH–left–to–right

Step 1: Begin the pattern by tying five DDHHs–right–to–left, going down. Use cord 6 as your filler cord, and cords 1–5 as working cords.

Step 2: Take the second cord now as your filler cord, and using cords 3–6 as working cords, tie four DDHHs–left–to–right, going up.

Step 3: Repeat step 2 twice.

Step 4: Using cord 6 as your filler cord and cords 2–5 as working cords, now tie four DDHHs–right–to–left, going down.

Step 5: Repeat step 4 twice.

Step 6: In order to complete the first leaf of our chain, tie five DDHHs–left–to–right, following the curve of the vine leaf. Take the first cord as your filler cord and cords 2–6 as working cords to do so.

Step 7: Repeat steps 1–6 as many times as you want until you reach your length of chain.

Running Weaving Diamond Chain

The **running weaving diamond chain** pattern mixes a common shape in macramé designs, the diamond, with a basic weaving technique. This particular pattern involves an uninterrupted line of diagonal double half hitches (DDHHs) running through the entire design. The weaving is added inside each of the diamonds using the tabby weave technique. This design is commonly seen in wall hangings, dream catchers, and hanging shelves. I use twelve cords in a vertical setup to demonstrate. You can practice this pattern in the Gila Dream Catchers and Cressida Hanging Shelf projects.

Knots Used:
Diagonal double half hitch (DDHH), see pages 62–63
Tabby Weave, see page 107

Knotting Sequence:
6 x DDHH–right–to–left / 5 x DDHH–left–to–right
 Tabby weave
5 x DDHH–left–to–right / 5 x DDHH–right–to–left
6 x DDHH–left–to–right/ 5 x DDHH–right–to–left
 Tabby weave
5 x DDHH–right–to–left / 5 x DDHH–left–to–right

Step 1: Begin the first diamond by tying six DDHHs–right–to–left, going down. Use cord 7 as your filler cord, and cords 1–6 as working cords.

Step 2: Now take cord 7 as your filler cord, and using cords 8–12 as working cords, tie five DDHHs–left–to–right, going down.

Step 3: Apply the tabby weave technique with cords 3–10 in the middle of the design.

Step 4: While holding all the cords in place, carefully tie five DDHHs–left–to–right, going down. Use the first cord as your filler cord, and cords 2–6 as your working cords.

Step 5: Next, tie five DDHHs–right–to–left, going down, with cord 12 as your filler cord and cords 7–11 as your working cords.

Step 6: To create the running effect in our pattern, we need an uninterrupted line that moves from diamond to diamond. To achieve this, use the technique explained in steps 1–5 in reverse. The second diamond of the pattern begins with six DDHHs moving down from left to right.

Step 7: To add additional diamonds to the pattern, keep repeating steps 1–6 until you reach the desired length of the chain.

15 Patterns & 4 Projects for Advanced Artists

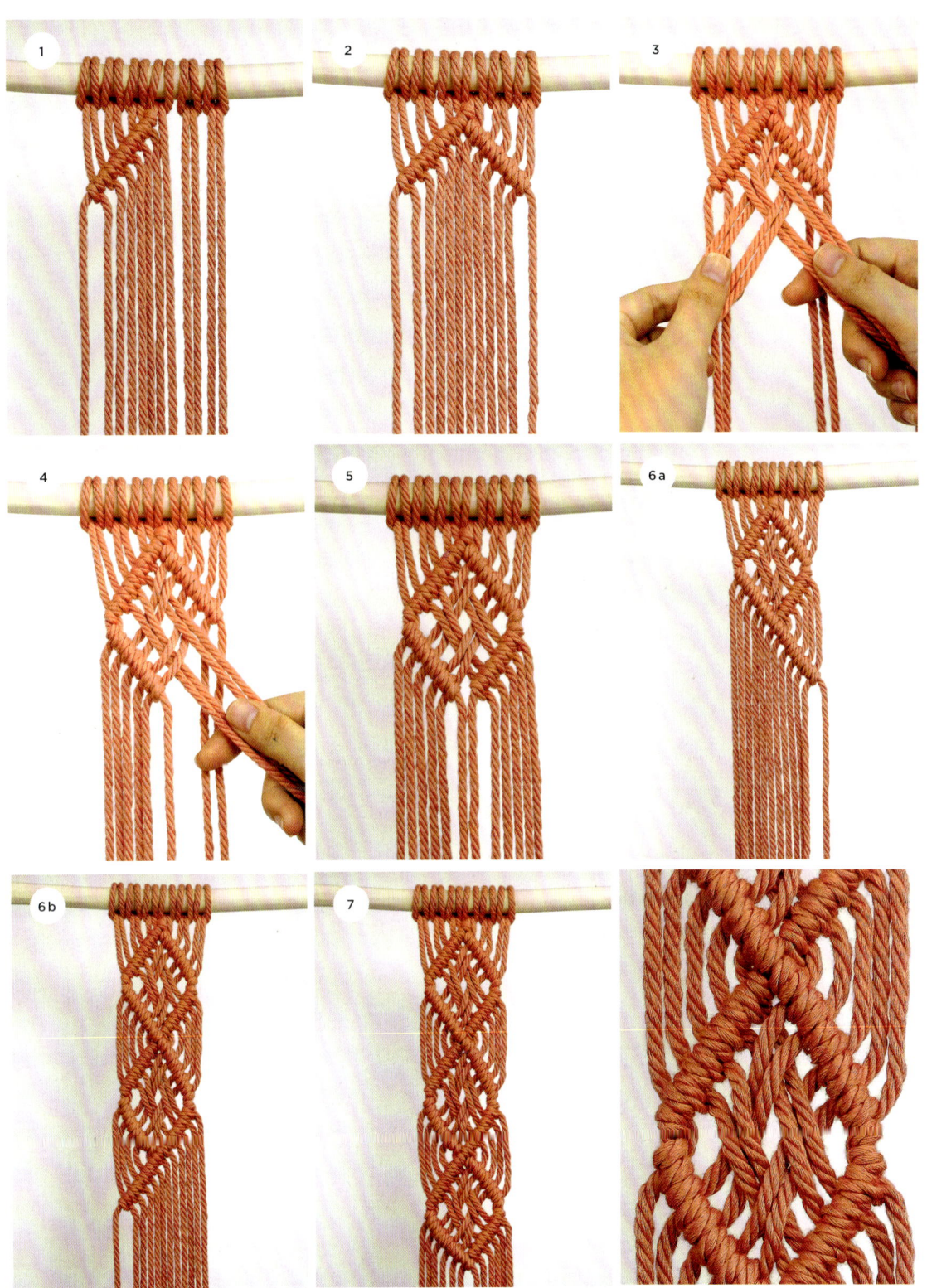

Macramé: The Power of Knots

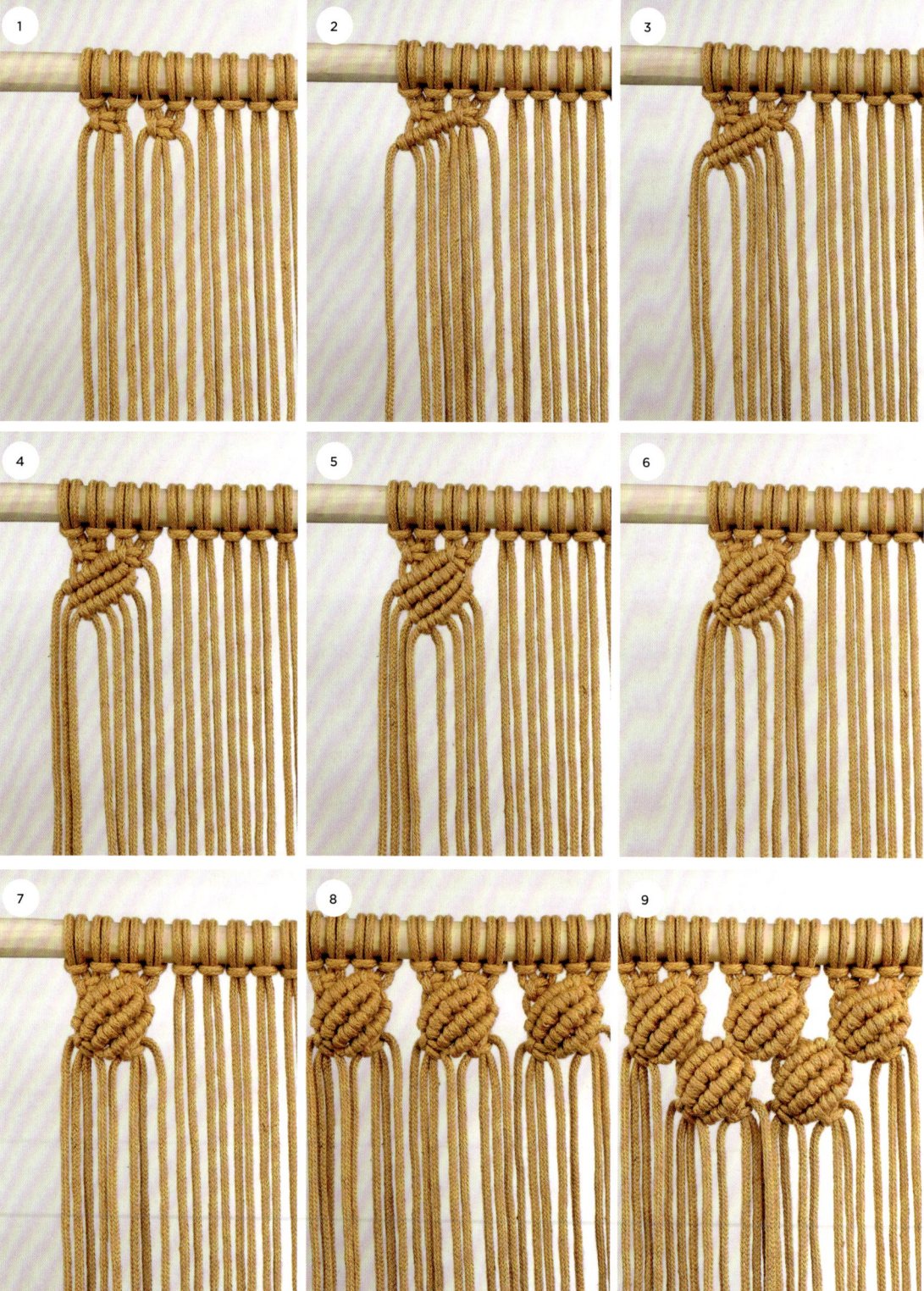

15 Patterns & 4 Projects for Advanced Artists

3D Shell Mesh

An intricate pattern that allows you to add depth and texture to your designs. The **3D shell mesh** uses diagonal double half hitch (DDHH) knots to form the bodies of the shells, while square knots (SKs) tighten and give the 3D effect. This pattern works beautifully in macramé bags and purses, as well as wall hanging designs. You need twelve cords arranged in a vertical setup to attempt this demonstration.

Knots Used:
Square knot (SK), see page 47
Diagonal double half hitch (DDHH), see pages 62–63

Knotting Sequence for One 3D Shell:
2 x SK
4 x (4 x DDHH–right–to–left)
2 x SK

Step 1: Begin the first shell of the pattern by tying two SKs with cords 1–8.

Step 2: Now use cord 5 as your filler cord and cords 1–4 as working cords to tie the first row of four DDHHs–right–to–left, going down.

Step 3: Now, using cord 6 as your filler cord and cords 2–5 as working cords, tie the second row of four DDHHs–right–to–left, going down.

Step 4: Now, using cord 7 as your filler cord and cords 3–6 as working cords, tie the third row of four DDHHs–right–to–left, going down.

Step 5: To tie the fourth and last row of four DDHHs–right–to–left, going down, use cord 8 as your filler cord and cords 4–7 as working cords.

Step 6: Now, tie one single SK using cords 1–4. Ensure your SK is tied following the shape of the shell tightly, and gently press the back of the design to give the body of the shell some curvature and thus create the 3D effect.

Step 7: Finish the first 3D shell by adding an extra SK using cords 4–8. Notice how this SK is diagonally tied following the shape of the shell. Once again, make sure to tie this knot tightly.

Step 8: Using the technique explained in steps 1–7, create two more shells to the right of the first one to complete the first row of your mesh.

Step 9: Alternate the pattern by creating two 3D shells underneath the first row. The shells of the second row are aligned between the shells of the first row. The bottom-right SK from one shell and the bottom-left SK from the following shell on the first row serve as the first knots of the alternating shells. This means you need to begin your alternating shells by directly adding rows of DDHHs to your design.

Running Diamonds Circle

The **running diamonds circle pattern** is best used to incorporate diamond shapes into circular frames. Each diamond in this pattern uses eight cords. You can make bigger diamond shapes by adding more cords to each group. If you wish to use a bigger ring, you would need to add extra groups of cords. In this example, using a horizontal setup, you need to mount ten groups of four mounting cords at least 1 m (3.3 ft) in length to a 15 cm (5.9 in) diameter ring. The Mandala Mirror project is a perfect example of how the running diamonds circle pattern is integrated into a gorgeous design.

Knots Used:
Lark's head knot (LHK), see page 41
Diagonal double half hitch (DDHH), see pages 62–63
Square knot (SK), see page 47

Step 1: Fold all forty cords in half and mount them to the ring with LHKs. Then divide all the cords into groups of eight.

Step 2: Starting from the left, take the eighth cord from each group as your filler cord, and cords 5–7 as working cords. Tie three DDHHs–right-to-left, going down.

Step 3: Now, take the first cord from each group as your filler cord, and using cords 2–5 as working cords, tie four DDHHs–left-to-right, going down.

Step 4: Take the first two cords of each group and the last two cords of the next group to the left and tie SKs around the design—ten SKs in total.

Step 5: Next, the groups of cords need to be rearranged. Create ten new groups of eight cords by adding two cords to the left and right of each SK.

Step 6: Using the new groups of cords, repeat steps 2 and 3. This step completes our first row of diamonds. Notice how each diamond contains a single SK.

Step 7: Keep repeating steps 4–6 to create two more rows of diamonds. Notice how uninterrupted lines of DDHHs run from the ring throughout the design.

15 Patterns & 4 Projects for Advanced Artists

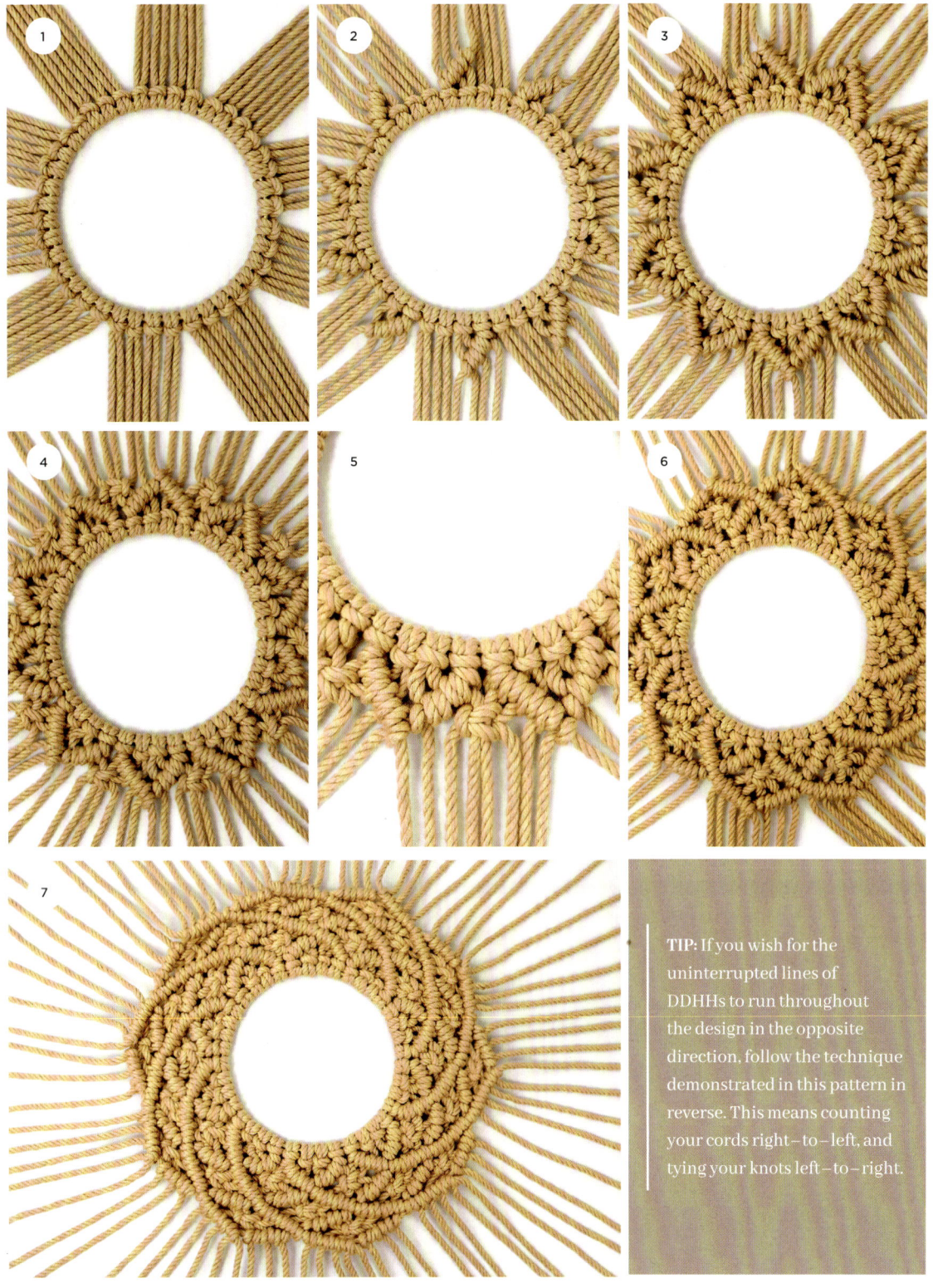

TIP: If you wish for the uninterrupted lines of DDHHs to run throughout the design in the opposite direction, follow the technique demonstrated in this pattern in reverse. This means counting your cords right–to–left, and tying your knots left–to–right.

Macramé: The Power of Knots

TIP: Bend the first line of DDHHs by hand to give it a curved shape before completing step 2.

//
Lily Mesh

This dazzling pattern is inspired by floral elements. The **lily mesh** is formed by creating petals using diagonal double half hitches (DDHHs). These petals are arranged together to create a lily flower, which could have a single diagonal double half hitch (DDHH) knot, a berry knot, or, as I demonstrate in this example, a square knot (SK), in the center of the flower as the ovule. The mesh is created by connecting flowers with square knots (SKs). I use a vertical setup and thirty-two cords to demonstrate. The lily mesh pattern is part of the Lilia Handbag project.

Knots Used:
Diagonal double half hitch (DDHH), see pages 62–63
Square knot (SK), see page 47

Knotting Sequence:
2 x (7 x DDHH–left–to–right)
2 x (7 x DDHH–left–to–right)
2 x (7 x DDHH–right–to–left)
2 x (7 x DDHH–right–to–left)
2 x SK
2 x (7 x DDHH–right–to–left)
2 x (7 x DDHH–right–to–left)
2 x (7 x DDHH–left–to–right)
2 x (7 x DDHH–left–to–right)
1 x SK

Step 1: Begin the first petal of each lily flower by tying seven DDHHs–left–to–right, going down. Use cords 1 and 17 as your filler cords, and cords 2–8 and 18–24 as working cords.

Step 2: To close off the petals, repeat step 1 using the same cords to create a second line of DDHHs. This time, leave some space between the first and second lines of DDHHs to make the petal shapes.

Step 3: Next, to create the second petal of each lily, follow the same technique, only this time tie seven DDHHs–right–to–left, going down. Use cords 16 and 32 as your filler cords, and cords 9–15 and 25–31 as your working cords.

Step 4: Create the ovule of each flower by connecting the petals with SKs. Use cords 7–10 for the first flower, and cords 23–26 for the second.

Step 5: To create the third petal of each lily, tie 7 DDHHs–right–to–left, going down. Cords 8 and 24 are your filler cords, and cords 1–7 and 17–23 are working cords.

Step 6: Now, the fourth petals are created by tying seven DDHHs–left–to–right, going down. Use cords 9 and 25 as your filler cords, and cords 10–16 and 26–32 as working cords. This step completes the first row of lilies.

Step 7: Connect the lilies of each row of flowers by tying an SK between each lily and the next using cords 15–18. Then, repeat steps 1–5 to create as many rows of lilies as you need for your mesh.

Alternating Half Hitch Six-Point Star

The **alternating half hitch six-point star** is a great way to incorporate a circular motif into a flat macramé design. It works wonderfully in pieces such as table mats or dream catchers. You have the chance to use this pattern in the Gila Dream Catchers project. I suggest starting with a six-point star shape first, and eventually add more points to your star. In order to do so, you would have to add more pairs of mounting cords to your anchor cord at the beginning of the process. For this demonstration, you need twelve cords of at least 1 m (3.3 ft) in length. A horizontal setup is the best way to approach this pattern.

Knots Used:
Lark's head knot (LHK), see page 41
Square knot (SK), see page 47
Alternating half hitch (AHH), see page 57

Step 1: Create a circumference with one of the cords by folding it so both ends face the same direction. Make sure that both ends are equidistant from the circumference.

Step 2: Fold eleven cords in half and mount them to the circumference using LHKs. Pull both ends of the anchor cord to close and tighten the circumference.

Step 3: Tie six SKs with all of the cords, including both ends of the anchor cord.

Step 4: Tie a three-AHHs chain using the last filler and working cords from one SK. Then, tie another three-AHHs chain with the next working and filler cords from the next SK.

Step 5: Connect both AHH chains with an SK.

Step 6: Repeat steps 4 and 5 with the rest of the cord. This completes the first layer of the alternating half hitch 6-point star pattern.

Step 7: Using the same technique, tie six AHHs per chain, and connect each chain with SKs. This completes the second layer of the pattern.

Step 8: To complete the third and last layer of your pattern, tie chains of nine AHHs each. Connect each pair of chains using single SKs once again.

15 Patterns & 4 Projects for Advanced Artists

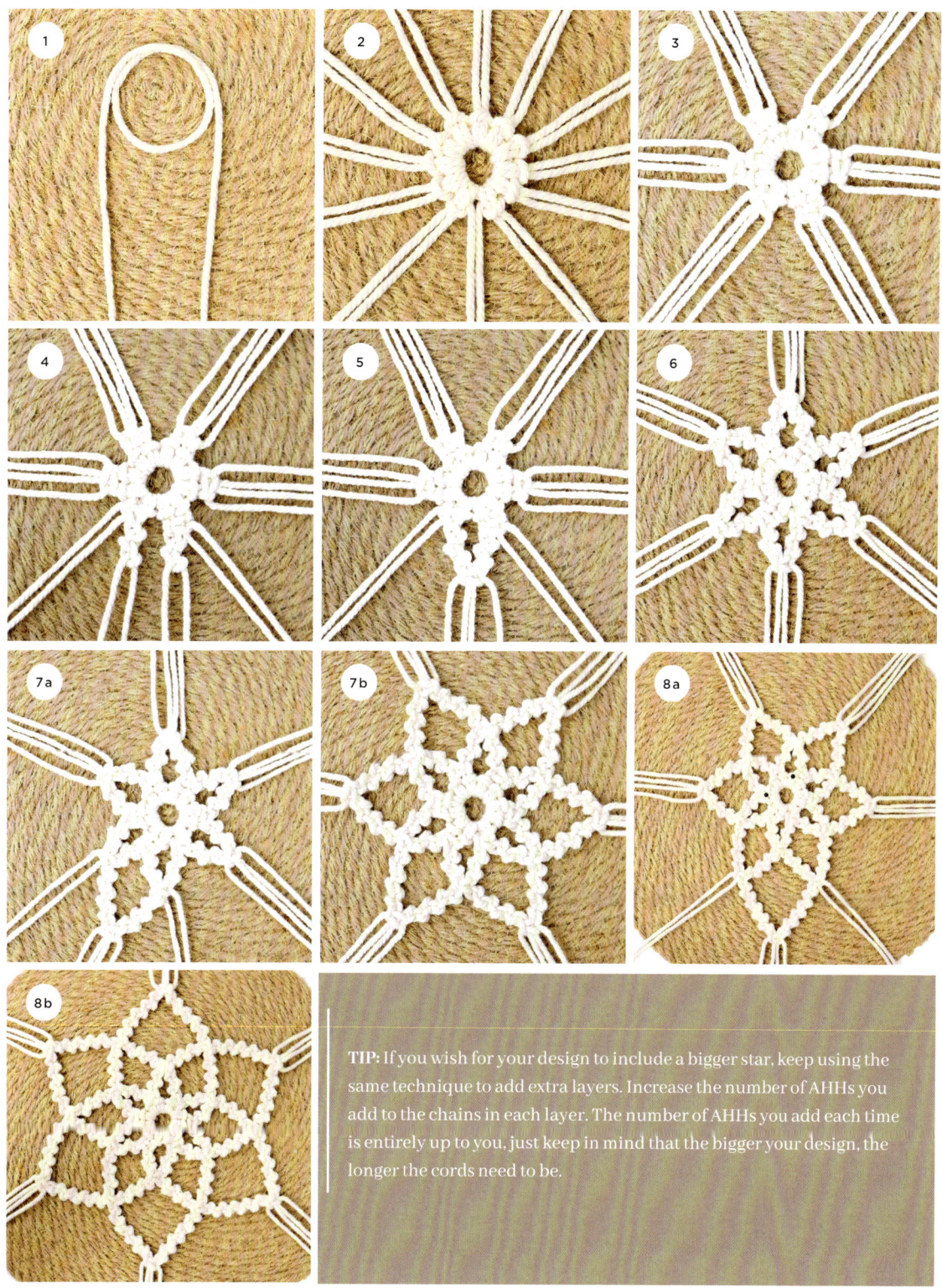

TIP: If you wish for your design to include a bigger star, keep using the same technique to add extra layers. Increase the number of AHHs you add to the chains in each layer. The number of AHHs you add each time is entirely up to you, just keep in mind that the bigger your design, the longer the cords need to be.

Macramé: The Power of Knots

Aztec Square Knot

This is a design that can easily be the centerpiece of any wall hanging or flat macramé artwork. The **Aztec square knot** is a stunning geometric design inspired by ancient Aztec tribal symbolism. A simple arrangement of diamond and triangle shapes is created by tying single square knots (SKs). To complete this striking pattern, you need forty-eight cords in a vertical setup. If you want to find out how powerful the Aztec square knot pattern can be, I apply this design, with a twist, in the Tayanna Wall Hanging project.

Knots Used:
Square knot (SK), see page 47
Alternating square knot (ASK), see page 51

Patterns Used:
Triangle square knot, see page 93
Square knot diamond with big square knot, see page 102

Step 1: Create one square knot diamond using cords 17–32. This is basically the square knot diamond with big square knot pattern, without including the big SK inside the diamond.

Step 2: Continue by tying two square knot triangle patterns right underneath the diamond—one triangle to the left, using cords 9–24, and another one to the right with cords 25–40.

Step 3: Next, you need to create another two square knot triangle patterns. One triangle is to the left, below the first triangle in step 2, and uses cords 1–16. The second one uses cords 33–48, and is to the right, below the second triangle from step 2. This step completes the top half of the pattern.

Step 4: To complete the bottom part of the pattern, you need to mirror (reverse) the design explained in the previous steps. This means following the directions in step 3 first, and then steps 2 and 1 consecutively. Keep in mind that the last two SKs of the triangles from step 3 are the opening knots of the first triangles in step 4. To properly mirror the design, you should also invert the direction of the triangles, thus increasing by one the number of ASKs, instead of decreasing it.

3D Flower

A sophisticated pattern inspired by nature, the **3D flower** can work as a single piece on its own, or it can be added to designs in which floral elements are meant to be strong statements. I personally love to use these as ornaments for wedding decor, or to add depth to flat decorative pieces. To follow this demonstration, you need six cords with a length of at least 1 m (3.3 ft) each. Approach this pattern using a horizontal setup.

Knots Used:
Vertical double half hitch (VDHH), see pages 67
Diagonal double half hitch (DDHH), see pages 62–63
Overhand knot, see page 38

Step 1: The 3D flower pattern consists of five individual petals gathered together. To create the first of the petals, fold one cord in half and secure it with a pin to your horizontal setup of choice. These cords will be your filler cords for steps 2 and 3.

Step 2: Take another cord and mount it to the filler cords with two VDHHs. Make sure both ends of the mounting cord are equidistant to the VDHHs.

Step 3: Repeat step 2 to mount four more cords. Notice how there are now twelve cords available to work with, five on each side of the column of VDHHs, and the two cords we were using as filler cords in the previous steps.

Step 4: From top to bottom, take the second cord from the left of the column as your filler cord and tie a DDHH going up using the first cord as working cord. Repeat this technique in reverse with the cords to the right of the column.

Step 5: Then, using the first cord to the left of the column as your working cord, tie five DDHHs–right–to–left, going down, with cords 2–6 as working cords. Use the same technique in reverse with the right side.

Step 6: Tie one single DDHH–right–to–left using the sixth cord of each side.

Step 7: Take the third cord from the left of the column as your filler cord and tie two DDHHs going up using cords 1 and 2 as working cords. Repeat this technique in reverse with the cords to the right of the column.

Step 8: Repeat steps 5 and 6.

Step 9: To close the first petal, we need to add the last two lines of DDHHs, one on each side of the design. These lines use DDHHs that gradually increase in size. To do this, start by tying a regular DDHH first. Then, in order to tie the next DDHH, take both the working and filler cords from the previous knot, and use them as your filler cords. With each DDHH you knot, a cord is added to the filler cords of the next knot. A total of five DDHHs need to be tied on each side.

Step 10: Repeat steps 1–9 four more times to make four more petals. To create the flower shape, gather the remaining cords of all the five petals together, and use one of the cords to tie an overhand knot.

15 Patterns & 4 Projects for Advanced Artists

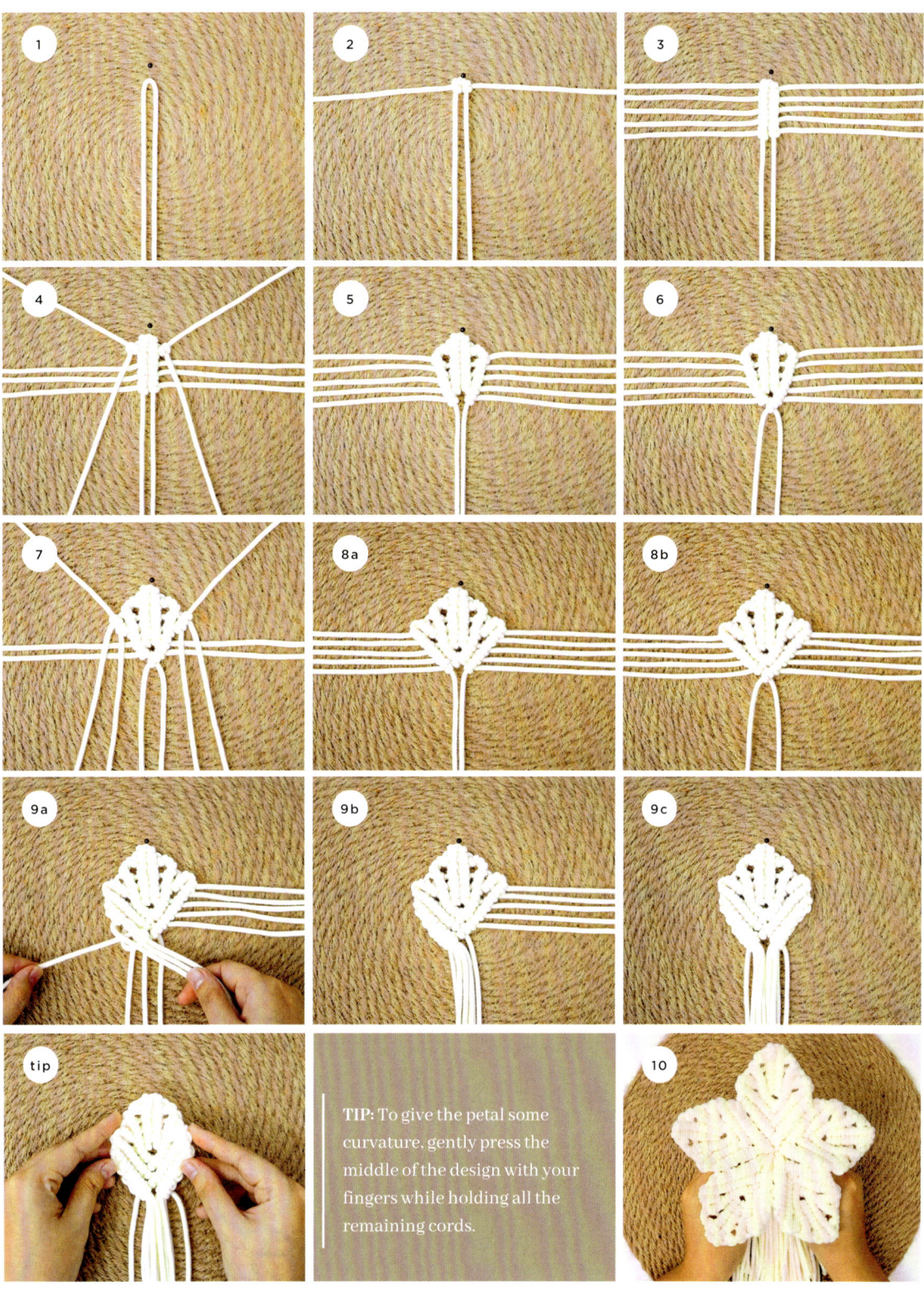

TIP: To give the petal some curvature, gently press the middle of the design with your fingers while holding all the remaining cords.

Reverse Arrows Mesh

If you have already practiced knotting simple arrows or meshes, this pattern is an excellent way to level up your macramé skills. The reverse arrows mesh combines lines of normal and reverse diagonal double half hitches (DDHHs), and incorporates big square knots (SKs) to fill and decorate the spaces between arrows. You need a minimum of thirty-two cords arranged in a vertical setup to attempt this pattern. You can see this gorgeous pattern included in the Tayanna Wall Hanging project.

Knots Used:
Diagonal double half hitch (DDHH), see pages 62–63
Reverse diagonal double half hitch (RDDHH),
  see pages 68–69
Square knot (SK), see page 47

Knotting Sequence:
2 x (7 x DDHH–left-to-right)
2 x (7 x DDHH–right-to-left)
2 x (7 x RDDHH–left-to-right)
2 x (7 x RDDHH–right-to-left)

Knotting Sequence (cont)
2 x (7 x DDHH–left-to-right)
2 x (7 x DDHH–right-to-left)
2 x DDHH–right-to-left
1 x SK
2 x (7 x DDHH–right-to-left)
2 x (7 x DDHH–left-to-right)
2 x (7 x RDDHH–right-to-left)
2 x (7 x RDDHH–left-to-right)
2 x (7 x DDHH–right-to-left)
2 x (7 x DDHH–left-to-right)

Step 1: Begin your pattern by tying two lines of seven DDHHs–left-to-right, going down. Use the first and the seventeenth cords as your filler cords, and cords 2–8 and 18–24 respectively as working cords.

Step 2: Now, use cords 16 and 32 as your filler cords to tie two lines of seven DDHHs–right-to-left, going down. Use cords 9–15 and 25–31 respectively as working cords.

Step 3: Using RDDHHs instead of DDHHs now, repeat steps 1 and 2.

Step 4: Switch back to DDHHs and then repeat steps 1 and 2 once again.

Step 5: To complete the top part of the pattern, you need to close each arrow with a single DDHH. Use cords 9 and 25 as your filler cords, and cords 8 and 24 as working cords.

Step 6: Use a big SK to connect the two arrows. To do so, take cords 11 and 22 as your working cords, and use cords 12–21 as filler cords.

Step 7: For the bottom part of the design, start by tying two lines of seven DDHHs–right-to-left, going down. Use cords 8 and 24 as your filler cords, and cords 1–7 and 17–23 as your working cords.

Step 8: Now, use cords 9 and 25 as your filler cords to tie two lines of 7 DDHHs–left-to-right, going down. Use cords 10–16 and 26–32 as working cords.

Step 9: Using RDDHHs instead of DDHHs now, repeat steps 7 and 8.

Step 10: Switch back to DDHHs and then repeat steps 7 and 8 once again to complete the pattern.

15 Patterns & 4 Projects for Advanced Artists

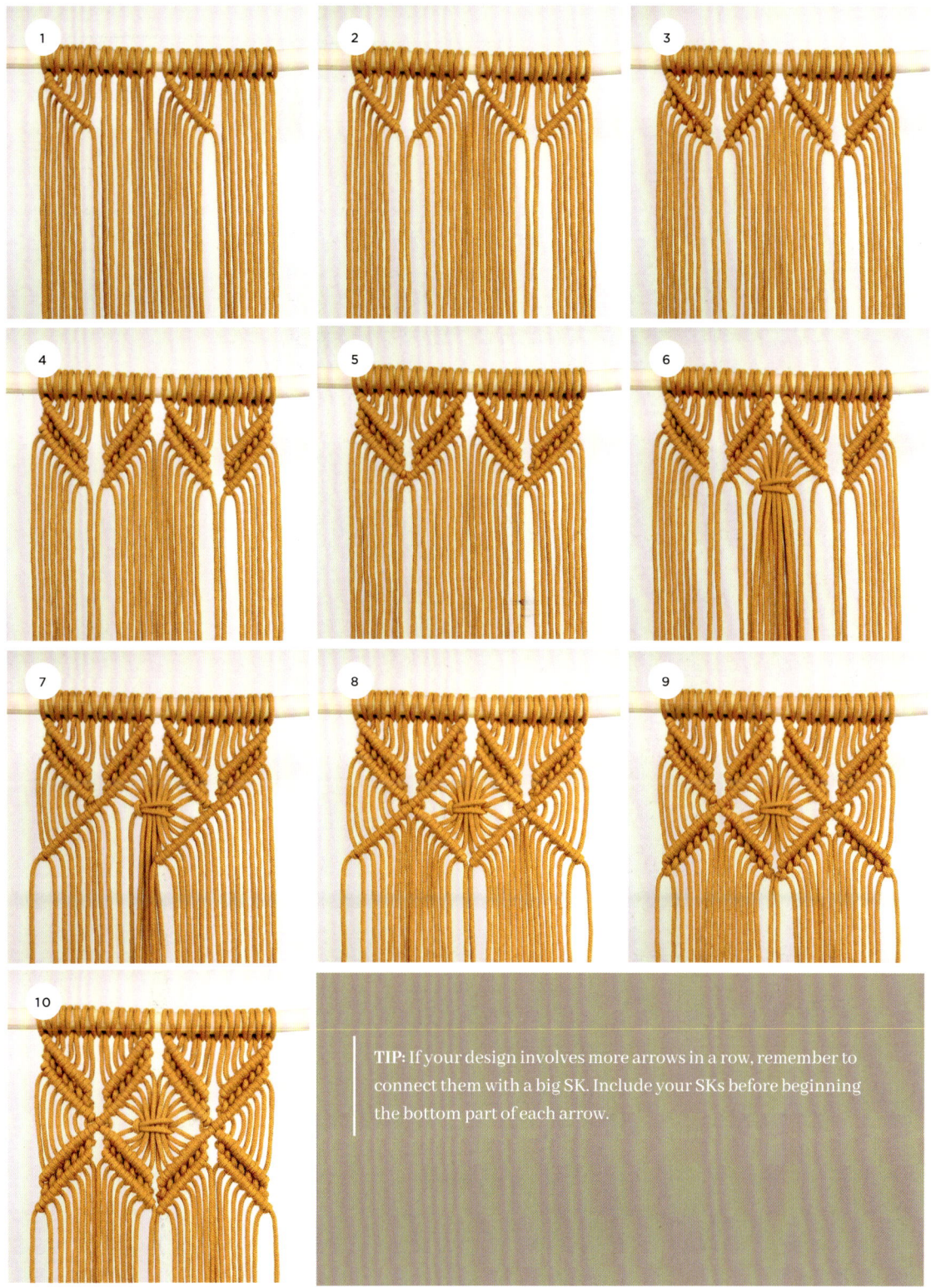

TIP: If your design involves more arrows in a row, remember to connect them with a big SK. Include your SKs before beginning the bottom part of each arrow.

Macramé: The Power of Knots

TIP: The tension of cords 15–19 should be enough to keep them straight and separated, but not so much that the shape of the diamond is affected. This is a tricky step to get right at first. Feel free to tie and untie your DDHHs until you are satisfied with the placement of the knots.

Infinity Diamond

Infinity patterns are used in this design to create a diamond shape. After you have completed the top part of the diamond, you will have to intertwine groups of cords to give a twisted effect in the middle. This makes for a very unique and pleasing way to fill diamond shapes, as you can see in the Gila Dream Catchers project in this book. A vertical setup is ideal to approach this pattern. You need twenty cords to complete the **infinity diamond**.

Knots Used:
Diagonal double half hitch (DDHH), see pages 62–63

Pattern Used:
Infinity, see page 146

Step 1: Begin by creating the first infinity pattern moving down from right to left. Use cords 1–10 to do so.

Step 2: Continue with a second infinity pattern, this time using cords 11–20 and moving down from left to right. This step completes the top part of the diamond.

Step 3: For the bottom part of the design, different sections of the third and fourth infinity patterns are tied in parallel. Start by taking the first cord as your filler cord, and cords 15–19 as working cords, to tie five DDHHs-left-to-right, going down. Notice that the working cords you are using belong to the second infinity pattern in step 2. This completes the first section of the third infinity pattern.

Step 4: Using the same technique in reverse, repeat step 3 to create the first section of the fourth infinity pattern. Notice how, in this step, your working cords belong to the first infinity pattern in step 1, and the last cord of the design is your filler cord.

Step 5: Use the first and last cords of the design as your filler cords to tie two separate lines of five DDHHs under the first section of the third and fourth infinity patterns respectively.

Step 6: Now, take the eight cords in the middle of the design and bring them forward. Grab the four cords from the left and twist them once with the four cords from the right.

Step 7: Keep using the same filler cords as in step 5 to add an extra four DDHHs to each line. Use the first and last four cords twisted in step 6 as working cords for each line respectively.

Step 8: To finish both the third and fourth infinity patterns, take cords 5 and 16 as your filler cords to tie two separate lines of five DDHHs under the lines tied in step 7. Use cords 6–10 as working cords to close the third infinity pattern, and working cords 11–15 to close the fourth one. This completes your infinity diamond pattern.

Open Diamond with Switch Knot Mesh

The **open diamond with switch knot mesh** pattern is a refreshing new take on what otherwise would be a simple diamond mesh. A series of uninterrupted and unconnected zigzag lines of diagonal double half hitches (DDHHs) are used to create a mesh of open diamond shapes. The pattern is then connected using several switch knots in the middle of those diamonds. You need to arrange twenty-four cords in a vertical setup for this demonstration.

Knots Used:
Diagonal double half hitch (DDHH), see pages 62–63
Switch knot (SWK), see page 52
Alternating square knot (ASK), see page 51

Step 1: Begin your pattern by tying two lines of five DDHHs-right-to-left, going down. Use cords 6 and 18 as your filler cords, and cords 1–5 and 13–17 as working cords.

Step 2: Now, use cords 7 and 19 as your filler cords to tie two lines of five DDHHs-left-to-right, going down. Use cords 8–12 and 20–24 as working cords.

Step 3: Tie a single SWK with cords 5–8.

Step 4: Tie two alternating SWKs underneath the previous SWK, using cords 3–6 and cords 7–10. For these knots, only the outer pair of working and filler cords are switched.

Step 5: Tie one ASK with cords 5–8 underneath the alternating SWKs.

Step 6: Now, use the first cord as your filler cord to tie five DDHHs-left-to-right, going down. Make sure to switch working cords 3 and 4, and working cords 5 and 6, while knotting the line DDHHs. This will ensure the arrangement of cords is consistent inside the open diamond.

Step 7: Use the same technique explained in step 6 in reverse with cords 9–12.

Step 8: Repeat steps 3–17 using cords 13–24.

Step 9: Now, repeat steps 3–17 again using cords 7–18.

Step 10: Continue alternating the pattern until you reach the desired length of your design.

15 Patterns & 4 Projects for Advanced Artists

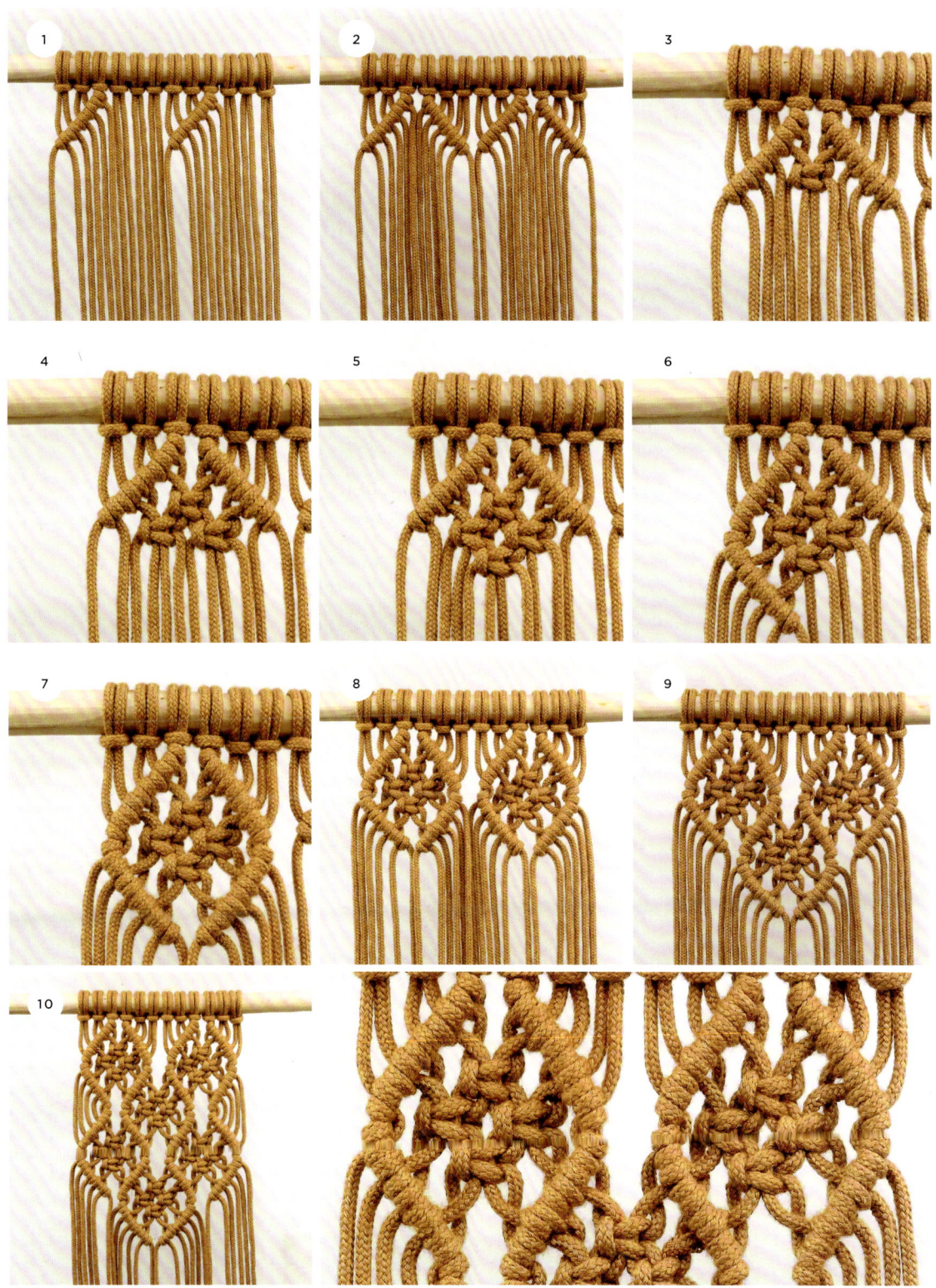

Macramé: The Power of Knots

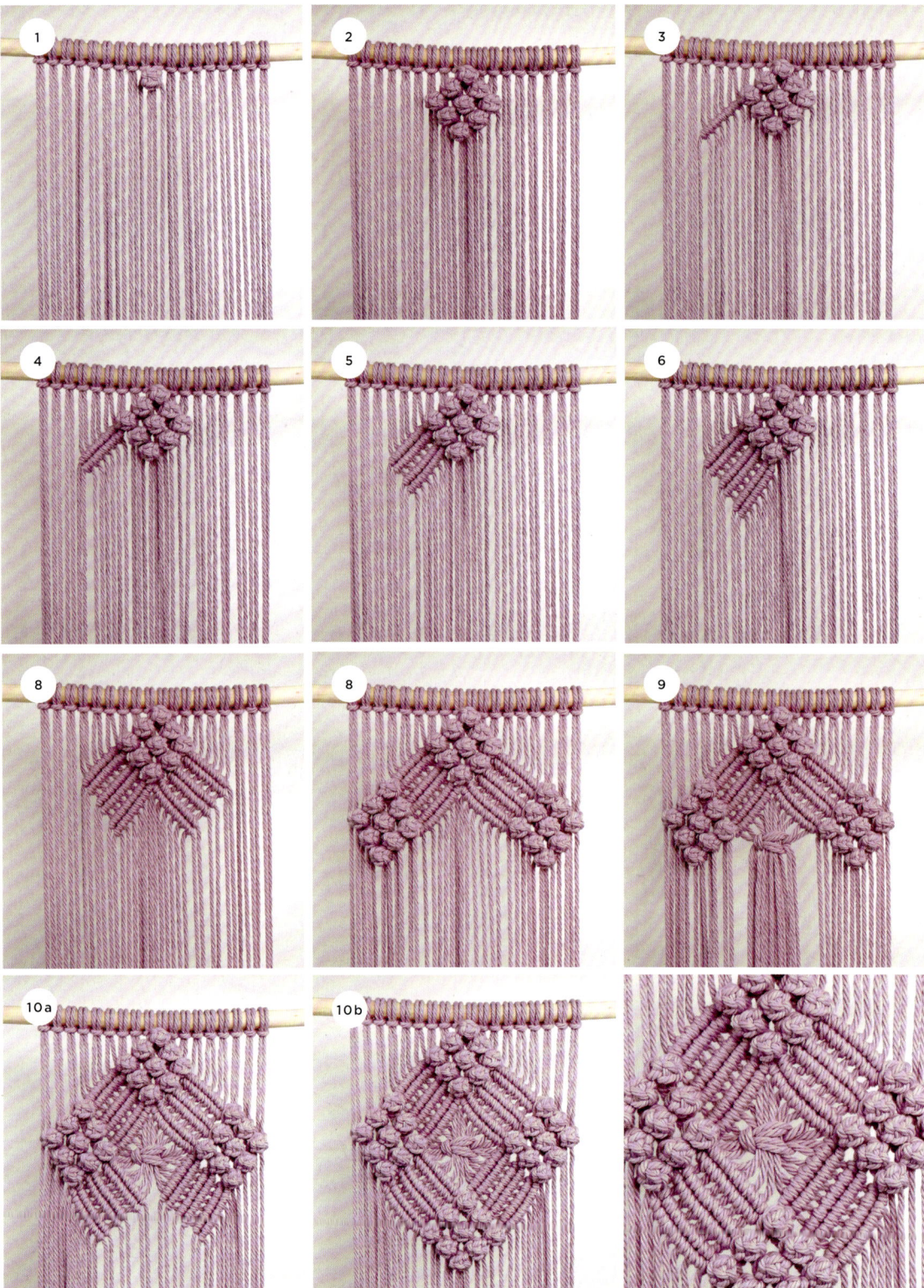

Berry Mesh

A combination of berry knots and diagonal double half hitches (DDHHs) is used to create this beautiful and intricate pattern. The **berry mesh** is a great choice for big macramé designs. I'm fond of the way this impressive pattern looks when it is featured in curtains and wedding backdrops. You need a minimum of thirty-six cords arranged in a vertical setup to attempt this demonstration.

Knots Used:
Berry knot, see page 72
Diagonal double half hitch (DDHH), see pages 62–63
Square knot (SK), see page 47

Step 1: Begin the pattern by tying a berry knot with cords 17–20.

Step 2: Continue tying rows of alternating berry knots with cords 13–24 until you form a diamond shape. Use two berry knots for the second row, three for the third, and then two and one for the fourth and fifth rows. This step completes the first berry knot diamond.

Step 3: Next, take the cord 13 as your filler cord, and tie six DDHHs–right-to-left, going down. Use cords 7–12 as working cords.

Step 4: Now take cord 14 as your filler cord, and tie six DDHHs–right-to-left, going down underneath the previous row of DDHHs. Use cords 8–13 as working cords.

Step 5: Leave a small gap before tying another two consecutive rows of six DDHHs –right-to-left, going down. Use cord 15 with cords 9–14, and cord 16 with cords 10–15, as filler and working cords, respectively, for each of the rows.

Step 6: Leave another small gap before tying the last two consecutive rows of six DDHHs –right-to-left, going down to the left of the diamond. Use cord 17 with cords 11–16, and cord 18 with cords 12–17, as filler and working cords, respectively, for each of the rows.

Step 7: Then you have to create three pairs of two consecutive rows of DDHHs to the right of the diamond. To do so, repeat the technique explained in steps 3–6 in reverse. This time, use cords 17–30 to tie rows of six DDHHs–left-to-right, going down.

Step 8: Using the technique explained in steps 1 and 2, create two separate berry knot diamonds. Use cords 1–12 to create the berry knot diamond to the left of the design, and cords 25–36 to create the one on the right.

Step 9: Continue the pattern by tying one SK in the middle of the design using cords 13–24. Use pairs of cords 13–14 and 23–24 as your working cords, and leave cords 15–22 as filler cords.

Step 10: To complete the berry mesh pattern, mirror the technique explained in the previous steps to create lines of DDHHs that meet in a berry knot diamond at the bottom of the design. You can repeat this pattern as many times as you want in order to create a bigger mesh.

Royal Diamond

The **royal diamond** pattern is a symmetrical design filled with details. It combines many lines of knots with two wooden beads to create an unusual and powerful looking diamond shape. You need two 20-mm (0.8-in) wooden beads and twenty cords to complete this demonstration. The best way to approach the royal diamond pattern is with a vertical setup.

Knots Used:
Diagonal double half hitch (DDHH), see pages 62–63
Square knot, see page 47

Step 1: The pattern starts with six DDHHs–right-to-left, going down. Use cord 11 as your filler cord, and cords 5–10 as working cords.

Step 2: Take cord 11 now as your filler cord, and tie five DDHHs–right-to-left, going down. Use cords 12–16 as working cords.

Step 3: Pass cords 10 and 11 through a 20-mm (0.8-in) wooden bead, and place it right underneath the lines of DDHHs.

Step 4: Then, take cord 5 as your filler cord, and use cords 6 and 7 as working cords to tie two DDHHs–left-to-right, going down. Repeat this step in reverse with cords 14–16 on the right side of the design.

Step 5: Using cord 5 as your filler cord now, take cords 3 and 4 as working cords, and tie two DDHHs–right-to-left, going down. Repeat this step in reverse with cords 16–18.

Step 6: Next, take cord 3 as your filler cord, and cord 4 as your only working cord, to tie a single DDHH–left-to-right. Repeat this step in reverse with cords 17–18.

Step 7: Take the third cord now as your filler cord, and using cords 1 and 2 as working cords, tie two DDHHs–right-to-left, going down. Repeat this step in reverse with cords 18–20.

Step 8: Now, take the second cord as your filler cord, and cord 1 as your only working cord to tie a single DDHH–left-to-right. Repeat this step in reverse with cords 19–20.

Step 9: Continue the pattern by tying a line of nine DDHHs–right-to-left, going down, starting from right under the wooden bead. Use cord 10 as your filler cord, and cords 1–9 as working cords. Repeat this step in reverse with cords 11–20.

15 Patterns & 4 Projects for Advanced Artists

Macramé: The Power of Knots

Step 10: Tie a single SK using cords 8 and 13 as working cords, leaving the cords between them as filler cords.

Step 11: Then, take cord 6 as your filler cord, and use cords 7–10 as working cords to tie four DDHHs–left–to–right, going down. Repeat this technique in reverse with cords 11–15.

Step 12: After that, tie two single SKs. Use cords 3 and 8, and cords 13 and 18, as working cords, leaving the cords in between each of those pairs (4–7 and 14–17) as filler cords.

Step 13: Now, tie four DDHHs–right–to–left, going down, using cord 10 as your filler cord and cords 6–9 as working cords. Repeat this technique in reverse with cords 11–15.

Step 14: Repeat step 10.

Step 15: To complete the bottom part of the pattern, you need to mirror the design explained in steps 1–9, working this time in reverse, starting with step 9.

Advanced Projects

15 Patterns & 4 Projects for Advanced Artists

Lilia Handbag

A project that shows how macramé pieces can be as functional as they are beautiful. The Lilia Handbag is a highly durable bag ideal for carrying all your groceries after a trip to the farmer's market. It's perfect to take as well all your essentials for a day out at the beach, or your laptop and books to a long study session at your favorite café. This washable macramé bag can stretch and adapt to fit anything you need inside. The Lilia Handbag is an elegant accessory perfect for everyday use, all year round.

♦ ♦ ♦

Finished project specs: length 50 cm (19.7 in) x width 40 cm (15.7 in)
Handle: 26 cm (10.2 in) long
Approximate completion time: 3 hours

Tools and Materials

Scissors
Measuring tape
Tapestry needle
Glue
Approximately 130 m (427 ft) brown 3 mm cotton braided rope
Approximately 10 m (33 ft) yellow 3 mm cotton braided rope

Knots and Patterns

Knots Used:
Left-facing half hitch (LFHH), see page 55
Diagonal double half hitch (DDHH), see pages 62–63
Vertical double half hitch (VDHH), see page 67
Berry knot, see page 72
Square knot (SK), see page 47
Alternating square knot (ASK), see page 51
Square knot sinnet (SKS), see page 50

Patterns Used:
Lily mesh, see page 193
Square knot net, see page 86

Preparation
Vertical setup

Cut the following:
24 cords, each 3 m (10 ft) long brown color
24 cords, each 2.4 m (7.9 ft) long brown color
2 cords, each 3 m (10 ft) long yellow color
16 cords, each 0.25 m (0.8 ft) long yellow color

Instructions

Step 1: Fold twelve brown cords, each 3 m (10 ft) long, in half. Move 10 cm (3.9 in) from the center point and use a yellow cord, 3 m (10 ft) in length, to wrap the twelve brown cords using a LFHH. Use the yellow cord as your working cord, and the twelve brown cords as your filler cords. Continue tying LFHHs until you run out of yellow cord. You should now have a 20-cm (7.9-in) yellow spiral.

Step 2: Cut both ends of the yellow cord at the end of the spiral, and use the fabric glue to secure them.

Step 3: Fold the spiral in half and hang it on an S-hook. Leave a 10-cm (3.9-in) gap from both ends of the spiral, and make a lily mesh pattern at each end. In these patterns, each petal is filled with VDHHs and the connected knots are berry knots.

To create a single filled petal, first complete one half by tying five DDHHs with the brown cords. Then, take one yellow cord, 0.25 m (0.8 ft) long, as your working cord and tie four VDHHs underneath the previous line of five DDHHs. Close the petal by tying another line of five DDHHs with the brown cords. Used the same technique to create all the petals on both lily mesh patterns.

Step 4: Tuck the ends of all yellow cords at the back of the design with a tapestry needle and use fabric glue to secure them.

Step 5: Now, in order to create the body of the bag, twelve new cords need to be added. To do so, take the first two cords as your filler cords and use an extra 2.4 m (7.9 ft) brown cord as your working cord to tie an SK. Use this technique to add the rest of the cords. Make sure all SKs are aligned under the lily mesh patterns. There are now six SKs under each pattern.

Step 6: Move down 1 cm (0.4 in) and tie a row of eleven ASKs. Notice how the sixth ASK connects the two sides of the design.

Step 7: Repeat steps 1–6 to create the other side of the Lilia Handbag.

Step 8: Hang both sides of the bag back-to-back on a single S-hook. Move down 1 cm (0.4 in) and tie two single ASKs to connect the sides. Continue tying ASKs until the row is complete.

Step 9: Create a square knot net pattern by tying twelve more rows of ASKs with all the cords.

Step 10: To close the body of the bag, first flip the design inside out and hang it on the S-hook again. Flatten the body of the bag, making sure the ASKs in the front are perfectly aligned with the ASKs at the back. Pair the first ASK from the front with the first ASK from the back and tie an SKS of two SKs. Use any cord as your working cords, and the rest as your filler cords. Keep pairing ASKs from the front and back of the design and continue making SKSs. You need a total of eleven SKSs to close the bag completely.

Step 11: Cut all the ends 5 cm (2 in) from the SKSs.

Step 12: To finish, flip the bag inside out one more time.

15 Patterns & 4 Projects for Advanced Artists

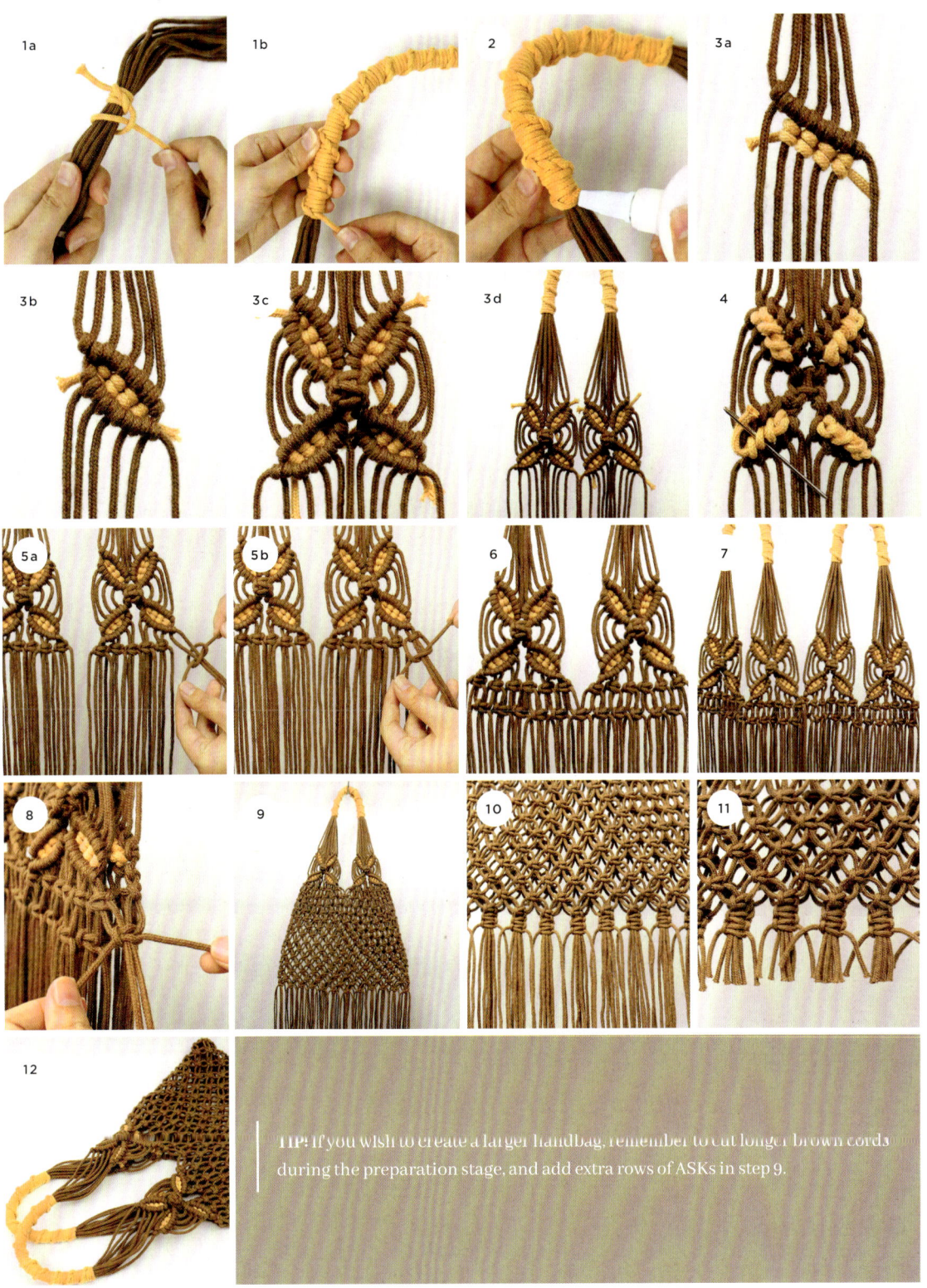

215

TIP! If you wish to create a larger handbag, remember to cut longer brown cords during the preparation stage, and add extra rows of ASKs in step 9.

15 Patterns & 4 Projects for Advanced Artists

Tayanna Wall Hanging

This is one of the most, if not the most, iconic macramé art piece there is. Macramé wall hangings are decoration statements that have been used for many generations to express one's artistic self. These pieces of wall tapestry are living proof of how macramé styles and techniques have evolved over time. The Tayanna Wall Hanging is a captivating and unique project with a modern bohemian spirit. I used an intricate geometric design with unique patterns to create a mesmerizing sense of style. This wall hanging is an astonishing piece of art that will brighten and bring to life any decor space.

♦ ♦ ♦

Finished project specs: length 90 cm (35.4 in) x width 40 cm (15.7 in)
Approximate completion time: 8 hours

Tools and Materials

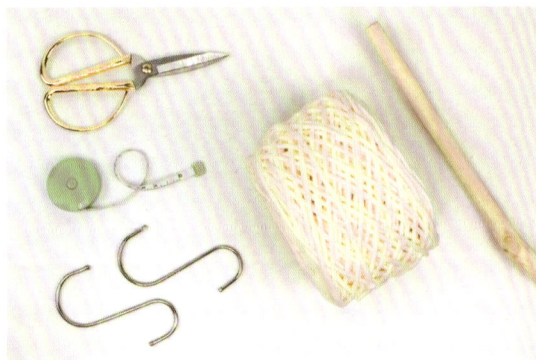

Scissors
Measuring tape
S-hooks
Approximately 184 m (604 ft) natural color 4 mm braided rope
1 wooden dowel, 40 cm (15.7 in) long

Knots and Patterns

Knots Used:
Lark's head knot (LHK), see page 41
Square knot (SK), see page 47
Alternating square knot (ASK), see page 51
Diagonal double half hitch (DDHH), see pages 62–63
Reverse diagonal double half hitch (RDDHH), see pages 68–69
Josephine knot, see page 80

Patterns Used:
Square knot net, see page 86
Reverse arrows mesh, see page 200
Aztec square knot triangles, see page 197
Square knot diamond with big square knot, see page 102
Decreasing arrows, see page 180
Rya knot weaving technique, see page 109

Preparation
Vertical setup
Cut the following:
40 cords, each 4.6 m (15 ft) long

217

Instructions

Step 1: Use two S-hooks to join the wooden dowel to your vertical setup. Then, fold the forty cords, 4.6 m (15 ft) long each, in half and mount them to the wooden dowel with LHKs.

Step 2: Create one row of SKs using all the cords.

Step 3: Tie four ASK rows underneath to create a square knot net pattern.

Step 4: After the square knot net, use all the cords available to create a reverse arrows mesh pattern. Use sixteen cords per arrow. There are five arrow sets with four SKs in between sets.

Step 5: Now, take cords 17–64 and create an Aztec square knot triangles pattern 4 cm (1.6 in) down from the reverse arrow mesh. After knotting the top half of the pattern, tie a Josephine knot using cords 33–48. Then, complete the bottom half of the Aztec square knot triangles pattern. Notice how the sixteen cords to the left and right of the pattern remain unknotted.

Step 6: Using the unknotted cords, tie two square knot diamonds with cords 5–12 and cords 68–76, 4 cm (1.6 in) from the reverse arrow mesh. Make sure these diamonds are aligned with the top part of the Aztec square knot triangles pattern.

Step 7: Now, make two bigger square knot diamonds with cords 1–16 and 65–80 respectively, 6 cm (2.4 in) down from the smaller square knot diamonds from the previous step.

Step 8: Move down 6 cm (2.4 in) and tie another two square knot diamonds using cords 5–12 and cords 68–76. Make sure these diamonds are aligned with the bottom part of the Aztec square knot triangles pattern.

Step 9: Next, move down 4 cm (1.6 in) and make six decreasing arrows patterns using all the cords. Use sixteen cords per decreasing arrow.

Step 10: Now, tie a row of SKs, using all the cords available, 4 cm (1.6 in) from the decreasing arrows patterns.

Step 11: Create a square knot net pattern by tying six ASK rows.

Step 12: Cut the ends of all cords at your desired length. In this piece I cut them at 20 cm (7.9 in).

Step 13: To finish the Tayanna Wall Hanging, add the tassels to our design by using the extra cords after cutting in the previous step. Each tassel is made of three cords, 20 cm (7.9 in) long. Add a total of twenty tassels between the decreasing arrows pattern from step 9 and the square knot net pattern from step 11. Each tassel passes through a group of four filler cords using the rya knot weaving technique.

15 Patterns & 4 Projects for Advanced Artists

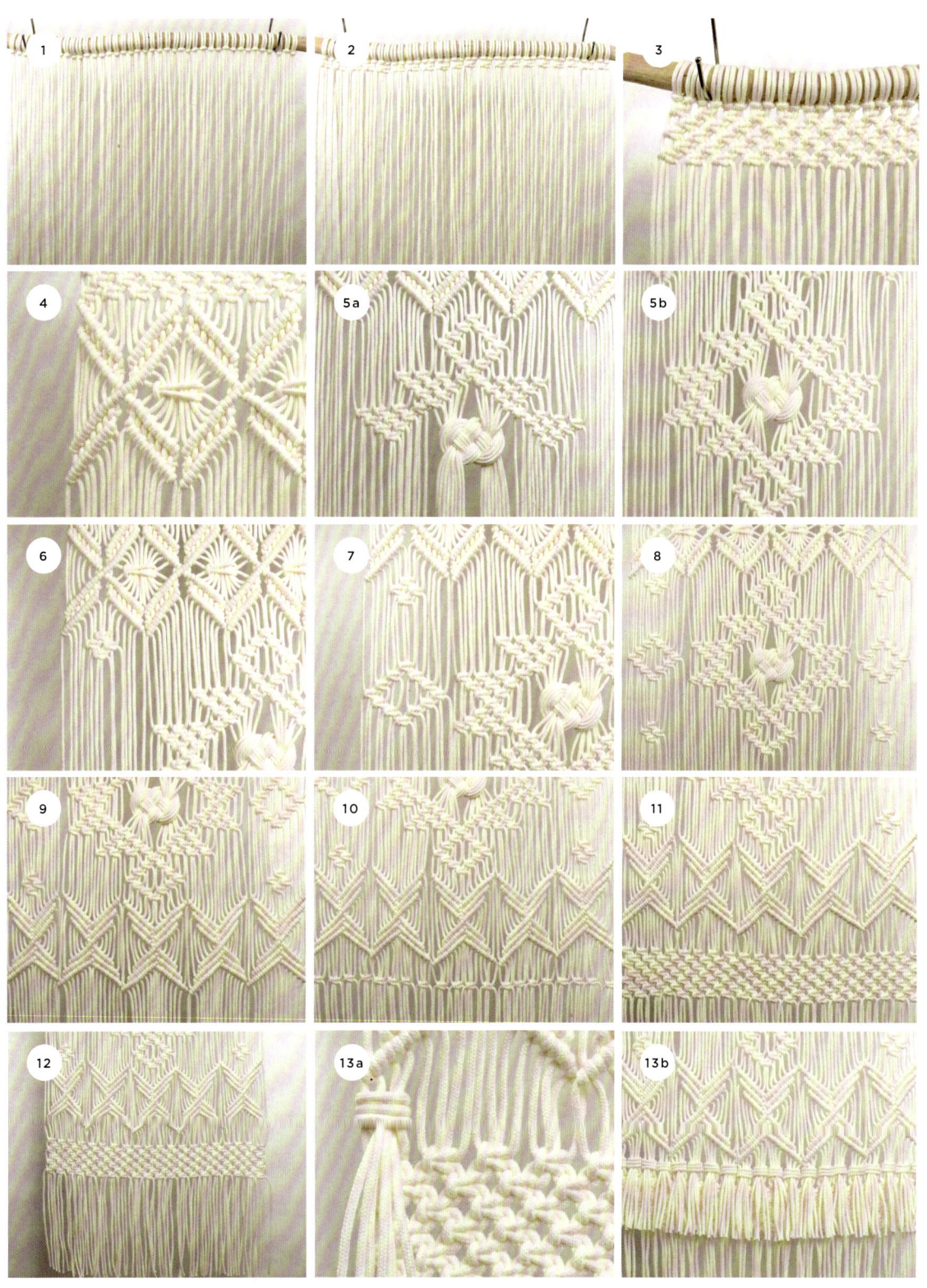

15 Patterns & 4 Projects for Advanced Artists

Mandala Mirror

The Mandala Mirror is an impressive project with its rustic, yet modern, look. This macramé design is a lovely decoration piece that can be placed at the entrance of your house, in the living room, over your bed, or even in your office. The Mandala Mirror includes bulky yarn weaving in order to add varying textures to the design, and is ideal to bring a boho vibe to any area around the house.

Apart from the tools and materials listed below, you need a 30–cm (11.8–in) diameter mirror to work on this project. I use the same tone for both the ropes and the yarn for a harmonious look. If you are looking to add some contrast, use a different color for each type of thread.

Finished project specs: 60 cm (23.6 in) diameter
Approximate completion time: 5 hours

Tools and Materials

Scissors
Measuring tape
Glue
Tapestry needle
Approximately 157 m (515 ft) sandstone 4 mm 3–ply twisted rope
Approximately 4 m (13 ft) sandstone bulky yarn
2 metal rings, 30 cm (11.8 in) diameter
1 metal ring, 40 cm (15.7 in) diameter

Knots and Patterns
Knots Used:
Lark's head knot (LHK), see page 41
Horizontal double half hitch (HDHH), see page 65
Berry knot, see page 72
Square knot (SK), see page 47
Reverse lark's head knot (RLHK), see page 43
Patterns Used:
Running diamond with square knot circle, see page 190
Tabby weave, see page 107
Preparation
Horizontal setup
Cut the following:
56 cords, each 1.8 m (5.9 ft) long
56 cords, each 1 m (3.3 ft) long

Macramé: The Power of Knots

Instructions

Step 1: Fold fifty-six cords, each 1.8 m (5.9 ft) long, in half and mount them to a 30-cm (11.8-in) diameter metal ring with LHKs.

Step 2: Place the mirror on top of the LHKs you previously mounted to the metal ring. The mirror's reflecting side should face upwards. Then, place the second 30-cm (11.8-in) diameter metal ring on top of it. To secure the mirror in place, now use all the cords from the first ring and mount them to the second ring with 112 HDHHs.

Step 3: Take the 40-cm (15.7-in) diameter metal ring and place it on top of the design. Gather all available cords in groups of four. To ensure the mirror is well centered inside the big ring, start by mounting four cords with HDHHs to one side of the big ring. Then, take the cords on the opposite side of the design and mount them to the ring with another four HDHHs. Continue by mounting the rest of the cords with HDHHs, leaving a 1.5 cm (0.6-in) gap between groups.

Step 4: Use the cords of each group from step 3 to tie twenty-eight individual berry knots.

Step 5: Fold fifty-six cords, each 1 m (3.3 ft) long, in half and mount them to the 40-cm (15.7-in) diameter metal ring with RLHKs. Mount two cords between each berry knot and the next.

Step 6: Use all the cords available to create a running diamond circle pattern around the design. Start the pattern with two of the newly added cords to the right of one of the berry knots. Tie this pattern with three rows of diamonds.

Step 7: Create fringes by cutting all cords evenly at 3 cm (1.2 in). Brush and trim all the fringes until you get the fluffy look you desire.

Step 8: Use the tabby weave technique to add the 4 m (13 ft) of sandstone bulky yarn to the space created between the small and big metal rings (steps 2 and 3). Use the groups of four cords to thread the bulky yarn all around the design. Tuck the end of the bulky yarn into the back of the design to finish the project.

> TIP: Use a tapestry needle to ease weaving.

Gila Dream Catchers

Dream catchers originated from Native American cultures. These beautiful decorative pieces are believed to filter dreams, allowing the good ones to go through their nets and gently down their feathers to reach the dreamer. It is also believed that nightmares are caught by dream catchers. They are also used as charms to bring good luck and harmony to whoever owns them. This is why they are such great gifts for family and friends.

The Gila Dream Catcher is a striking project that consists of three pieces hanging from a wooden dowel. One unique design is used in the big centerpiece, while a simpler design is replicated in both of the smaller supporting pieces. Amaze your loved ones with a thoughtful and meaningful present, perfect for decorating bedrooms and living rooms, or to be used as wedding or event backdrops.

15 Patterns & 4 Projects for Advanced Artists

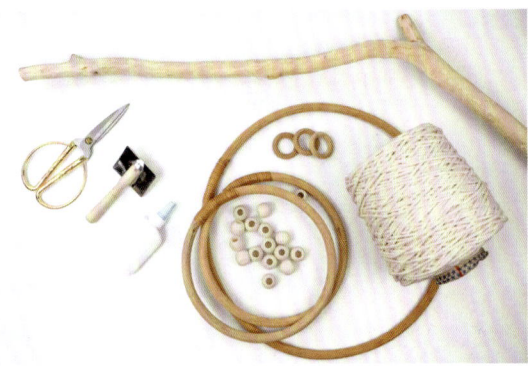

Finished Project Specs:
Centerpiece length 100 cm (39.4 in) x width 35 cm (13.8 in)
Side pieces length 70 cm (27.5 in) x width 20 cm (7.9 in)

Approximate completion time: 7 hours

Tools and Materials

Scissors
Measuring tape
Glue
Tapestry needle
Approximately 205 m (672 ft) natural color 3 mm 3-ply twisted rope
3 wooden rings, 4 cm (1.6 in) diameter
1 wooden ring, 35 cm (13.8 in) diameter
2 wooden rings, 20 cm (7.9 in) diameter
16 large-hole wooden beads, 20 mm (0.8 in) diameter
1 wooden dowel, 90 cm (35.4 in) long

Knots and Patterns

Knots Used:
Lark's head knot (LHK), see page 41
Alternating half hitch (AHH), see page 57
Square knot (SK), see page 47
Horizontal double half hitch (HDHH), see page 65
Overhand knot, see page 38
Diagonal double half hitch (DDHH), see pages 62–63
Left-twist spiral knot (LSPK), see page 59
Reverse lark's head knot (RLHK), see page 43

Patterns Used:
Alternating half hitch six-point star, see page 194
Zigzag, see page 104
Infinity diamond, see page 203
Decreasing arrows, see page 180
Running weaving diamond chain, see page 186
Tassels, see page 152

Preparation

Horizontal setup (centerpiece and supporting ring designs)
Vertical setup (decorative hanging design)

Cut the following for the centerpiece:
6 cords, each 1.5 m (4.9 ft) long
6 cords, each 2.7 m (8.8 ft) long
12 cords, each 2 m (6.6 ft) long
4 cords, each 1.4 m (4.6 ft) long
12 cords, each 2.6 m (8.5 ft) long
36 cords, each 1 m (3.3 ft) long
4 cords, each 2.3 m (7.5 ft) long
18 cords, each 0.3 m (1 ft) long

Cut the following for 2 supporting pieces:
12 cords, each 1 m (3.3 ft) long
12 cords, each 2 m (6.6 ft) long
20 cords, each 1.5 m (4.9 ft) long

Macramé: The Power of Knots

1

1.5m (4.9ft)

2.7m (8.8ft)

Instructions

Step 1: Using a horizontal setup, begin the centerpiece of the dream catchers by folding in half six cords, 1.5 m (4.9 ft) long, and mounting them to the top part of a 4-cm (1.6-in) wooden ring. Then, mount another six cords, 2.7 m (8.8 ft) long, to the bottom part of the same wooden ring.

Step 2: Create an alternating half hitch six-points star pattern with three layers using all the cords. Make sure the first SK in this step is tied using the first pair of cords of the top part of the ring [1.5-m (4.9-ft) long mounted cords], and the next pair of cords from the bottom [2.7-m (8.8-ft) long mounted cords].

Step 3: Take the four cords of each of the six pointy ends of the star, and pass them through a 20-mm (0.8-in) wooden bead. Tie SKs to secure each of the six beads tightly in place.

Step 4: Place and center the 35-cm (13.8-in) wooden ring on top of the design. Use the remaining cords to mount your design to the ring using twenty-four HDHHs. The bottom part of the design is where the remaining cords are longer, as they will be used as part of the decorative hanging design at a later stage in the project.

Step 5: Cut the short cords of the top part of the design as close as possible to the HDHHs, and use glue to secure the ends. Notice how at the bottom of the design there are now three separate groups of four cords. We will refer to them as Groups 1, 2, and 3, going from left to right, in the next steps.

Step 6: To begin adding the decorative elements of the hanging part of the design, now take the cords from Group 1 and pass them through five 20-mm (0.8-in) wooden beads. Do the same with the cords from Group 3. Tie an overhand knot to secure the beads in place.

Step 7: Fold twelve cords, 2 m (6.6 ft) long, in half. Now, using RLHKs, mount six cords to each side of the ring of Group 2.

Step 8: Make two zigzag patterns with cords 1–4 and cords 25–28. Use cords 1 and 28 as filler cords for each zigzag pattern, and cords 2–4 and 25–27 respectively as working cords.

Step 9: Now, using cords 5–23, create an infinity diamond pattern in the center of the design, between the zigzags.

Step 10: Then, fold four cords, 1.4 m (4.6 ft) in length, and mount two of them to each side of the zigzag patterns in Group 2. Use RLHKs to do so. These cords' main and only purpose is to add body to our centerpiece, and will remain unknotted.

Step 11: Now is the time to add cords to Groups 1 and 3 of our centerpiece. First, fold six cords in half, 2.6 m (8.5 ft) long, and mount them to ring using RLHKs to the right of Group 1. Use the same technique to add another six cords to the left of Group 3.

Step 12: Working with the cords just added to Group 1, tie a straight line of five DDHHs-left-to-right, going down. Use the first cord as your filler cord, and cords 2–6 as working cords. Now, create a running weaving diamond chain pattern starting with six DDHHs-left-to-right, going down, continuing the line of five DDHHs previously explained in this step. The chain will be completed after four diamond shapes.

Step 13: Repeat step 12 with the newly added cords to Group 3. Use the same technique, this time in reverse, to ensure a symmetrical design. Notice how the DDHHs are now tied from right to left.

Step 14: In this step, we are going to connect the running weaving diamond chains. Use cords 7–12 from the pattern in Group 1, and cords 1–6 from Group 3, to create a single decreasing arrow pattern.

Step 15: Fold thirty-six cords, 1 m (3.3 ft) long, in half. Using RLHKs, mount six cords to the outer working cords between the diamonds of each chain.

Step 16: The last two decorative hanging elements of our centerpiece are two LSPKs. To create these spirals, continue by folding four cords, 2.3 m (7.5 ft) in length. Fold the cords at 1.8 m (5.9 ft) from one of the ends. Mount two cords to the left of Group 1, and two cords to the right of Group 3, following this sequence of lengths: first cord, 1.8 m (5.9 ft)–0.5 m (1.6 ft), and second cord, 0.5 m (1.6 ft)–1.8 m (5.9 ft).

Step 17: Now, tie seventy LSPKs for each spiral. Use the 0.5-m (1.6-in) cords as your filler cords, and the 1.8-m (5.9-ft) cords as working cords.

Step 18: It's time to add the tassels to our design. Each tassel is made by untwisting and brushing six 0.3-m (1-ft) long cords. Using the attached tassel technique, add two tassels at the end of each of our spirals, and one tassel at the end of the decreasing arrow. Remember to brush and trim the ends of the tassels to give them an even finish.

Step 19: To complete the centerpiece, cut all the remaining cords in a V-shape, at the length you desire.

Step 20: Both supporting ring pieces of the dream catchers are identical but simpler versions of the centerpiece. Start by mounting cords to the small wooden rings following the technique explained in step 1, only this time, the top mounted cords are 1 m (3.3 ft) long, and the cords mounted to the bottom part of the ring are 2 m (6.6 ft) in length.

Step 21: Create simpler and smaller alternating half hitch six-points star patterns, one for each supporting piece, by knotting only the first two layers of the stars. To begin this step, this time tie three SKs for the top part of the ring, using only the 1-m (3.3-ft) long mounted cords. And for the bottom part, do the same with the 2-m (6.6-ft) long cords.

Step 22: Use the techniques demonstrated in steps 4 and 5 to mount both designs to your 20-cm (7.9-in) diameter wooden rings.

Step 23: Fold ten cords, 1.5 m (4.9 ft) long, in half. Using RLHKs, mount five cords to the ring between Groups 1 and 2, and another five cords between Groups 2 and 3.

Step 24: Cut all the remaining cords on both supporting pieces in a V-shape at your desired length.

Step 25: To complete the project, hang the dream catchers onto a 90-cm (35.4-in) wooden dowel.

15 Patterns & 4 Projects for Advanced Artists

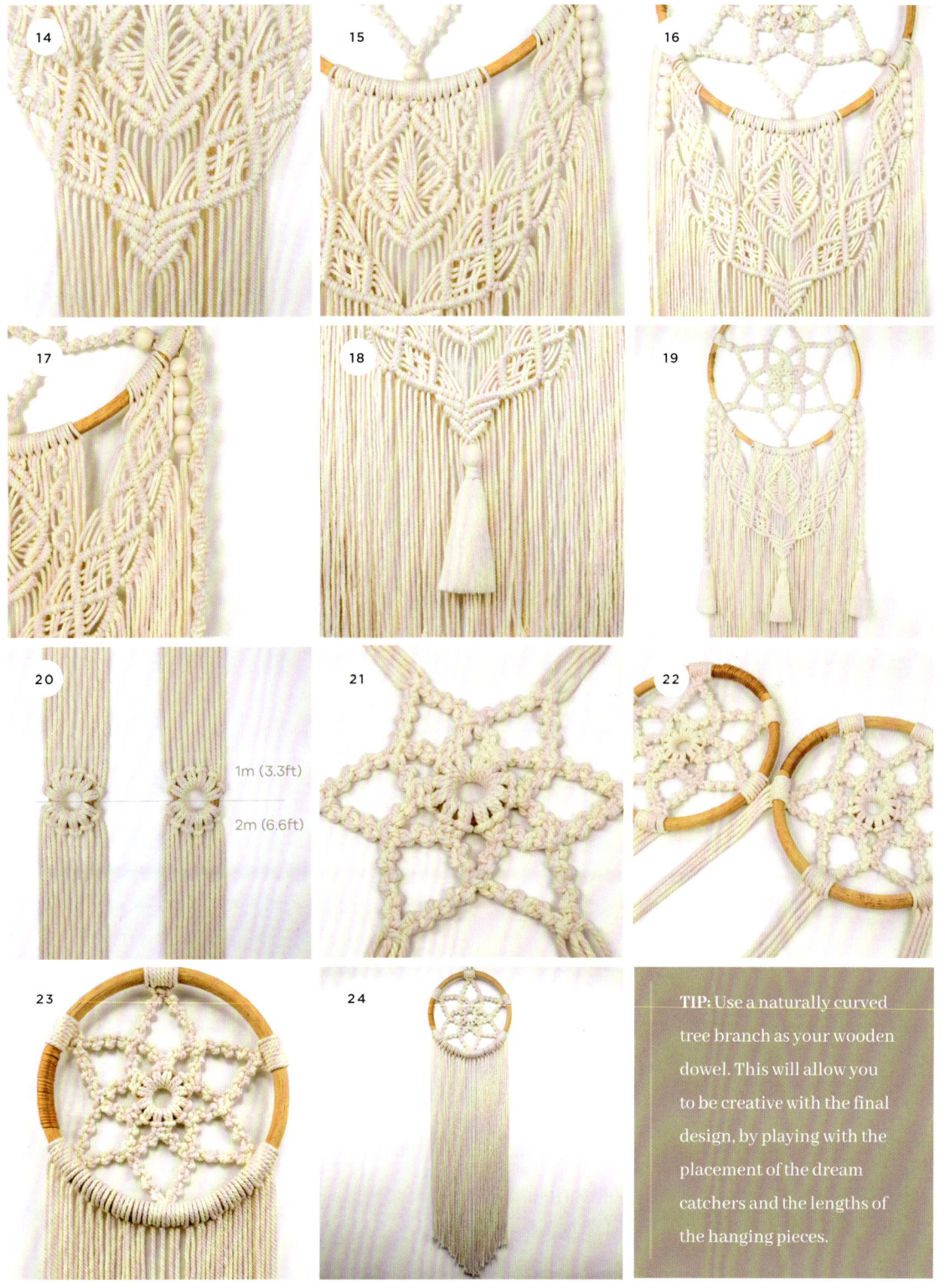

TIP: Use a naturally curved tree branch as your wooden dowel. This will allow you to be creative with the final design, by playing with the placement of the dream catchers and the lengths of the hanging pieces.

Resources

To get the macramé materials and tools needed to get you started, I'd like to invite you to check out my online macramé supply store: www.missknottiemacrame.store

In addition, let me share with you some of my favorite alternatives to get supplies from:

- Ganxxet.com (USA)–eco-friendly cords
- Niromastudio.com (USA)–cords only
- Larksheadshop.com (USA)–cords only
- Etsy.com/ca/shop/UnfetteredCo (CANADA)–cords and frames
- Marymakerstudio.com.au (AUSTRALIA)–cords and tools
- Jachomeheart.com.au (AUSTRALIA)–cords and tools
- Shop.bobbiny.com (EUROPE)–cords only
- Createholic.se (EUROPE)–cords only
- Macramespaghetti.com (EUROPE)–cords and tools

Acknowledgments

I would like to start by thanking my awesome husband, Fernando, for supporting and spending hundreds of hours with me in order to finish the manuscript. He is as important to the completion of this book as I am. Thank you, Fernando, for believing in me, comforting me when I needed it, and providing me with incredible advice. You pushed me to be the best I could and helped me to grow every day. Thank you for everything. I could not have done it without you.

I would like to extend my sincere thanks to my family. Thank you to my sister, Tran, for all her support and for helping me create a worldwide presence for Miss Knottie Macrame. And to my parents, for always encouraging me to follow my passion and supporting me in my pursuit of a crafting career.

My sincere thanks to everyone on the Mango Publishing team. Thank you for providing me with an incredible opportunity to inspire people all over the world with my craft. Special thanks to Lisa, Jessica, Meloni, and Yaddyra, who from the beginning were there to help shape and put this book together.

I very much appreciate DG Photography for capturing some astonishing photos for this book. Thank you, Pupi and Hang, for all your incredible contributions during the photoshoot.

Finally, my deepest gratitude goes to all my followers and supporters. Thank you for being there from the beginning. You have kept me motivated and wanting to work harder every day. This book is dedicated to you!

About the Author

Nghi Ho is a successful self-taught macramé artist and content creator. As a kid, she was amazed by how using your hands and a bit of creativity one could create something beautiful. One of her fondest memories as a child is making lanterns for the Mid-Autumn Festival.

Nghi followed her passion and received her bachelor's degree in fashion design. After graduating, she got a job as a graphic designer. She then decided to become a freelancer, in order to have more artistic freedom, and to be able to choose projects she was really passionate about. After a while, Nghi began to show interest in other types of digital businesses. She's self-taught in basic coding/programming, recording/editing content, image compositions, web development, and building a social media presence.

It took Nghi a while to learn the art of macramé. And during that time, at some point, she got frustrated with some of the options available to do so. It was then that she decided to give it a try and began creating her own content. Since then, she has built a presence in the online macramé community, and uses platforms like Instagram, YouTube, and Pinterest to inspire others to take on the craft. She creates easy-to-follow tutorials with the goal to spark people's creativity as well as artistic self-expression. Apart from creating content and managing her social media channels, Nghi has developed her own brand of macramé supplies, Miss Knottie Macrame. Her online store has allowed people from all over the world to get everything they need to start tying knots.

Discover more about Nghi's work at:

- Instagram: @missknottie.macrame
- Pinterest: @missknottiemacrameus
- YouTube: Miss Knottie Macrame
- Online Store: www.missknottiemacrame.store
- Etsy: MissKnottieMacrame
- Contact Nghi directly at missknottiemacrame@gmail.com

Yellow Pear Press, established in 2015, publishes inspiring, charming, clever, distinctive, playful, imaginative, beautifully-designed lifestyle books, cookbooks, literary fiction, notecards, and journals with a certain *joie de vivre* in both content and style. Yellow Pear Press books have been honored by the Independent Publisher Book (IPPY) Awards, National Indie Excellence Awards, Independent Press Awards, and International Book Awards. Reviews of our titles have appeared in Kirkus Reviews, Foreword Reviews, Booklist, Midwest Book Review, San Francisco Chronicle, and New York Journal of Books, among others. Yellow Pear Press joined forces with Mango Publishing in 2020, both with the vision to continue publishing clever and innovative books. The fact that they're both named after fruit is a total coincidence.

We love hearing from our readers, so please stay in touch with us and follow us at:

Facebook: Mango Publishing
Twitter: @MangoPublishing
Instagram: @MangoPublishing
LinkedIn: Mango Publishing
Pinterest: Mango Publishing

Newsletter: mangopublishinggroup.com/newsletter